The Global Age-Friendly Community Movement

Life Course, Culture and Aging: Global Transformations
General Editor: Jay Sokolovsky, University of South Florida St. Petersburg

Published by Berghahn Books under the auspices of the Association for Anthropology and Gerontology (AAGE) and the American Anthropological Association Interest Group on Aging and the Life Course.

The consequences of aging will influence most areas of contemporary life around the globe, from the makeup of households and communities and systems of care to attitudes toward health, disability, and life's end. Engaging a cross-cultural framework, this series publishes monographs and collected works that examine these widespread transformations with a perspective on the entire life course and a particular focus on mid/late adulthood.

Volume 1
TRANSITIONS AND TRANSFORMATIONS
Cultural Perspectives on Aging and the Life Course
Edited by Caitrin Lynch and Jason Danely

Volume 2
UNFORGOTTEN
Love and the Culture of Dementia Care in India
Bianca Brijnath

Volume 3
AGING AND THE DIGITAL LIFE COURSE
Edited by David Prendergast and Chiara Garattini

Volume 4
CARE ACROSS DISTANCE
Ethnographic Explorations of Aging and Migration
Edited by Azra Hromadžić and Monika Palmberger

Volume 5
THE GLOBAL AGE-FRIENDLY COMMUNITY MOVEMENT
A Critical Appraisal
Edited by Philip B. Stafford

THE GLOBAL AGE-FRIENDLY COMMUNITY MOVEMENT

A Critical Appraisal

Edited by

Philip B. Stafford

NEW YORK • OXFORD
www.berghahnbooks.com

First published in 2019 by
Berghahn Books
www.berghahnbooks.com

© 2019, 2020 Philip B. Stafford
First paperback edition published in 2020

All rights reserved. Except for the quotation of short passages
for the purposes of criticism and review, no part of this book
may be reproduced in any form or by any means, electronic or
mechanical, including photocopying, recording, or any information
storage and retrieval system now known or to be invented,
without written permission of the publisher.

Library of Congress Cataloging-in-Publication Data

A C.I.P. cataloging record is available from the Library of Congress
Library of Congress Cataloging in Publication Control Number: 2018039453

British Library Cataloguing in Publication Data

A catalogue record for this book is available from the British Library.

ISBN 978-1-78533-667-6 hardback
ISBN 978-1-78920-799-6 paperback
ISBN 978-1-78533-668-3 ebook

CONTENTS

List of Illustrations and Figures	vii
List of Tables	viii
Acknowledgments	ix
Preface	xi

Introduction: Theorizing and Practicing Age-Friendly Development   1
Philip B. Stafford

PART I. Equity and Sustainability

1. Creating Age-Friendly Communities in Urban Environments: Research Issues and Policy Recommendations   15
Tine Buffel and Chris Phillipson

2. Training Advocates to Undertake Livable Community Initiatives: A Pilot Program   31
Sharon A. Baggett

3. Public Places, Community, and the Physical and Mental Health of Children and Elders   54
Suzanne H. Crowhurst Lennard

4. The Intersection between Sustainable and Age-Friendly Development   78
Alan DeLaTorre

PART II. Age-Friendly Neighborhoods

5. Accessibility, Participation, Networking: The Impact of a Local Network on the Environment and the Life Relationship of Older People   105
Birgit Wolter

6. Assessing the Aging-Friendliness of Two New York City
   Neighborhoods: A Case Study   127
   Mia R. Oberlink and Barbara S. Davis

PART III. Collaboration across Generations

7. Communities for All Ages: Reinforcing and Reimagining
   the Social Compact   139
   Corita Brown and Nancy Henkin

8. Ibasho Café: Giving Elders a Role to Play in Making
   Communities More Resilient   169
   Emi Kiyota

9. Youth and Older Persons as Agents for Change: Creating
   an Inclusive and Age-Friendly Society for All   188
   Arthur Namara and Kristin Bodiford

PART IV. Rural Aging

10. Retrofitting Small Towns: How Aging in Place Could
    Transform Rural America   211
    Zachary Benedict

11. Creating an Age-Friendly Community in a Depopulated Town
    in Japan: A Search for Resilient Ways to Cherish New
    Commons as Local Cultural Resources   229
    Nanami Suzuki

PART V. Being Well Enough in Old Age

12. Relational Well-Being and Age-Friendly Cities   249
    Marian Barnes

Index   269

ILLUSTRATIONS AND FIGURES

Figure 0.1	The WHO age-friendly cities and communities domains (source: WHO)	8
Figure 3.1	Humans are social beings (photo by author)	55
Figure 3.2	Building a social immune system (photo by author)	60
Figure 3.3	Children learn social skills through participation, observation, and reenactment (photo by author)	62
Figure 3.4	Elders walk if this offers social interaction (photo by author)	63
Figure 3.5	Mixed-use human-scale urban fabric fosters social life (photo by author)	66
Figure 3.6	Community social life is generated in multifunctional neighborhood squares (photo by author)	69
Figure 5.1	Focus group using balloons and stones method (source: IGF)	110
Figure 5.2	Märkisches Viertel (source: IGF)	111
Figure 5.3	Neighborhood fete in Märkisches Viertel (source: IGF)	115
Figure 5.4	Shopping center plaza (Brunnenplatz) (source: IGF)	117
Figure 6.1	The four domains of an age-friendly community (source: VNSNY)	129
Figure 8.1	Ibasho café framework (chart by author)	172
Figure 10.1	Indiana small-town summary (source: U.S. Census)	215
Figure 10.2	Correlation between successful aging and community engagement (source: AARP/Roper Public Affairs & Media group of NOP World, *Beyond 50.05 Survey* [2004], 44)	217
Figure 10.3	Lifetime Community District concept plan, Bloomington, Indiana (source: MKM architecture + design)	224

TABLES

Table 2.1	Knowledge and Skills Pre- and Post-Survey (n = 92)	42
Table 2.2	Trainee Report on Progress toward Goals for Attending Sessions	43
Table 2.3	Post-Training Assessment of Training Quality	44
Table 2.4	Follow-Up Survey: Post-Training Actions	46
Table 4.1	Proposed Guiding Principles of Sustainable Development for an Aging Society	94
Table 4.2	Corresponding Elements of Sustainable Development and Portland's Age-Friendly Communities	97
Table 10.1	LCD District Components and Considerations (in relation to the "age-friendly city topic areas" defined by the World Health Organization's *Global Age-Friendly Cities: A Guide*)	221

ACKNOWLEDGMENTS

LONG TIME COMING, THIS BOOK has nevertheless been a labor of love. It grew from a symposium on age-friendly communities held at the 2013 Congress of the International Union of Anthropological and Ethnological Sciences in Manchester, England. Several of the chapter authors participated and were kind enough to expand and enrich their papers for this volume.

To achieve one of the first three or four book-length volumes on the age-friendly community movement required reaching out to several outstanding researchers and practitioners involved with the movement. I am deeply indebted to both the original contributors and the "added bonus" colleagues for the time, effort, and excellence they provided to this work. I have known and worked with multiple chapter authors over several years, and they have inspired, energized, and challenged me in ways that have made a significant positive difference in my thinking and practice.

My fascination with the subject of aging and old age goes back six decades, to a time when I sought to be with elders in their homes and tape-record their stories. I have always cautioned students to avoid careers in gerontology if they don't maintain an abiding interest in history and a deep appreciation for the unique biographical experience of every person. While every biography is unique, it is those very same old people I have been privileged to know over sixty years who have taught me that there is, in fact, no such thing as an individual apart from relationships. If there are unique stories, they are about how we are in the world as *social* beings, not atomized individuals. This revelation, learned directly from those friends, has led me to value the work of scholars that have focused on intersubjectivity, folklorists of performance, practitioners of participatory research and development, and those who lean toward a belief in the social construction of reality. This has led me away from positivist social science and often landed me in the realm of literature, arts, and humanities as tools for both understanding and social change.

At the time this book began, I was nearing retirement from the Indiana Institute on Disability at Indiana University, and I owe a debt of gratitude for the provision of support from my co-retiring director, David Mank. At our Center on Aging and Community, I had the unmatched pleasure of working with creative, fun, and supportive colleagues Jane Harlan-Simmons, Peg Holtz, Matt Norris, Jennie Todd, and Lora Wagers. They developed with me a somewhat atypical (note I don't say warped) but joyful environment, which we shared for over sixteen years. Jennie played a key role in helping develop the advocacy training project so well described and researched by Sharon A. Baggett in chapter 2.

I'd like to call out Jay Sokolovsky for special mention, as he is admirably creating and nurturing, as general editor, the growing Berghahn Press *Life Course, Culture and Aging* series, of which this volume is a part. I've been fortunate to know Jay for forty years, more or less. His contributions to the anthropology of aging as a scholar, teacher, and friend/encourager to virtually *everyone* in the field are well known and appreciated.

My loving and understanding wife, Linda Stafford, is largely responsible for any success I have, by encouraging and tolerating me for nearly fifty years. I have the great good fortune to have both daughters (Libby and Abby) living near and the grandparent's dream of playing with three delightful and really smart grandkids (Jayden, Mya, and little Brylee) every single week. It only reinforces my good choice to study and live with an appreciation for place and for relationships that thrive over time. It is to them that I dedicate this volume.

—Philip B. Stafford

PREFACE

Without relationships, I'm a dead man . . .

WITH THIS QUOTE, MILTON FIGEN at age eighty-five put his finger on the theme of this volume. The changes associated with our aging bodies, to be sure, represent an individual challenge. Yet, the Madison Avenue image of the aging individual striving for (and paying for) unending youth is a fiction. It is a fiction to think that we exist outside of the complex net of relationships in which we are embedded—relationships with others close, not so close, or even those who preceded us (forebears) or who will succeed us (successors), as described by the phenomenologist Alfred Schutz (1967). It is not antithetical to reject individual choice. As one Schutz commentator pointed out, in a world of blue jeans, one can still wear red jeans (as the iconoclastic former mayor of Bristol, England, George Ferguson, does daily).[1] (This is not meant to make light of the reality of choice-limiting environments occupied by the vulnerable among all societies.) It is the attention to this *social* reality, the lifeworld, that provides the foundation for the age-friendly community movement, insofar as it can reject the psychological reductionism so dominant in the study of aging (Moody 1986). Seeing aging, health, illness, and disability as relational phenomena, deeply social and interactional in their essence, certainly points us in new directions (Verbrugge and Jette 1994). It turns us to the quotidian social life of ordinary elders "carrying on" as well as to the high-level policy and practices in human and health services that carve out individual bodies for treatment as economically efficient units of service.

It should be noted (I should say, argued) that our existence as individuals *against* nature (which perhaps underlies our cult of youth) is also a fiction. While the argument ventures into the spiritual, it need not. Gregory Bateson, in *Steps to an Ecology of Mind* (1999), provides a stepstone. In a lovely little parable about a blind man with a white cane, he explains that while we of course have a physically real brain, the brain only becomes mind when looped into its surrounding environment. (This is a useful way to think about the distinction between Alzheimer's disease and dementia, and the risks of viewing the villain as Alzheimer's disease [the deficit] and not dementia [a form of social isolation].)

This focus on the preeminence of the social over the individual may be an ex post facto theoretical defense of the age-friendly movement, not usually foregrounded in the work we see in the field. Indeed, in the age-friendly movement itself, proponents sometimes present goals and solutions organized around overly individualized models of well-being. It is not unusual, fortunately, to discover that the construction of a fitness trail, the creation of an exercise group, or the provision of a nutritious meal (common age-friendly community innovations) is only successful *because* of the social benefits that emerge—not because people want to exercise for its own sake nor eat alone. Within the field of gerontology, it is the subfield of environmental gerontology and its focus on person-environment interaction that holds the most promise, in my view, and age-friendly proponents do indeed make that connection. Yet, I would hope that the subfield would delve even more deeply into the irreducible nature of our intersubjective reality and lose the hyphen!

This book is intended to provide a critical appraisal of the age-friendly community movement—where the term *critical* means neither oppositional nor polemic. The authors uniformly see promise in the movement, while hoping to address some of its shortcomings: its lack of attention to inequities and social justice and the obverse, an overreliance on the concept of livability; its too-ready attempts to employ clean, abstract models of the age-friendly community to complex social environments that don't fall neatly into separate categories. Authors also provide us with some wonderful examples of development work that is age-friendly but doesn't call itself such. Success in these cases comes not from branding the work as "age-friendly," but instead finding and collaborating with those institutions that can benefit the work by virtue of their own similar goals—goals related to sustainable development, agricultural and economic development, even social work education. There is a basic theme here that rejects the needs- and deficiencies-based model of response to our rapidly aging world . There is a long way to go, but with these contributions in mind, I feel this book moves the field forward. It has been a privilege to assemble this group of scholars, practitioners, and humanists.

Note

1. Ferguson is an active participant in the International Making Cities Livable movement and steered his city to be named the European Green Capital in 2015.

References

Bateson, Gregory. (1972) 1999. *Steps to an Ecology of Mind.* Chicago: University of Chicago Press.

Moody, Harry (Rick). 1986. "The Meaning of Life and the Meaning of Old Age." In *What Does It Mean to Grow Old? Reflections from the Humanities,* ed. Thomas. R. Cole and Sally Gadow, 9–40. Durham, NC: Duke University Press.

Schutz, Alfred. (1932) 1967. *The Phenomenology of the Social World.* Evanston, IL: Northwestern University Press.

Verbrugge, Lois, M., and Alan M. Jette. 1994. "The Disablement Process." *Social Science and Medicine* 38(1): 10–14.

INTRODUCTION
Theorizing and Practicing Age-Friendly Development

Philip B. Stafford

Background

IN HIS PRESIDENT'S MESSAGE TO prospective attendees of the twelfth annual International Federation on Ageing (IFA) conference held in Hyderabad, India, Dr. K. R. Gangadharan quotes Klauss Schwab, founder and executive chairman of the World Economic Forum: "Ageing is widely seen as one of the most significant risks to global prosperity in the decades ahead because of its potentially profound economic, social, and political implications. Global ageing, in developed and developing countries alike, will dramatically alter the way that societies and economies work."

The World Heath Organization (WHO) reports that from 2000 to 2050, the proportion of the world's population over sixty years will have doubled from 11 percent to 22 percent. The number of people aged sixty years and over is expected to increase from 605 million to 2 billion over the same period. In so-called developed countries, the size of the elderly population has already surpassed that of the twelve to twenty-four age group. Eighty percent of older people will live in low- and middle-income countries. Chile, China, and the Islamic Republic of Iran will have a greater proportion of older people than will the United States of America. The number of older people in Africa will grow from 54 million to 213 million (World Economic Forum 2012).

At the global level, there are two factors that, combined, have led to the current demographic shift: declining birth rates and increased life expectancy. Across the world, from 1970 to 2013, the average number of children per woman declined from 4.7 to 2.5. While in Europe and North America fertility is approaching no net replacement, significant drops have been recorded also in Asia and in Latin America and the Caribbean, with a reduction of 5.4 to 2.2 in the former and 5.3 to 2.2 in the latter (Population Reference Bureau 2014).

The trends with life expectancy are also truly global and not restricted to the developed world. Global life expectancy increased by about six years from 1990 to 2013. In Japan, average age at death in 1990 was seventy-three years. By 2013 it had climbed to eighty-one, leading the planet. These gains, worldwide, are attributable to significant drops in deaths caused by several major diseases: diarrheal diseases, neonatal diseases, lower respiratory infections, cardiovascular diseases, and cancers (WHO 2005).

At the local level there is another reason that communities grow older—perhaps just as significant. It is the combined phenomenon of a growing population of elders and the out-migration of the young. According to the United Nations, 3.2 percent of the world's population are international migrants (232 million individuals). Of these, 30 percent are below the age of thirty. In addition, another 740 million young people migrate within their own national borders. In either case, young people are leaving their home communities (whether urban or rural), and older people are left behind, creating "naturally occurring retirement communities" (NORCs). The true impact of this global phenomenon has been inadequately studied, and it would be premature to define the elders as "abandoned," since young people experiencing success in migration may very well be channeling resources back to their home communities. In 2013, an estimated $414 billion in remittances flowed back to developing countries, in some cases representing a significant portion of GDP (WHO 2013).

In the United States, mayors and other public officials in rural and small-town communities regularly cite the outflow of youth as a major threat to the basic fabric of their communities. As Carr and Kefalas (2009) note, "This so-called rural 'brain drain' isn't a new phenomenon, but by the twenty-first century the shortage of young people has reached a tipping point, and its consequences are more severe now than ever before. Simply put, many small towns are mere years away from extinction, while others limp along in a weakened and disabled state."

The cost of addressing the demographic change is often characterized as a potentially catastrophic "silver tsunami" that will overwhelm world economies. The demographics of aging are undeniable and possibly world-changing. Whether this change is for the good or instead portends a looming catastrophe is a subject of current debate. Klauss Schwab, echoing many world leaders, notes that the lack of institutionalized pension systems is a chief barrier to the well-being of elders, especially in light of changing family patterns and the loss of traditional supports. The Melbourne Mercer Global Pension Index uses three subindices—adequacy, sustainability, and integrity—to measure retirement income systems against more than forty indicators. The 2012 report viewed eighteen systems, twelve of which scored average or below with respect to their long-term and, in four cases, short-term sustainability. All were cases of developed countries. In the developing world, government pension systems are either scant or nonexistent. Two strategies are presented to address the coming needs, including greater levels of funding (doubtful for many nations) and the extension of working years by individuals. The latter provides reason for some optimism as long as health as well can be extended in time.

The cost of health care is typically cited as the second major challenge associated with the demographic revolution. Only in Western Europe, North America, and Australia (with small exceptions) does general government expenditure as a percentage of overall expenditure reach 15 percent. In much of the world, expenditures are far less, as little as 5 percent in parts of Central Africa and South Asia (WHO 2013b).

With respect to health-care expenditures it is important to note that already, even in the poorest countries, the biggest killers are not communicable disease, but heart disease, stroke, and chronic lung disease, while the greatest causes of disability are visual impairment, dementia, hearing loss, and osteoarthritis (WHO 2005) The WHO reports that "from a projected total of 58 million deaths from all causes in 2005, it is estimated that chronic diseases will account for 35 million, which is double the number of deaths from all infectious diseases (including HIV/AIDS, tuberculosis and malaria), maternal and perinatal conditions, and nutritional deficiencies combined." Moreover, 80 percent of worldwide deaths from noninfectious diseases occur in low- and middle-income countries (WHO 2010). In much of Africa, more than 30 percent of females age eighteen and above experience raised blood pressure. In North America, Europe, Russia, and much of South America, more than 60 percent of adult males are overweight (body mass greater than 25 kg/m^2). In Russia and much of South Asia, tobacco use rates exceed 36 percent. Moreover, tobacco use is shifting from developed countries to the developing world. In the twenty-first century, there will be one billion tobacco-related deaths, with 70 percent from the developing world and 30 percent developed—a complete reversal of twentieth-century rates. In 2005, 61 percent of fifty-eight million deaths worldwide were attributed to chronic diseases such as cardiovascular diseases, diabetes, and chronic respiratory diseases (WHO 2005).

Unhealthy diet, physical inactivity, and tobacco use are key factors in the development of chronic disease. The treatment of intermediate risk factors such as prediabetes, hypertension, and obesity will require mobilizing primary care resources in the developing world. This will be extremely costly. However, given that these intermediate risk factors are preventable through primary prevention, it is quite clear that public health, not biomedicine, is the way out of the silver tsunami. Focusing on the development of healthy *environments*, including age-friendly ones, is the path to take.

From the Individual to the Social

Focusing on environments for aging presents its own set of challenges. The dominant discourse on healthy aging, modeled after Western biomedicine, is about individual aging bodies and not communities or environments. Individual lifestyle and personal responsibility are offered as the ticket to "successful aging."

In their critique of the lifestyle discourse in American culture, Howell and Ingham (2001) quote former surgeon general Louis Sullivan on how to improve the nation's health: "First, personal responsibility, which is to say responsibility and enlightened behavior by each and every individual, truly is the key to good health." In talking of the disparity of health between "those of lower socio-economic status," the "disadvantaged," and the "poor of society" Sullivan continued:

> If we are to extend the benefits of good health to all of our people, it is crucial that we build in our most vulnerable populations what I have called a "culture of character," which is to say a culture, or a way of thinking and being, that actively promotes responsible behavior and the adoption of lifestyles that are maximally conducive to good health. This is "prevention" in the broadest sense.

The notion that health is primarily an issue of personal responsibility has clearly fueled the explosion of commercial attention to what is called "lifestyle." Howell and Ingham (2001) attribute the development of the lifestyle craze to a changing relationship among labor, capital, and government introduced during the Reagan years, changes favoring capital, of course. They describe the transformation of "public issues into personal troubles and problems of lifestyle" (331) and the redefinition of illness, health care, and unemployment as private issues of character (330). As the call for personal responsibility became ubiquitous, there arose a rich opportunity for the corporatization of wellness and the commodification of the body. Public governance became operative through the virtual redefinition of the self (after Foucault 1973). Given its numbers, it was no coincidence that the exploding baby boom generation became a prime target for the commodification of the self.

One could argue that the movement away from care and cure to illness prevention represents a step toward awareness of the environmental determinants of health, and indeed it does. Yet, the medical model has its own approach to prevention and, as above, still involves intervention at the level of the individual. Hartman-Stein, Potkanowicz, and Bierman (2003) provide an exemplary review of the many regimens available to be adopted by older adults:

> The news for the baby boomer generation is indeed positive regarding their upcoming late life years. Behaviors, thinking patterns, and emotional and spiritual lifestyles in middle age, factors over which individuals have significant control, have much more impact on health and satisfaction in the seventh and eighth decade of life than was once believed possible. Successful or healthy aging is a goal within reasonable reach.

While personal behavior and health care have been demonstrated to play a role in population health, the contribution is moderate but not dominant. Environmental factors, broadly defined, play the major role in community health. It can be argued that investing in environmental interventions should be at least on par with the huge investments made in medical care and personal wellness.

Since the publication of Lawton and Nahemow's seminal article on "person-environment relationships" (1973) a thriving subfield within gerontology (environmental gerontology) has amassed an impressive literature on the influence of environmental factors on health and well-being in later life. It is well beyond the scope of this introduction (and the knowledge of its author) to adequately portray the history and current state of the art in environmental gerontology, which itself found earlier roots in Kurt Lewin's theory of behavior, where $B = f(P,E)$—behavior is a function of the person in his or her environment (1936).

In 2003, Hans-Werner Wahl and Gerald D. Weisman authored a major review of the field of environmental gerontology, tracing its roots and summarizing its successes and limitations at the beginning of the new millennium (Wahl and Wiesman, 2003). They characterize the field as pluralistic, gently pointing to the fuzzy nature of essential definitions such as environment itself and the paradox of attempting to evaluate the influences of environment without accommodating subjective, psychological processes such as cognition, perception, and affect. They note that much of the research to that point focused on housing—the home environment, planned residential environments and institutions. Researchers often focused on relocation and transitions across those boundaries as a methodological tool to illuminate the impact of these environments on behavior. Of course, much of the empirical research was motivated by a goal of improving practice—designing new or sustaining current environments that support well-being, leaving behind the goal of developing a solid and agreed-upon theoretical base to guide the effort.

Since the 2003 summary, the field of environmental gerontology has benefited from an explosion of research in the field of public health. Research on the relationships between the built environment and such outcomes as obesity, reductions in pedestrian and motorist mortality, nutritional status, mental health, perceptions of safety, diabetes, chronic obstructive pulmonary disease (COPD), asthma, and many other health- and mental-health-related outcomes has filled multiple journals in public health and related fields. The weight of this research effort has resulted in the popular claim that the most prominent determinant of health in the United States is nothing less than one's zip code. While often targeted to non-elderly populations, such research has stimulated and informed its application to the field of environmental gerontology.

It is perhaps not surprising that the more recent focus on these obdurate realities of the built environment has moved environmental gerontology away from its roots in social psychology and behavioral outcomes toward a political economy model of explanation. This is in part likely due to an increasing call for attention to structural forces that transcend individual psychology—forces defined by race, income, and, more recently, globalism, migration, and forced relocation. It is notable that the age-friendly movement has experienced this same tension and that some of the more recent critiques of the age-friendly movement echo the tension seen in the broader field of environmental gerontology. Chapters in this volume contribute to the resolution of some of these tensions through critique and through offering suggestions for change. It is perhaps appropriate to begin with a brief review of just what the age-friendly movement is all about.

The Age-Friendly Community Movement

Shifting focus from the individual to the matrix of community, the age-friendly community movement is rapidly growing throughout the world under such rubrics as elder-friendly communities, communities for all ages, and, here, age-friendly communities (after the WHO nomenclature), examples of which are found in this volume. The explosion of interest in age-friendly communities is reflected in the very recent appearance of peer-reviewed articles and book-length treatments (Buffel, Handler, and Phillipson 2018; Moulaert and Garon 2016; Scharlach and Lehning 2016; Greenfield et al. 2015) and specific research articles that attempt to describe and assess the attributes of success, when found.

While the elements of an age-friendly community are stated in various ways, the first comprehensive model was developed as the AdvantAge Initiative (see https://apps.vnsny.org/advantage/), a nationwide community planning and development project of the Center for Home Care Policy and Research (Feldman and Oberlink 2003). The AdvantAge Initiative organizes the elements of an "age-friendly" community into four domains, as illustrated in figure 6.1. An age-friendly community:

- Adresses basic needs
- Optimizes physical and mental health and well-being
- Promotes social and civic engagement
- Maximizes independence for the frail and people with disabilities

The domains themselves were derived from a series of focus group discussions with elders and community leaders in four diverse U.S. communities. Each domain, as pictured in chapter 6, includes several subsidiary "dimensions," and the dimensions further subsume thirty-three "indicators" of an age-friendly community that are measured through random telephone surveys and employed as data for citizen participation planning efforts. The survey has been conducted in over sixty-three U.S. communities and neighborhoods and with a national sample, providing a wealth of comparative data that enables communities to "benchmark" themselves against others and establish their own goals and objectives. A valuable case study of the employment of the AdvantAge Initiative model is provided in chapter 6, authored by Mia R. Oberlink and Barbara S. Davis. Other descriptive articles have demonstrated its use in other communities in the United States (Hanson and Emlet 2006; Oberlink and Stafford 2009).

On a more global basis, the United Nations has also shifted focus to the environmental aspects of aging. It declared 1999 as International Year of Older Persons: Towards a Society for All Ages, and since that time, it has organized international conferences and research initiatives designed to increase the quality of elder environments in both rural communities and urban areas in support of "active aging." The Madrid International Action Plan on Aging 2002 recommended "creating enabling and supportive environments" as a key focus area, and this is currently being implemented through the World Health Organization Age-Friendly Cities initiative. A framework similar to the Advantage Initiative identifies *eight* domains around which participating communities can assess their needs and organize work (WHO 2007).

The WHO has used this framework to develop a "certification" program that incentivizes communities around the world to plan age-friendly development. As of 2018, the website for the WHO Global Network of Age-Friendly Cities and Communities reports the involvement of "541 cities and communities in 37 countries, covering over 179 million people worldwide" (WHO 2007).

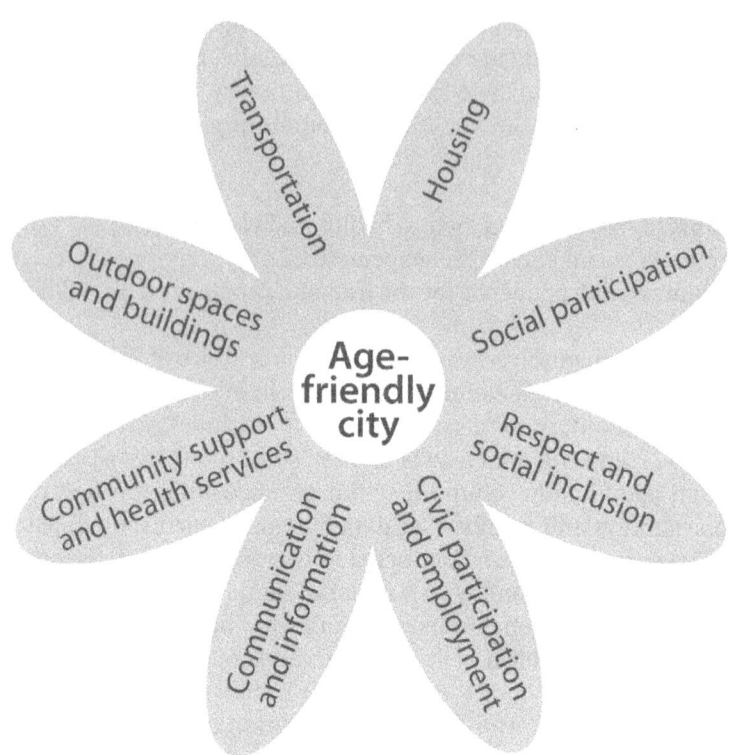

FIGURE 0.1. The WHO age-friendly cities and communities domains (source: WHO)

In 2013 the WHO program arrived on the shores of the United States as the first major city sought certification and developed a comprehensive age-friendly community plan—Portland, Oregon (Portland State University 2013). Subsequent to the acceptance of the WHO program in Portland and then New York City, AARP (American Association of Retired Persons), the largest organization of and for older adults in the world, with a membership of over thirty-seven million, formally adopted the WHO framework and offered support to U.S. communities that sought to participate in the certification process. By 2016, three dozen U.S. towns and cities were seeking certification. By December of 2018, this number had grown to two hundred. This AARP initiative aligned well with the organization's major commitment to broader issues of livability.

The AARP website has become a rich resource of research publications, planning guidelines, policy recommendations, and links to funding sources sponsored by the organization. In a major livable communities project, AARP spent several years developing the Livability Index, a massive database on selected indicators that enables communities (down to the level of the household address) to score themselves across a set of key factors. An overall score can be provided, as can scores in specific areas of focus, including housing, neighborhood, transportation, environment, health, engagement, and opportunity—areas that have a major impact on the quality of life for older adults (any age, actually) (AARP 2015).

In the United States, other major national organizations have taken up this age-friendly community approach with enthusiasm. The National Association of Area Agencies on Aging (2007; with partners) produced the *Blueprint for Action: Developing a Livable Community for All Ages* and piloted age-friendly work in six towns and cities from 2013 through 2014 (https://www.n4a.org/livablecommunities). The Environmental Protection Agency (EPA) ramped up its efforts to help create age-friendly communities through its initiative entitled Building Healthy Communities for Active Aging, though the program has faltered under the current administration. In addition, the Centers for Disease Control (CDC) has developed a focus on healthy environments for aging, with special emphasis on the built environment and public health, tying research, policy, and practice recommendations to the National Prevention Strategy—the surgeon general's commitment to health for all ages and groups (CDC 2011). Grantmakers in Aging, the lead organization for philanthropy in the field of aging, organized Community AGEnda, a three-year national demonstration project in five sites to assist communities with becoming good places to grow up and grow old. The project developed a wide range of tools and resources to help other communities in their age-friendly work (Grantmakers in Aging 2015). The formerly titled Administration on Aging (now part of the Administration for Community Living of Health and Human Services) developed a three-year national aging-in-place demonstration entitled Community Innovations for Aging in Place (2009–12), supporting fourteen diverse communities to create plans and action steps targeting aging-in-place goals (Community Innovations for Aging in Place 2012).

The True Value of the Age-Friendly Community Movement

It seems clear to me that the most valuable contribution of the age-friendly movement, and the encompassing work in evironmental gerontology, can be the radical transformation of the fundamental model of healthy and "successful" aging itself—a critical repositioning of aging as primarily a cultural, not a physical phenomenon. Even dementia is subject to such a critical turn in scholarship (Stafford 1991, 1992). It moves the discourse away from the focus on individual aging bodies and personal responsibility and toward a model that integrates aging and community.

Wendell Berry (2002) offers a useful framework for rethinking the notion of health in such fundamental terms: "To be healthy is literally to be whole. . . . Our sense of wholeness is not just the completeness in ourselves but also is the sense of belonging to others and to our place. . . . I believe that the community, in the fullest sense: a place and all its creatures . . . is the smallest unit of health and that to speak of the health of an isolated individual is a contradiction in terms." Zachary Benedict returns to this theme in chapter 10.

In suggesting that community is the smallest unit of health, we are drawn to an entirely new model of health in old age, one organized around the notion of the age-friendly community. In short, aging (and disability) is not about the body nor about chronological age, rather about place and relationships. It is timely to assess the current state of the age-friendly community movement to see if it does, indeed, part company with the dominant cultural discourse around healthy aging. Ordering and labeling the chapters in this volume was a difficult task, as several themes, challenges, critiques, and suggestions cut across the entire set. Tine Buffel, Chris Phillipson, and Sharon A. Baggett address social iniquities and the political economy. Birgit Wolter, Buffel, and Phillipson discuss urbanism and address the issues surrounding diversity in the everyday life of elders. Zachary Benedict and Nanami Suzuki explore rural aging. Suzanne H. Crowhurst Lennard, Corita Brown, Nancy Henkin, Emi Kiyota, Kristin Bodiford, Arthur Namara, and Luke Nchichupa all address intergenerational design and community development. Alan DeLaTorre, Baggett, and Benedict describe the role of municipal planning for age-friendly communities. Benedict and Nanami Suzuki explore the economic development implications of age-friendly communities. Bodiford, Namara, and Nchichupa provide an outstanding example of participatory research and community development for health and well-being in intergenerational communities. Finally, Marian Barnes tackles the major challenge of the movement—redefining healthy aging as a social phenomenon.

Sharon Baggett has asked of the age-friendly community movement, "Is it a movement?"—a very valid question. While this book does not adequately address the true scope of the work, it seems clear that if it is to be a movement, it must be based on solid theory and manifested in creative, participatory, and structural change. The authors of this volume move us in that direction in very effective ways. There is little discussion of livability, which risks touching on well-being as lifestyle, and a good deal of discussion about the generational structure of society and local communities, cultural difference, income disparities, social justice, urban planning, and communities that have been left behind. That sets an important tone for the movement as it goes forward.

Philip B. Stafford is adjunct professor of anthropology at Indiana University in Bloomington, retiring in 2017 as director of the Indiana University Center on Aging and Community. Focusing on aging and sense of place, his research has been primarily ethnographic and participatory. He has employed the arts and humanities as tools for achieving a greater public understanding of the lifeworld experiences of older adults, and as a consultant, speaker, and writer he has built a wide international audience. He received the Blackburn Award from the Indiana chapter of the American Institute of Architects for contributions to architecture by a non-architect and is a member of the board of the American Society on Aging. He is the author/editor of numerous articles and two books on aging in institutional environments, small towns, and urban neighborhoods.

References

AARP. 2015. "AARP Livability Index." Accessed 19 February 2018. https://www.livabilityindex.aarp.org.

Ball, M. Scott. 2012. *Livable Communities for Aging Populations: Urban Design for Longevity*. Hoboken, NJ: Wiley.

Berry, Wendell. 2002. "Health is Membership." In *The Art of the Commonplace*, 146. New York: Counterpoint.

Buffel, Tine, Sophie Handler, and Christopher Phillipson. 2018. *Age-Friendly Cities and Communities: A Global Perspective*. Bristol: Policy Press.

Carr, Patrick J., and Maria J. Kefalas. 2009. *Hollowing Out the Middle: The Rural Brain Drain and What It Means for America*. Boston: Beacon Press.

CDC (Centers for Disease Control and Prevention). 2011. "National Prevention Strategy." Accessed 2 September 2018. https://www.surgeongeneral.gov/priorities/prevention/strategy/index.html.

Community Innovations for Aging in Place. 2012. Accessed 19 February 2018. http://www.ciaip.org.

Feldman, Penny H., and Mia Oberlink. 2003. "The AdvantAge Initiative: Developing Community Indicators to Promote the Health and Well-Being of Older People." *Family and Community Health* 26(4): 268–74.

Foucault, Michel. 1973. *The Birth of the Clinic: An Archaeology of Medical Perception*. London: Tavistock.

Golant, Stephen M. 2014. *Age-Friendly Communities: Are We Expecting Too Much?* IRPP Insight 5. Montreal: Institute for Research on Public Policy.

Grantmakers in Aging. 2015. Community AGEnda. https://www.giaging.org/initiatives/age-friendly/.

Greenfield, Emily, Mia Oberlink, Andrew E. Scharlach, Margaret B. Neal, and Philip B. Stafford. 2015. "Age-Friendly Community Initiatives: Conceptual Issues and Key Questions." *Gerontologist* 55(2): 191–98. /https://doi.org/10.1093/geront/gnv005.

Hanson, David, and Charles A. Emlet. 2006. "Assessing a Community's Elder-Friendliness: A Case Example of the AdvantAge Initiative." *Family and Community Health* 29(4): 266–78.

Hartman-Stein, Paula E., Edward S. Potkanowicz, and Jeanette S. Bierman. 2003. "Behavioral Determinants of Health Aging: Good News for the Baby Boomer Generation." *Online Journal of Issues in Nursing* 8(2): manuscript 5. Accessed 19 February 2018. www.nursingworld.org/ojin/topic21/tpc21_5.htm.

Howell, Jeremy, and Alan Ingham. 2001. "From Social Problem to Personal Issue: The Language of Lifestyle." *Cultural Studies* 15(2): 326–351.

Lawton, M. Powell, and Lucille Nahemow. 1973. "Towards an Ecological Theory of Adaptation and Aging." *Environmental Design Research* 1(1): 32.

Lewin, Kurt. 1936. *Principles of Topological Psychology*. New York: McGraw-Hill.

Moulaert, Thibauld, and Suzanne Garon, eds. 2016. *Age-Friendly Cities and Communities in International Comparison*. New York: Springer.

National Association of Area Agencies on Aging. 2007. *Blueprint for Action: Developing a Livable Community for all Ages*. https://www.n4a.org/files/07-116-N4A-Blueprint4ActionWCovers.pdf.

Oberlink, Mia, and Philip B. Stafford. 2009. "The Indiana AdvantAge Initiative: Measuring Community Elder-Friendliness and Planning for the Future." *Generations* 2: 91–94.

Population Reference Bureau. 2014. *Total Fertility Rates Have Declined in All Regions 1970–2013*. Population Reference Bureau. http://www.prb.org/Publications/Datasheets/2014/2014-world-population-data sheet/data-sheet.aspx.

Portland State University. 2013. *Action Plan for an Age-Friendly Portland*. Portland, OR: Portland State University. Accessed 19 February 2018. https://www.pdx.edu/ioa/sites/www.pdx.edu.ioa/files/Age-Friendlypercent20Portlandpercent20Actionpercent20Plan percent2010-8-13_0.pdf.

Scharlach, Andrew E., and Amanda Lehning. 2016. *Creating Aging Friendly Communities*. New York: Oxford.

Stafford, Philip B. 1991. "The Social Construction of Alzheimer's Disease." In *Bio-Semiotics: The Semiotic Web*, ed. Thomas A. Sebeok, 393–406. Berlin: Mouton de Gruyter.

———. 1992. "The Nature and Culture of Alzheimer's Disease." *Semiotica* 92: 167–76.

Wahl, Hans-Werner, and Gerald D. Weisman. 2003. "Environmental Gerontology at the Beginning of the New Millennium: Reflections on Its Historical, Empirical, and Theoretical Development." *Gerontologist* 43(5): 616–27.

WHO (World Health Organization). 2005. *Preventing Chronic Diseases: A Vital Investment*. WHO Global Report. Accessed 19 February 2018. http://www.who.int/chp/chronic_disease_report/en/.

———. 2007. *Global Age-Friendly Cities: A Guide*. Accessed 19 February 2018. https://extranet.who.int/agefriendlyworld/.

———. 2013a. *World Youth Report: Youth and Migration*. Accessed 14 July 2018. http://www.unworldyouthreport.org/images/docs/fullreport.pdf.

———. 2013b. *World Health Statistics*. WHO Global Health Observatory. Accessed February 2018. http://www.who.int/gho/publications/world_health_statistics/2013/en.

World Economic Forum. 2012. *Global Population Ageing: Peril or Promise?* Accessed 19 February 2018. https://www.weforum.org/reports/global-population-ageing-peril-or-promise.

PART I
Equity and Sustainability

PART I ADDRESSES ONE OF the major criticisms of the age-friendly movement—that it falls short in addressing the political and economic conditions that favor the privileged position of certain segments of the older adult population and fails to benefit those challenged by lower incomes and other associated forms of difference such as race, ethnicity, gender, and geography.

We start with the big picture. Tine Buffel and Chris Phillipson (chapter 1) ground an understanding of the age-friendly movement within the broadest context of global changes affecting not only older adults but multiple populations. Moreover, they trace the influence of these forces (migration, crime, industrialization and deindustrialization, disinvestment in certain urban spaces, privatization of public space, and others) to the neighborhood level. They surface and reveal the structural inequities particularly burdensome on elderly individuals and groups—inequities not typically addressed through soft, more passive calls for livability that fall short in the face of austerity-driven policies. While acknowledging the pertinence and contributions of environmental gerontology as a platform for age-friendly research, they argue for a more effective extension of the research into policy and action.

This necessary linkage between theory and action is well demonstrated by Sharon A. Baggett (chapter 2), who seeks to embed age-friendly work within the broader context of theories of urban change. She extends Buffel's and Phillipson's focus on the "right to the city" and reviews significant traditions in urban studies such as the just city, urban citizenship, and models of community change such as exemplified by the Industrial Areas Foundation. While she is not reliant on environmental gerontology as a theoretical platform, she, refreshingly, uses the concept of urban citizenship to develop a practical outcome of municipal policy influence actually led by older adults and people with disabilities in alliance. Moreover, she does not assume that without "training," any group of citizens can effectively mount a social change effort. She describes a project developed with Jennie Todd that equips older adults with a knowledge base that elevates their capacity to converse with planning technocrats, city leaders, and the general public. Moreover, she effectively demonstrates the power of identifying the common strengths and challenges faced not only by older adults but by another marginalized group—people with developmental and cognitive disabilities. With this, Baggett and Todd provide an innovative model for an alliance between elders and people with disabilities, a major limitation of current advocacy efforts in both aging and disability silos.

Insofar as both chapters 1 and 2 emphasize the importance of access to public spaces as a matter of social justice and equity, in chapter 3 Suzanne H. Crowhurst Lennard provides a practical segue into the manner in which the design of those spaces can, in fact, lead to improvements in the quality of social life and mental health of both older adults and children. She provides a comprehensive overview of the genius of public spaces in old world cities, where plazas, piazzas, squares, and parks support a rich and vibrant social life across generational differences. Moreover, she provides an incisive critique of public spaces (if they exist at all) in a post-automobile, privatized world.

Alan DeLaTorre (chapter 4) extends the discussion of equity by building a bridge to the sustainable development movement, which, within the field of planning, is more pervasive than the age-friendly thread. He argues that attention to issues across the life span has not been a prime feature of the sustainable development movement, but that doing just that—incorporating an age-friendly approach—will strengthen the sustainability movement itself. He demonstrates how the use of green building technologies, durable materials, and accessibility and affordability features of housing for seniors is a central value totally aligned with the movement toward more sustainable communities. In his research he documents this blind spot in the sustainability movement and, as a positive contribution, describes the work in Portland, Oregon, meant to integrate these two major movements through public policy. If the age-friendly movement is to gain traction within the much larger field of urban planning and design, the Portland initiative points to the necessary elements.

1 CREATING AGE-FRIENDLY COMMUNITIES IN URBAN ENVIRONMENTS
Research Issues and Policy Recommendations

Tine Buffel and Chris Phillipson

Introduction

TWO MAJOR FORCES ARE SET to shape the quality of daily life in the twenty-first century: population aging on the one side and urbanization on the other. Both have become dominant concerns for public policy, with significant implications for all types of communities—from the most isolated to the most densely populated. By 2030, two-thirds of the world's population will be residing in cities; at that point many of the major urban areas in the developed world will have 25 percent or more of their populations aged sixty and over. Katz, Altman, and Wagner (2008: 474) view the present century as the "urban age," one that is unfolding at a "dizzying pace and with a scale, diversity, complexity, and level of connectivity that challenges traditional paradigms and renders many conventional needs and practices obsolete." Cities are now regarded as central to economic development, attracting waves of migrants and supporting new knowledge-based industries (Burdett and Hall 2017). However, the extent to which the new "urban age" will produce "age-friendly" communities, creating opportunities for older people as well as strengthening ties across different age and social groups, remains uncertain. Such concerns may also be linked with the emergence of conflicts within urban space arising from inequalities in access and influence among different social and generational groups.

This chapter examines some of the research and policy issues that arise from attempts to build age-friendly communities. The discussion begins by reviewing some of the factors driving the age-friendly debate, with a focus on issues relating to urban change and population aging. The chapter reviews some of the research literature available for assessing age-friendly issues, focusing on debates in environmental gerontology and urban sociology. The chapter then provides a critical assessment of some of the limitations of the age-friendly debate before moving to a consideration of some alternative policy options and recommendations.

Factors Influencing the Development of the Age-Friendly Approach

Although aging and urbanization can rightly be viewed as major trends for the present century, they have been separated in the field of research. This has happened despite urging from pioneer researchers of urban society such as Lewis Mumford (1956) that we should be seeking "age integration" rather than "age segregation" in our cities. Against this, the direction of policy over the postwar period appears to have been largely in the opposite direction, with the focus on developing age-segregated provision such as sheltered housing (in the United Kingdom in the 1950s and 1960s) through to retirement communities and the more recent evolution of urban retirement villages. An alternative approach, however, has stressed the importance of developing what has been termed by the World Health Organization (WHO 2007) as "age-friendly communities." Accordingly, "it should be normal in an age-friendly city for the natural and built environment to anticipate users with different capacities instead of designing for the mythical 'average' (i.e. young) person. An age-friendly city emphasizes enablement rather than disablement; it is friendly for all ages and not just 'elder-friendly'" (WHO 2007: 72; see also Fitzgerald and Caro 2014; Buffel, Handler, and Phillipson 2018). In 2010, the WHO launched the Global Network of Age-Friendly Cities in an attempt to encourage implementation of policy recommendations from the 2006 project. By 2018 there were over six hundred participating cities and communities across thirty-seven countries worldwide.

A number of factors may be cited as influencing the development of the age-friendly approach: first, the global impact of demographic change, with a wide range of housing and community needs emerging among those aged fifty and over (Menec et al. 2011); second, the policy goal of supporting people in their own homes for as long as possible—the idea of "aging in place" (Wiles et al. 2012); third, awareness of the impact of urban change on the lives of older people, notably in areas experiencing social and economic deprivation (Buffel, Phillipson, and Scharf 2013); and fourth, debates about "good" or "optimal" places to age, these stimulated by the growth of retirement housing and recognition of what has been termed "naturally occurring retirement communities" (Scharlach and Lehning 2013).

The drive to create age-friendly cities may also be placed in the context of attempts to improve the quality of life for people living in urban environments. This was reflected in new perspectives influencing urban development over the course of the 1990s and early 2000s—for example, ideas around "sustainable" (Satterthwaite 1999) and "harmonious cities" (UN-Habitat 2008). The former raised questions about managing urban growth in a manner able to meet the needs of future as well as current generations. The idea of "harmonious" development emphasized values such as "tolerance, fairness, social justice and good governance" (UN-Habitat 2008), these regarded as essential principles of urban planning. Such themes were also influential in the elaboration of ideas (as noted above) associated with "lifetime homes" and "lifetime neighburhoods" (Department of Community and Local Government 2008; Atlanta Regional Commission 2009), which emerged alongside recognition of the need for more systematic interventions to support population aging at a community level. The key issue behind the "lifetime" concept was an understanding that effective support for older people within neighborhoods would require a range of interventions linking different parts of the urban system—from housing and the design of streets to transportation and improved accessibility to shops and services.

These developments took place against a backdrop of radical change affecting many urban environments. Among the most important of these have been widening economic inequalities within cities (Wacquant 2008; Burdett and Hall 2017); the impact of rural migration on urban environments and the displacement of traditional sources of support for older people (Lloyd-Sherlock, Barrientos, and Mase 2012); the influence of economic globalization and the rise of "world cities" (Sassen 2012); and, finally, increasing inequality between cities affected by either rapid industrialization or deindustrialization in the case of many medium-sized cities (Hall 2014). As will be argued at different points in this chapter, such developments have received only limited acknowledgment within the age-friendly movement, hence the need for the critical perspective developed in this chapter. Moreover, much of the debate about age-friendly cities remains disconnected from the pressures on vulnerable groups given the range of changes affecting cities. While the dominant approach has been toward encouraging what came to be termed "aging in place" (Wiles et al. 2012), the places in which older people were aging often proved hostile and challenging (Buffel et al. 2013). The next section of this chapter examines this point in relation to research in the field of environmental gerontology, reviewing findings that highlight the pressures on developing an age-friendly approach within urban environments.

Environmental Gerontology and Age-Friendly Cities

An important disconnect in the age-friendly debate has been with trends in the field of environmental gerontology, an approach that has emphasized the need for an in-depth understanding of both the objective and subjective processes of aging individuals interacting with their physical-social settings (Wahl and Oswald 2010). Four different approaches have contributed to the advancement of environmental gerontology (Peace et al. 2007; Wahl and Oswald 2010; Phillipson 2011): "integration" versus "segregation" debates in the field of housing; theoretical models examining the person-environment fit; research on place attachment and the construction of identity; and studies examining the impact of neighborhood and community change.

Work relating to housing provided the initial focus for research on environmental issues, with studies in the 1950s and 1960s using this topic to explore arguments around "age integration" versus "age segregation" (Kleemier 1956). Such debates reflected two competing theories that dominated research in social gerontology during this period—activity and disengagement theory (Havighurst and Albrecht 1953; Cumming and Henry 1961), each presenting contrasting views about the extent to which older people wish to be "integrated" into or "segregated" from mainstream society. An additional factor influencing this work, however, was the rise of retirement communities in North America, from the 1950s onward. Such developments raised several questions about the (dis)advantages of "same-age" communities, especially regarding security, social, physical and mental well-being, and recreational facilities. This debate was subsequently extended through research exploring the benefits of different types of age mix within residential settings for friendship formation and social integration (Rosow 1967).

By the 1970s, researchers shifted their focus to examining the reasons why some physical contexts achieved a better "fit" with the needs and abilities of older residents than others, with the Press Competence (PC) model (Lawton 1980) emerging as a dominant framework for understanding person-environment relationships. The underlying assumption of this approach is that individual behavior is a result of congruence between the demand character of the environment (environmental press) and the capabilities of the person to deal with that demand (personal competence) (Lawton 1980; see also Wahl and Oswald 2010). *Personal competence* is generally recognized as a characteristic of the individual, typically defined as internal (e.g., personality, physical and mental health, skills, and cognitive ability) and external (e.g., financial status and social networks), and is viewed on a continuum from low to high. *Environmental press* examines the contextual demands of the environment, such as aesthetic appearance, walkability, amenities, and fear of crime, and how people respond to these based on their competence level (Lawton 1980). As with personal competence, environmental press is measured on a scale from low to high. With this approach, individuals with low competence encountering strong environmental press are more likely to have maladaptive behavior compared with those showing high competence encountering weak environmental press, where behavior is likely to be adaptive or positive. The PC model has been especially influential in showing how mismatches between personal needs and environmental options to fulfill these needs can undermine well-being and mental health (Wahl and Oswald 2010).

New approaches emerged through the 1980s and 1990s focusing on experiential perspectives relating to aging and the environment (Rowles 1978, 1983; Rubinstein and Parmelee 1992). These raised issues about the meanings associated with places such as the home and neighborhood. In contrast to earlier perspectives that focused mainly on the role of the objective, physical-spatial environment, research on place attachment addresses affective, cognitive, and behavioral ties that people develop with their physical surroundings, thereby transforming "space" into "place" (Peace et al. 2007; Wahl and Oswald 2010). More recent work has focused on the importance of neighborhood and community change for understanding the dynamics of aging in place. Such themes have been developed through, for example, work by Scharf et al. (2002, 2005) in deprived urban communities in England. The researchers took the concept of social exclusion—the extent of participation or no participation in mainstream institutions—to explore issues facing older people in deprived urban communities. The authors identified five forms of social exclusion relevant to the circumstances of older people living in inner-city areas: exclusion from material resources, social relations, civic activities, basic services, and neighborhood ties. Linking theoretical ideas about space and place with the concept of social exclusion, Scharf et al. (2005) suggested that attachment to the environment might be compromised or diminished by structural challenges affecting communities, these increasing the vulnerability of older people aging in place. This approach has been further developed with studies examining the impact of gentrification on aging populations living in urban environments (Ogg 2005; Phillipson 2007; Burns, Lavoie, and Rose 2012).

Community studies involving older people suggest that they may be especially affected by processes associated with social exclusion. Research suggests that older people derive a strong sense of emotional attachment from both their home and the surrounding community (Phillipson et al. 2001; Rowles and Chaudhury 2005; Buffel et al. 2013). Indeed, Rowles

(1978: 200) suggests that "selective intensification of feelings about spaces" might represent "a universal strategy employed by older people to facilitate maintaining a sense of identity within a changing environment." While this may be possible in relatively secure and stable neighborhoods, some residential settings impede the maintenance of identity in old age. The argument, which requires detailed empirical testing, is that this is much more likely in certain types of urban environments than in others or in rural areas. It may, for example, be especially the case in the "zones of transition" marked by a rapid turnover of people and buildings and in unpopular urban neighborhoods characterized by low housing demand and abandonment by all but the poorest and least mobile residents (Rogers and Power 2000; Newman 2003). Disadvantaged urban neighborhoods, and the people who reside in them, may also be prone to "institutional isolation" (Gans 1972) as services and agencies withdraw, resulting in restricted access to basic facilities such as grocery stores, telephones, and banking (Scharf et al. 2002).

Urban areas also host a growing number of first-generation migrants who experience especially acute problems of poverty and poor housing. The study by Scharf et al. (2002) found that almost eight out of ten older Somali migrants and nearly seven out of ten older people of Pakistani origin found it very difficult to manage on their current incomes. Many of them had to cut back on essentials, including food, and had to limit their social activities. Similarly, Becker (2003: 135) highlighted the precariousness of the living conditions of older migrants living in inner-city neighborhoods in Northern California. This study found that many older people belonging to minority ethnic groups lived in rooms without bathrooms or kitchens, and many others lived in overcrowded apartments. The neighborhoods in which they lived were areas with a long history of illegal activities such as drug dealing, prostitution, and gambling, these presenting challenges to create a sense of home in old age (see, further, Buffel et al. 2013).

High rates of crime in deprived neighborhoods may also contribute to feelings of insecurity in old age (Smith 2009; Livingston, Bailey, and Kearns 2010). The experience of crime and the perceived risk of criminal victimization may act as psychological barriers that deter older people from leaving their homes, especially after dark (Scharf et al. 2002). Evidence from the Belgian Aging Studies (De Donder et al. 2012) demonstrates that neighborhoods with poor physical environments and limited access to services also increase feelings of insecurity. Conversely, older people who enjoy living in their neighborhood and who influence the design of their neighborhood (e.g., through political participation) express fewer problems relating to lack of safety and security. Pain (2000: 365) makes the point here that fear of crime should be seen as "inseparable from a range of social and economic problems concerned with housing, employment, environmental planning and social exclusion."

Critical Issues for Developing Age-Friendly Cities

Building on the review of the research literature, what are some of the main challenges to be faced in respect to building age-friendly environments? Several issues can be identified. First, as Golant (2014: 13) observes, it is important to "ask whether communities have acquired the structural capacity—that is, resources and opportunities—to accommodate the needs and goals of their aging populations and to help improve their physical and psychological well-being." In fact, as already highlighted, many of the neighborhoods in which older people live may have been destabilized through global economic change. Where this is the case, interventions may be required that raise the level of resources within communities before age-friendly policies can begin to be implemented. Developing a related theme, Scharlach (2012: 28) observes that "social policy and discourse regarding the needs of older persons pay little attention to quality of life, social integration, community participation, and other non-economic outcomes of helping elders to remain in familiar homes and neighborhoods." Reflecting on this, he argues for a shift from the traditional focus around "aging in place" to one of "aging in community" (see, further, Stafford 2009).

Second, greater attention needs to be given to the tension between the social needs associated with old age and the private ownership of public space. Logan and Molotch (cited in Zukin 2010) make the point here that "city dwellers want to enjoy the use-values of their communities and homes, but developers are interested in maximizing exchange values—in making money." This disconnect has become especially important in the context of meeting the needs of groups—notably older people—for whom the neighborhood plays a central role in shaping the quality of daily life (Gardner 2011). Tonkiss (2005: 74) makes the point that "the political economy of the city is not confined ... to questions of who owns what, but with how this spatial economy is regulated in terms of access, exclusion and control."

Third, implementing the age-friendly approach may encounter obstacles arising from policies associated with economic austerity (Clark 2014). Here, there are significant pressures to reduce funding for the type of activities associated with the WHO model. Buffel et al. (2014) highlighted this in their assessment of age-friendly policies in Brussels and Manchester—both members of the WHO Global Network. In the case of the former, recessionary pressures meant that the council had been unable to increase public spending on community health and social care in line with increases in demand. A consensus had emerged that more investment was required to improve support to carers, as well as develop more flexible and culturally sensitive services in response to the challenges posed by increasing diversity in the older population. In the case of Manchester, plans to promote age-friendly neighborhoods have been affected by budget cuts that reduce public services such as libraries, information and advice centers, and day care facilities for groups such as older people. Threats to services may lead to a public perception that the "age-friendly" brand is unrealistic and unlikely to be implemented given restrictions on public spending.

Fourth, given the global ambitions of the age-friendly movement, priority must be given to supporting older people displaced from their homes through civil wars and conflicts between nation-states. In the second decade of the twenty-first century, elderly people in countries such as Sierra Leone, Syria, and Ukraine have found themselves to be disproportionately at risk of forced evacuation and in need of humanitarian assistance (Adele 2013; Marzouk 2013; Gillam 2015). Laudable though the ambition to support aging in place may be, many of the communities in which older people live are being progressively undermined through political strife and the speed of economic change—the latter through accelerated industrialization (as in China) or the collapse of core industries affecting many communities in the Global North.

New Policies to Promote Age-Friendly Environments

For all their limitations, adapting urban living to aging populations will be a key issue for public policy. And urban environments do have numerous benefits for older people: as centers for creativity and innovation, providing facilities that raise the quality of daily living, and delivering specialist resources for minority groups. The key challenge thus becomes ensuring that older people are recognized as having a central role to play in the cultural, economic, and social life of cities. Implementing this agenda will, however, require changes to the age-friendly model, with four major areas discussed below: first, recognizing the diversity of cities and the implications for the age-friendly approach; second, developing new forms of "urban citizenship" that support changing needs across the life course; third, understanding changes affecting the body in late old age; and fourth, creating opportunities to involve aging populations more effectively in the planning and regeneration of neighborhoods.

The first issue concerns applying age-friendliness in a way that recognizes the complexity of the urban environment. The techniques for ensuring an age-friendly approach will vary considerably depending on the characteristics of urban change and development. While the trend toward urban living is worldwide, the pattern of urban growth demonstrates huge variation: shrinking city populations in the developed world (Europe especially); and accelerating urbanization in Africa and Asia, with both continents demonstrating a mix of rapidly expanding cities in some cases, declining ones in others (UN-Habitat 2010). Age-friendly approaches will also need to vary according to the size of a city. The approach might, for example, be different in Europe, where small cities with fewer than five hundred thousand residents are the norm, as compared with the United States, where large urban agglomerations (with populations of between two and five million) are much more common. Securing age-friendliness in the context of the rise of "megacities" and "hyper-cities" (the latter with populations of twenty million or more) provides another variation. At the same time, processes for developing age-friendliness will need radical adaptation given the slum cities prevalent in Southern Asia and sub-Saharan Africa (UN-Habitat, 2012). The bulk of population growth in these continents has taken place largely through the rise of slums, many of these located on the periphery of capital cities (Davis 2006). The problem of reaching older people and migrants who are aging in place and housed in temporary accommodation bereft of basic facilities underlines the need for new models of intervention that can respond to the highly unequal contexts experienced by the urban elderly across the world.

A second issue concerns the need to link the debate about developing age-friendly cities to ideas about urban citizenship and the right to make full use of the city (Baggett, chapter 2 in this volume). The concept of "the right to the city" is closely associated with the work of Lefebvre (1991) and has been used in debates around access to public space—or, in Harvey's terms (2009: 315), the right to "make and remake our cities and ourselves under circumstances in which private capital is dominating the urban process." Commenting on Lefebvre's work, Purcell (2003: 577–78) argues that "the right to the city" implies two main rights for its inhabitants. The first is to *appropriate* urban space; the right to "full and complete usage" of the city. The second concerns the right to *participate* centrally in decision-making surrounding the production of urban space. These issues may be of importance for older people who become reliant upon their immediate environment for achieving a fulfilling existence in old age. However, the so-called "paradox of neighborhood participation" (Buffel, Phillipson, and Scharf 2012) applies especially well to older people, that is, they tend to spend a lot of time in their neighborhood (*being part of the city*), but are often among the last to be engaged when it comes to decision-making processes within their neighborhood (*taking part in the city*). While cities are increasingly viewed as key drivers of a nation's economic and cultural success, their reconstruction is often to the detriment of those outside the labor market, especially those with low socioeconomic status. Achieving recognition of the needs of different generations within cities and exploiting the potential of the city for groups of whatever age will be central to the process of making cities more age-friendly.

A third observation is that linking age-friendliness with urban citizenship also draws attention to changing needs associated with age and recognition of the frailty of the human body. Geographical perspectives on cities assert that "all urban dwellers have to negotiate the city *practically* [author's emphasis], and work through the dilemmas, problems and possibilities of 'getting by' in the city" (Hubbard 2006: 113; see also Skinner, Andrews, and Cutchin 2017). And feminist perspectives on the use of urban space highlight the way in which "women's spatial practice is constrained by geographies of violence and fear" (Tonkiss 2005: 94–95). Such ideas and the extent to which older people are to some degree "prisoners of space" (Rowles 1978) are especially relevant to aging in the city—both in global cities undergoing accelerated change and those cities facing deindustrialization. Both contexts raise dilemmas in the context of mental and physical vulnerabilities. Older men and women may find difficulties "creating" space within cities: global cities raise tensions between a "hyper-mobile" minority and those aging in place; deindustrializing cities (with shrinking populations) create problems arising from the withdrawal of an economic base that can maintain sustainable networks for different social groups. The challenge here then is creating an urban environment that supports the autonomy of the aging body and the equal rights of older people with others to a share of urban space. This issue will be especially important to implement at a local level, with a focus on improving the quality of urban design and promoting safety and inclusion as key features of urban living (Buffel, Handler, and Phillipson 2018; Lennard, chapter 3 in this volume).

Fourth, and following the above, making cities more age-friendly will require radical interventions in terms of involving older people as well as the generation that is approaching old age as key actors in setting the agenda for future urban development. Urban regeneration policies, for instance, can benefit from the skills and experience of older people and the attachment and involvement they bring to their communities (Simpson 2010). Policy strategies for making cities more age-friendly will therefore require a clear assessment of the (structural) barriers and vehicles to engaging older people in community redevelopment. At the same time, there is also a need to develop strategies targeted at different groups within the older population, with awareness, for example, of contrasting issues faced by different ethnic groups, people with particular physical or mental health needs, and those living in areas with poor housing alongside high population turnover (Kelly-Moore and Thorpe 2012).

Fifth, developing the age-friendly approach requires a clearer focus on the importance of the neighborhood in the lives of older people (Gardner 2011). Neighborhoods that are designed to make it easy and enjoyable to go outdoors can help people attain recommended levels of physical activity. Access to natural environments and green, open spaces are themselves important in promoting health and well-being (Stafford 2009). Extending the range of housing options within communities is another important element in an age-friendly approach. To date progress has been slow in increasing choice, beyond specialist provision such as retirement villages and extra-care housing. The reality, however, is that older people will continue to prefer to live in communities with a mix of ages. Interest in a greater variety of housing options (such as cooperative housing and house sharing) is likely to grow given the growth of single-person households. Meeting this demand will require a creative partnership between older people, housing associations, building companies, and other relevant groups. In many cases, groups of older people will themselves want to take control in developing new types of housing more directly tailored to the needs and aspirations they bring to daily life (Brenton 2013). Finally, creating safe spaces within neighborhoods is an important part of an age-friendly approach. In some cases, this will draw on existing resources such as libraries, community centers, colleges, and sheltered housing schemes. Work is needed to ensure that groups of older people in areas of high economic deprivation have access to spaces that allow full participation within the community. Outreach activities to those in residential homes, befriending schemes for those who are housebound, and extending access to educational programs are also important areas for expansion within communities (Achenbaum 2005).

Conclusion: Planning Cities for All Ages

Developing cities that meet the interests of all generations remains an important goal for economic and social policy. The future of communities across the world will in large part be determined by the response made to achieving a higher quality of life for their older citizens. A crucial part of this response must lie in creating supportive environments providing access to a range of facilities and services. However, the research and policy agenda will need to change in significant ways if this is to be realized. First, the issues raised by developing age-friendly communities within complex urban environments will require a more coherent link between research and policy than has thus far been achieved. Research on environmental aspects of aging has an impressive literature to its name, yet it remains detached from analyzing the impact of powerful global and economic forces transforming the physical and social context of cities. To remedy this will require, as has been argued in this chapter, closer integration with developments in disciplines such as urban sociology, urban economics, and human geography. Developing optimum environments for aging must be regarded as an interdisciplinary enterprise requiring understanding of the impact on older people of developments such as the changing dynamics of urban poverty, the impact of urban renewal and regeneration, the influence of transnational networks, and changing relations between different class-, gender-, ethnic-, and age-based groups.

Second, in keeping with the approach taken in this chapter, given the rapid changes affecting many urban areas, new approaches to understanding older people's relationship to urban change—and city development in particular—is urgently required. In particular, there is a strong case for more research in urban ethnography to capture the disparate experiences of those living in cities that are now experiencing intense global change and that are strongly influenced by complex patterns of migration on the one side and population aging on the other. Sassen (2000: 146) pointed to the need for detailed fieldwork as a "necessary step in capturing many aspects of the urban condition" (see also Wacquant 2008); such work will be especially important for understanding the impact of urban growth on groups such as migrants aging in place, single people, and those on low incomes. Urban sociology was founded (through the work of the Chicago School from the 1920s) upon detailed studies of experiences of urban life, especially of disadvantaged and insecure people from different migrant populations. Ethnographies would bring to the surface the attitudes, motivations, and experiences of older people who are aging in place and will deepen our understanding about the way in which cities are changing and about the positive and negative contributions that the changes have on the quality of daily life in old age.

Finally, incorporating issues about aging in urban environments with the wider debate concerning spatial justice is also essential. Here, we would underline the relevance of Soja's (2010: 19) argument that the "geographies in which we live can have both positive and negative effects on our lives.... They are not just dead background or a neutral physical stage for the human drama but are filled with material and imagined forces that can hurt us or help us in nearly everything we do, individually and collectively." He concludes, "This is a vitally important part of the new spatial consciousness, making us aware that the geographies in which we live can intensify and sustain our exploitation as workers, support oppressive forms of cultural and political domination based on race, gender, and nationality, and aggravate all forms of discrimination and injustice." Ensuring spatial justice for older people is now a crucial part of this debate, with developing an integrated approach to demographic and urban change representing a key task for research and public policy.

Tine Buffel is Senior Research Fellow in the School of Social Sciences at the University of Manchester, United Kingdom. Dr. Buffel is funded through the Economic and Social Research Council Future Leaders Scheme on a project that involves a comparative study of social exclusion among older people living in three urban areas in three European national states. She has published extensively on a range of social and urban policy issues. Before coming to Manchester, Dr. Buffel was a research associate and lecturer in educational sciences at the Free University of Brussels (VUB). Her latest (coedited) book is *Age-Friendly Cities and Communities: A Global Perspective* (Policy Press, 2018)

Chris Phillipson is professor of sociology and social gerontology at the University of Manchester. He was the director of the Manchester Institute for Collaborative Research into Ageing (2013–16). He is a past president of the British Society of Gerontology. He has published extensively in the field of social aging. His latest (coedited) book is *Age-Friendly Cities and Communities: A Global Perspective* (Policy Press, 2018).

References

Achenbaum, W. Andrew. 2005. *Older Americans, Vital Communities: A Bold Vision for Societal Aging*. Baltimore: John Hopkins University Press.
Adele, Fidelis. 2013. "From Valuable to Vulnerable." Accessed 31 January 2017. http://www.dandc.eu/en/article/after-civil-war-many-old-people-must-fend-themselves-sierra-leone.
Atlanta Regional Commission. 2009. *Lifelong Communities: A Framework for Planning.* Accessed 28 January 2017. http://www.atlantaregional.com/aging-sources/life longcommunities/lifelongcommunities}.
Becker, Gay. 2003. "Meanings of Place and Displacement in Three Groups of Older Immigrants." *Journal of Aging Studies* 17(2): 129–49.
Brenton, Maria. 2013. *Senior Co-housing Communities: An Alternative Approach*. York: Joseph Rowntree Foundation.
Buffel, Tine, Sophie Handler, and Chris Phillipson, eds. 2018. *Age-Friendly Cities and Communities: A Global Perspective*. Bristol: Policy Press.
Buffel, Tine, Paul McGarry, Chris Phillipson, Liesbeth De Donder, Sara Dury, Nico De Witte, and Ann Sofie Smetcoran. 2014. "Developing Age-Friendly Cities: Case Studies from Brussels and Manchester and Implications for Policy and Practice." *Journal of Aging and Social Policy* 26(1–2): 52–72.

Buffel, Tine, Chris Phillipson, and Thomas Scharf. 2012. "Ageing in Urban Environments: Developing 'Age-Friendly' Cities." *Critical Social Policy* 32(4): 597–617.

Buffel, Tine, Chris Phillipson, and Thomas Scharf. 2013. "Experiences of Neighborhood Exclusion and Inclusion among Older People Living in Deprived Inner-City Areas in Belgium and England." *Aging & Society* 33(special issue 01): 89–109.

Burdett, Ricky, and Suzanne Hall. 2017. *The Sage Handbook of the 21st Century City*. London: Sage Books.

Burns, Victoria F., Jean-Pierre Lavoie, and Damaris Rose. 2012. "Revisiting the Role of Neighbourhood Change in Social Exclusion and Inclusion of Older People." *Journal of Aging Research*. Accessed 4 March 2017. http://www.hindawi.com/journals/jar/2012/148287/.

Clark, Tom, and Anthony Heath. 2014. *Hard Times: The Divisive Toll of the Economic Slump*. New Haven, CT: Yale University Press.

Cumming, Elaine, and William E. Henry. 1961. *Growing Older: The Process of Disengagement*. New York: Basic Books.

Davis, Mike. 2006. *Planet of Slums*. London: Verso Books

De Donder, Liesbeth, Nico De Witte, Tine Buffel, Sara Dury, and Dominique Verté. 2012. "Social Capital and Feelings of Unsafety in Later Life." *Research into Aging* 34(2): 425–48.

Department of Community and Local Government. 2008. *Lifetime Homes and Lifetime Neighbourhoods: A National Strategy for Housing in an Aging Society*. London: Department for Communities and Local Government.

Fitzgerald, Kelly G., and Frank Caro. 2014. "An Overview of Age-Friendly Cities and Communities around the World." *Journal of Aging and Social Policy* 26(1–2): 1–18.

Gardner, Paula. 2011. "Natural Neighbourhood Networks: Important Social Networks in the Lives of Older People Aging in Place." *Journal of Aging Studies* 25(3): 263–271.

Gillam, Sarah. 2015. "Ukraine Crisis Has Huge Impact on Older People." Accessed 1 January 2018. http://www.helpage.org/newsroom/latest-news/ukraine-crisis-has-huge-impact-on-older-people/.

Golant, Stephen. 2014. *Age-Friendly Communities: Are We Expecting Too Much?* Montreal: Institute for Research on Public Policy.

Hall, Peter. 2014. *Good Cities, Better Lives*. London: Routledge.

Harvey, David. 2009. *Social Justice and the City*. Revised ed. Athens, GA: University of Georgia Press.

Havighurst, Robert J., and Ruth Albrecht. 1953. *Older People*. New York: Longmans, Green.

Horgas, Ann L., Hans-Ulrich Wilms, and Margret M. Baltes. 1998. "Daily Life in Very Old Age: Everyday Activities as Expressions of Daily Life." *Gerontologist* 38(5): 556–68.

Hubbard, Phil. 2006. *City*. London: Routledge.

Katz, Bruce, Andy Altman, and Julie Wagner. 2008. "An Agenda for the Urban Age." In *The Endless City*, ed. Ricky Burdett and Deyan Sudjic, 474–81. London: Phaidon.

Kelly-Moore, Jessica, and Roland Thorpe. 2012. "Age in Place and Place in Age: Advancing the Inquiry on Neighborhoods and Minority Older Adults." In *Handbook of Minority Aging*, ed. Keith Whitfield and Tamara Baker, 497–506. New York: Springer.

Kleemier, Robert. 1956. "Environmental Settings and the Aging Process." In *Psycho-

logical Aspects of Aging, ed. John Anderson, 105–116. Washington, DC: American Psychological Association.

Lawton, M. P. 1980. *Environment and Aging*. Pacific Grove, CA: Brooks/Cole Publishing.

Lefebvre, Henri. 1991. *The Production of Space*. Oxford: Blackwell.

Livingston, Mark, Nick Bailey, and Ade Kearns. 2010. "Neighbourhood Attachment in Deprived Areas: Evidence from the North of England." *Journal of Housing and the Built Environment* 25: 409–27.

Lloyd-Sherlock, Peter, Armando Barrientos, and Julia Mase. 2012. "Social Inclusion of Older People in Developing Countries: Relations and Resources." In *From Exclusion to Inclusion in Old Age: A Global Challenge*, ed. Thomas Scharf and Norah Keating, 51–70. Bristol: Policy Press.

Marzouk, Sarah. 2013. "Help Age Concerned about Old People Affected by Syria Crisis." Accessed 30 January 2017. http://www.helpage.org/newsroom/latest-news/helpage-concerned-about-older-people-affected-by-syria-crisis/.

Menec, Verena H., Robin Means, Norah Keating, Graham Parkhurst, and Jacquie Eales. 2011. "Conceptualizing Age-Friendly Communities." *Canadian Journal on Aging* 30(3): 479–93.

Mumford, Lewis. 1956. "For Older People—Not Segregation but Integration." *Architectural Record* 119: 109–16.

Newman, Kathleen. 2003. *A Different Shade of Gray*. New York: New Press.

Ogg, Jim. 2005. *Heat Wave*. London: Young Foundation.

Oswald, Frank, and Hand-Werner Wahl. 2005. "Dimensions of the Meaning of Home in Later Life." In *Home and Identity in Later Life: International Perspectives*, ed. Graham Rowles and Habib Chaudhury, 21–46. New York: Springer.

Pain, Rachel. 2000. "Place, Social Relations and the Fear of Crime: A Review." *Progress in Human Geography* 24(3): 365–87.

Peace, Sheila, Hans-Werner Wahl, Heidrun Mollenkopf, and Frank Oswald. 2007. "Environment and Aging." In *Aging in Society*, ed. John Bond, Sheila Peace, Freya Dittmann-Kohli, and Gerben Westerhof, 209–34. London: Sage.

Phillipson, Chris. 2007. "The 'Elected' and the 'Excluded': Sociological Perspectives on the Experience of Place and Community in Old Age." *Aging & Society* 27: 321–42.

———. 2010. "Growing Old in the 'Century of the City.'" In *The Sage Handbook of Social Gerontology*, ed. Dale Dannefer and Chris Phillipson, 597–606. London: Sage.

———. 2011. "Developing Age-Friendly Communities: New Approaches to Growing Old in Urban Environments." In *Handbook of Sociology of Aging*, ed. J. L. Angel and R. Settersten, 279–293. New York: Springer Verlag.

Phillipson, Chris, Miriam Bernard, Judith Phillips, and Jim Ogg. 2001. *The Family and Community Life of Older People*. London: Routledge.

Purcell, Mark. 2003. "Citizenship and the Right to the Global City: Reimagining the Capitalist World Order." *International Journal of Urban and Regional Research* 27(3): 564–90.

Rogers, Richard, and Ann Power. 2000. *Cities for a Small Country*. London: Faber.

Rosow, Irving. 1967. *Social Integration of the Aged*. New York: Free Press.

Rowles, Graham. 1978. *Prisoners of Space? Exploring the Geographical Experience of Older People*. Colorado: Westview Press.

———. 1983. "Place and Personal Identity in Old Age: Observations from Appalachia." *Journal of Environmental Psychology* 3(3): 299–313.

Rowles, Graham, and Habib Chaudhury, eds. 2005. *Home and Identity in Later Life: International Perspectives.* New York: Springer.
Rowles, Graham, Frank Oswald, and Elizabeth G. Hunter. 2004. "Interior Living Environments in Old Age." In *Annual Review of Gerontology and Geriatrics: Aging in Context; Socio-Physical Environments,* ed. Hans-Werner Wahl, Rick Scheidt, and Paul Windley, 167–94. New York: Springer.
Rowles, Graham, and John F. Watkins. 2003. "History, Habit and Hearth: On Making Spaces into Places." In *Aging Independently: Living Arrangements and Mobility,* ed. K. Warner Schaie, Hans-Werner Wahl, Heidrum Mollenkopf, and Frank Oswald, 77–96. New York: Springer.
Rubinstein, Robert L., and Patricia A. Parmelee. 1992. "Attachment to Place and the Representation of the Life Course by the Elderly." In *Handbook of the Sociology of Aging, Place Attachment,* ed. Irwin Altman and Setha M. Low, 139–64. New York: Plenum Press.
Sassen, Saskia. 2000. *Cities in a World Economy.* London: Sage.
Satterthwaite, David, ed. 1999. *The Earthscan Reader on Sustainable Cities.* London: Earthscan.
Scharf, Thomas, Chris Phillipson, and Allison Smith. 2005. *Multiple Exclusion and Quality of Life amongst Excluded Older People in Disadvantaged Neighbourhoods.* London: OPDM and Social Exclusion Unit.
Scharf, Thomas, Chris Phillipson, Allison Smith, and Paul Kingston. 2002. *Growing Older in Socially Deprived Areas: Social Exclusion in Later Life.* London: Help the Aged.
Scharlach, Andrew. 2012. "Creating Age-Friendly Communities in the United States." *Aging International* 37: 25–38.
Scharlach, Andrew E., and Amanda J. Lehning. 2013. "Ageing-Friendly Communities and Social Inclusion in the United States of America." *Ageing & Society* 33: 110–136.
Simpson, Charles. 2010. "Older People and Engagement in Neighbourhood Renewal: A Qualitative Study of Stoke-on-Trent." Unpublished Ph.D. thesis. Keele, UK: Keele University.
Skinner, Mark, Gavin Andrews, and Malcolm Cutchin, eds. 2017. *Geographical Gerontology: Perspectives, Concepts, Approaches.* London: Routledge.
Smith, Allison. 2009. *Aging in Urban Neighbourhoods.* Bristol: Policy Press.
Soja, Edward. 2010. *Seeking Spatial Justice.* Minneapolis: University of Minnesota Press.
Stafford, Phil. 2009. *Elderburbia: Aging with a Sense of Place in America.* Oxford: Praeger.
Tonkiss, Fran. 2005. *Space, the City and Social Theory.* Cambridge: Polity Press.
UN-Habitat. 2008. *State of the World's Cities 2008/2009.* London: Earthscan.
———. 2010. *State of the World's Cities 2010/2011—Cities for All: Bridging the Urban Divide.* London: Earthscan.
Wacquant, Louis. 2008. *Urban Outcasts: A Comparative Sociology of Advanced Marginality.* Cambridge: Polity.
Wahl, Hans-Werner, and Frank Oswald. 2010. "Environmental Perspectives on Aging." In *The Sage Handbook of Social Gerontology,* ed. Dale Dannefer and Chris Phillipson, 111–24. London: Sage.
Wiles, Janine, Annette Leibing, Nancy Guberman, Jeanne Reeve, and Ruth Allen. 2012. "The Meaning of 'Aging in Place' to Older People." *Gerontologists* 52(3): 357–66.
World Health Organization. 2007. *Global Age-Friendly Cities: A Guide.* Geneva: WHO.
Zukin, Sharon. 2010. *The Naked City: The Death and Life of Authentic Urban Places.* New York: Oxford University Press.

2 TRAINING ADVOCATES TO UNDERTAKE LIVABLE COMMUNITY INITIATIVES
A Pilot Program

Sharon A. Baggett

Introduction

SUPPORT FOR DEVELOPING LIVABLE COMMUNITIES has grown rapidly over the last decade, both in the United States and across the globe. Driven by the demographic changes of global aging, much of this support has focused on assisting communities to plan effectively for successful aging in place and for meeting the needs of residents of all ages without fostering competition between them (Ghazaleh et al. 2011; Henkin et al. 2005; Kennedy 2010; Plouffe and Kalache 2010; Stafford 2009). However, no consensus exists about broadening the age-friendly focus for a more inclusive model of social change. Those promoting or researching age-friendly community initiatives (AFCIs) acknowledge the lack of agreement on age-specific terminology and whether AFCIs should be separated from other community change efforts (Lehning and Greenfield 2017). However, current AFCIs do not appear to have been intentionally guided by urban theory or other successful community change movements, yet learning from earlier urban social change efforts is needed if AFCIs and other livability[1] initiatives are to develop successful strategies. Indeed, urban theory and some successful community social movements support models that argue for a more inclusive community movement, and they expand ownership by empowering advocates with the knowledge and skills needed to lead. Yet while a model of age- and ability-friendly advocacy fits well within the goals of many AFCIs, use of such a model may raise universal justice and equity issues, which are of special importance as aging-focused initiatives face funding and support challenges.

This chapter reports on a pilot program where urban and community change theories and an effective community change strategy were used to develop a livability advocacy initiative. The pilot centered on bringing a broader base to AFCIs by developing a citizen advocacy corps that would bring age- and ability-friendly concepts to the larger community. Our pilot did not test a specific theory nor did its outcomes suggest a single social change model. Rather we offer the project outcomes to inform assumptions about these theories and existing social change models and their applicability to AFCIs. For the age-friendly cities movement to thrive, achieve success, and be sustained, a wider range of highly trained, citizen advocates are needed, who can push forward a livable-for-all agenda while also recognizing unique needs of key population groups.

Project Foundation: Theory and Effective Models

The Just City

Writings on the just city and successful community change models provided the foundation for our training project. In response to perceived failures of previous planning theories and ideologies (Castells 1977; Harvey 1973, 1992), just-city scholars such as Sandercock (2004) and Fainstein (2010) began to elaborate a more inclusive planning theory. Fainstein's work "increasingly emphasizes society's stake in better services, amenities and other collective goods for everyone" (Friedmann 2008: 31), and this strong vein of social justice flows through her defense of the just-city model and its political economy approach to analysis (Fainstein 2000). She cautioned that participative democracy alone does not guarantee that minorities and all parties will benefit. "City building for the benefit of non-elite groups requires empowering those who are excluded not just from discussions but from structural positions that allow them genuine influence" (18). They must not only be empowered to participate but also be supported by other resources such as access to expertise and effective organization.

Fainstein (2010) identified three main strands in recent writing on justice in the city: democracy, diversity, and equity. Just-city writings relative to democracy and diversity were most salient to our project. Planners and policy scientists disagree as to the value of deliberative democracy, in which planners listen to citizens in dialogue with policy decisions, assuming that broader participation will lead to more "just" or redistributive outcomes. Critics argued that while democratic engagement may be inspiring and "liberating and creative," it may also serve to oppress those who are relatively disadvantaged from the beginning (Campbell and Marshall 2006; Healey 2003; Huxley and Yiftachel 2000). This does not disappear in some ideal goal of "achieving consensus and/or the common good"; only through mobilizing citizens, exploring their common interests, and practicing "consciousness" formation will just outcomes occur (Fainstein 2010). Fainstein has noted there are examples where this assumption of just outcomes has not occurred, but this does not mean there is not a role for greater mobilization, ownership, and empowerment to act collectively in creating just cities.

In developing our pilot project, just-city writings and debates informed three guiding questions. Could citizen advocates' determination of *livable* be combined with best practices from AFCIs and broader livability concepts to identify priority livable-for-all actions in local settings? Second, could these citizen advocates be given resources, such as access to expertise and effective organization, to move beyond a simple deliberative model of democracy? That is, could they develop the knowledge and skills not only for communicating with decision makers but to engage in creating livability projects on their own and with local policy makers, thus exerting some control over their environment? Third, could the unique needs and voices of competing groups—who often advocate for their group's needs—be empowered so they can be heard and act in livable community efforts as a voice both common and distinct?

Models of Community Change

Community change has been conceptualized as a multistage process that involves everyone and embraces diversity, bringing community stakeholders together to share knowledge, resources, power, and decision-making in order to effect specific social, political, and policy changes (Everyday Democracy: n.d.). Lehning, Scharlach, and Wolf (2012) emphasized access to sufficient resources to effect social change and broad community involvement as key components of a theory of change. Diversity, access to resources, capacity development, and social advocacy were all integrated into the livable communities' intervention described in this chapter.

While Lehning and Greenfield (2017: 182) noted that "the broader scholarship on community change approaches could offer guidance to identifying best practices and overcoming challenges to age-friendly community development," to date little research has connected these ideas of social change to livability initiatives. Recent exceptions include use of a framework developed by the International Association for Public Participation, in which a five- point continuum of engagement, from information to co-production, is discussed for older persons' engagement in AFCIs (Buffel and Phillipson 2012; Rémillard-Boilard, Buffel, and Phillipson 2017). Perhaps this lack of connection is not surprising given the array of relationships, actors, directions, and foci of change in various initiatives for livable communities. Yet one necessary component of effective community change, the involvement of *everyone*, and especially those who will most benefit from a community change initiative, is lacking in many livability initiatives. In a study of 124 community aging initiatives in thirty-four U.S. states, Lehning et al. (2012) found that those that could be identified as "consumer-driven support networks" and "cross-sector systems change" showed the highest level of elder involvement. But many of the initiatives lacked elder involvement at the level of decision-making.

Foster-Fishman et al. (2001) argued that collaborative capacity is essential for successful community change, identifying four critical levels of collaborative capacity for effective collaboration: member capacity, relational capacity, organizational capacity, and programmatic capacity. *Member capacity* involves having the skills to work collaboratively with others, to create effective programs, and to build and maintain a coalition infrastructure with existing skills or with technical assistance. *Relationship capacity* implies that members must be committed to the benefits of collaborative effort; must view the other members as valuable, experienced, and needed; and must view their own role in a positive light. In building *organizational capacity*, coalitions with diverse membership are more likely to have the range of skills needed for effective collaborative action. Structures must also be there to support the full engagement of those with diverse needs. Members should be supported through training and technical assistance, by ensuring that logistical barriers are addressed (e.g., transportation, child care, need for financial reimbursement), and through provision of translation, personal assistance, or other supports to encourage engagement in meetings. *Relational capacity* underlies all later aspects of the collaborative effort. Members may not know each other, may have no history (or a history of conflict), or may never have worked collaboratively with others, especially to create community-wide change. So attention to building relationships, to finding ways to help members unite around a shared vision, and to building structures where everyone is engaged in the work and in decision-making helps to ensure effectiveness.

An Example of Leadership for Cooperative Action

No example more clearly and effectively incorporates the relational components of organizing than the Industrial Areas Foundation (IAF). IAF, which grew out of Alinksy's community organizing work in Chicago and beyond, centers on the idea that "providing leadership to develop cooperative action requires more than having the skills to advocate for a group or issue. Leaders require the capacity to build relationships with and among others, relationships that can lead to a politics of collective action" (Warren 2001: 24). This concept of bridging social capital, originally focused on issues of race and class segregation, can be broadly applied. Warren observed that bridging social capital is essential if we are to come to an understanding of the common good and address problems in America (27).

Founded in 1940, and still active around the United States, the IAF includes some key strategies for building social capital and organizing across lines of race, class, or other factors (e.g., age, ability). Among the most important are relational organizing and broad-based representation of individuals/organizations as a framework. In relational organizing, rather than being mobilized around predetermined issues, community residents first come together to discuss the needs of their community and to find common ground for action. Through ten-day training sessions and five-day regional leadership training events, the IAF also focuses on leadership development and building skills in research, public speaking, mobilization of residents, relationship building, negotiation, and compromise. The IAF encourages leaders from a broad range of communities and "draws upon the strengths of group identity, while working to overcome the weaknesses of isolation and narrow group outlook" (Warren 2001: 32). Leaders are expected, once action is taken, to reflect on the experience, assessing their own leadership and effectiveness of the action, and to use the process to improve future efforts. Finally, leaders are expected to recruit and build new leaders and are held accountable for growing the base of skilled organizers.

The social change models above, especially that of Foster-Fishman et al. (2001) and the IAF, informed our advocacy training project in three key ways. First, we posited that effective social change comes when a group moves from "providing information" toward "co-production" (and beyond to citizen-led initiatives) on the continuum of participation. Second, Foster-Fishman et al.'s four capacities must be expanded among citizen groups with a stake in livability (age- and ability-friendly) outcomes. Third, advocacy development models like the IAF, when extensive and sustained, can guide training and sustaining a corps of age- and ability-friendly advocates.

Pilot Project: Training Advocates for Livable Communities

In 2011, the Indiana Governor's Council for People with Disabilities (GCPD) invested in a statewide effort to bring more people with disabilities into the livable communities "conversation."

Integration of the disability perspective into the healthy community movements and livable community movements has been quite recent (Vanags 2010). In addition, persons with disabilities have not, until lately, been included in the assessment of public spaces that are often the focus of livability design and enhancement (Mathers 2008). Persons with physical, intellectual, and learning disabilities were noticeably absent from some of the prior livability efforts, under the assumption that communities livable for the elderly, or for children, or for (fill in the blank) would be livable for all. This assumption is still being made. Yet all groups affected must be engaged in livable assessment, planning, and advocacy. When change is projected under the auspices of one group, even while arguing loudly that their view will benefit everyone, exclusion still exists and issues of power are ignored. For example, in a "walkabout" assessment of a newly built "rails to trails" project, built to current standards for accessibility (ADA) and meant to be friendly for all ages, a group of disabled adults, younger to older, found numerous barriers to full use of features of the trail.[2] While many components of livable community planning—for example, complete streets ordinances, affordable housing, access to health, social supports, and recreation—do enhance the lives of all, these areas of focus and advocacy for change must include the views and needs of all ages and abilities. This does not imply that needs of specific groups be subsumed, rather that policies and practices in livable community initiatives be viewed through the lens of the specific *and* the common good. In our project, we focused on bringing together at least two citizen groups, older adults and adults with disabilities, as the base for a trained corps of livable community advocates in order to broaden the voices engaged in planning in the state and to provide advocates with skills to take on leadership roles in determining livability priorities and actions.

The GCPD commissioned the Center on Aging and Community at Indiana University and the Center for Aging and Community at the University of Indianapolis to develop, deliver, and evaluate a curriculum, *Advocates for Livable Communities: Working Together for Change*. The five-day training program was delivered in six communities in Indiana between fall 2013 and May 2017, with 114 graduates.

One premise of the training was that through developing relational capacity and increasing knowledge and skills, two groups that more often worked toward their individual interests would develop that wider lens through which to advocate for change. They would also engage in collective action on common livability issues while maintaining respect for individual group needs. The target trainee groups had not always wanted to be identified as having common cause. Persons with disabilities have not wanted their message "diluted" by association with the needs and issues of the elderly, while advocates for older adults, including older persons themselves, have argued that advanced age should not be identified with assumed disability.[3]

However, it is important that we have community residents across ages and abilities trained to act as effective advocates for the broad range of issues involved in community livability and to advocate for issues within the context of creating communities and neighborhoods that work for all. For example, while seniors are known to attend hearings and zoning meetings more often than other age groups, most are there to make their voices heard on single, personal issues rather than on issues facing broader elder-friendly or inclusive communities (K. Holdsworth and M. Peoni, personal communication, 3 May 2011). Peoni noted, "We would love to ask for educated advocates to attend our community hearing and forums since most cannot get above their personal interests." Having a corps of citizen activists who can articulate common good as well as specific goods in policy debates is likely to be essential, considering the resource challenges of most of our cities and communities.

The elderly are not alone in their single-issue and age-specific focus. As Sites et al. (2007) noted, while new kinds of planned communities are being envisioned, and new concepts of community are being put forward (e.g., social capital, assets-based), "community in the broader sense of shared interests or solidarities appears to be under unrelenting attack, as traditional notions of collective action and inclusive modes of social development are challenged by sociopolitical forces (globalization, social-welfare retrenchment, religious sectarianism, [and I would add ageism]) and by intellectual currents that seem to point toward more fragmented social orders" (519–20). Late twentieth-century economic and political pressures have pushed many organizations toward community development and planning in pursuit of interest-group strategies to secure support, while others seek to build new coalitions and movements to promote social ends. Communities for all ages are an example of the latter. But if we are going to move toward community renewal for all—across the life span and across abilities—we must find new and effective ways to train and engage advocates who can lead action while representing the needs and desires of their specific age or group within the larger context of everyone in the community and not relinquishing power held through single-group identity. Under the broad umbrella of livability, advocates must also identify and work toward issues *they* identify as important rather than reacting to pre-identified issues as they arise.

Specific goals of the project included the following:

- Engaging new citizens in the livability effort
- Empowering often unheard citizens to identify their priorities for livability and ideas for addressing local livability issues

- Enhancing capacity of these citizens through providing content, language, and tools of livability advocacy and effective community change
- Building relational capacity among these advocates
- Training advocates who are ready to lead as well as collaborate in livability efforts in their communities

Community Selection and Recruitment

Five of the six communities were selected for the project because of previous interest in age-friendly or community improvement initiatives; in the remaining community, a local senior services leader requested that her community be a training site. Most of the six were recipients of Indiana Office of Community and Rural Affairs' Stellar Communities Designation grants, a multi-agency partnership that provides resources for "transformative quality of place community improvements." In the designated communities, there was evidence of commitment to improving livability by local leadership, and thus these communities could provide fertile ground for advocates to engage in community improvement, furthering the likelihood of success for advocacy efforts. In each community a local planning committee representing older adults, adults with disabilities, aging and disability advocates, livable community advocates, and other interested leaders was convened and developed a recruitment plan. In some cases this committee became the link to media to promote the importance of the training to the community and cover the outcomes of the training. Additionally, stipends were provided to trainees, acknowledging the importance of their time and, in some cases, for time away from employment. Personal care attendants or family member assistants were also reimbursed as needed.

Training Content

The training content was divided into two sections. Section one covered best-practice approaches to creating more livable communities in six key areas: mobility (transit, pedestrian, biking); housing (affordability, visitability, universal design); social and cultural opportunities; health and support services (including food and nutrition); recreation; and work, education, and civic engagement. Section one also included a unit in which trainee groups identified assets and challenges to livability in their communities and identified their priorities for livability efforts. Section two focused on developing advocacy skills in six areas: advocate (being an advocate); educate (framing and beyond); unite (collaboration); engage (venues for advocacy and understanding the planning process); speak out (gathering evidence; testimony); and serve (engaging with local committees, boards, commissions, leading citizen actions). The content is designed to empower advocates to use the language, tools, and current knowledge of best practices not only in dialogue with decision makers engaged in livability efforts but also to take direct action using the knowledge and tools gained and to work on a par with collaborative partners.

Training Approach

Five days of training was delivered in three units: an initial two days followed two weeks later by another two days, followed two weeks later by a final day. Core concepts of information, application, practice, reflection, and engagement guided the active learning approach. Within each session, a range of learning activities was used, including visual presentations, small- and large-group discussions, and short projects. The consistent focus was on engaging trainees in active learning exercises designed to build relationships and shared vision and on their interacting with the trainers as they applied what was learned to their local communities. The trainees were encouraged to challenge and debate the concepts based on their experience and in the context of their communities.

Some of the learning exercises were outlined in a 130-page workbook developed specifically for the training.[4] Each workbook chapter included an introduction, a brief outline of key topics, topical content, actual scenarios, a get-started exercise, and selected tips and resources. The workbook was designed to support the training sessions but was not strictly followed. The live training session on housing, for example, is short, and only one or two housing topics included in the workbook could be covered. Trainers referred trainees to the additional material in the workbook as a resource.

In other training sessions, unique activities were used to involve trainees in applying the concepts to their home communities and in reflecting on that experience. These types of activities and reflections were used specifically in two assignments trainees completed between the first two-day session and the second, and between the second session and the final day of training. These assignments required pairs or groups of older adults and persons with disabilities to partner to complete a project in their home community, based on specific components of the training. Given the short time frame, two weeks between sessions, the first assignment was simply doing a mini-assessment of the walkability of a street or small, bounded destination (i.e., a park or a block), determining if the community had a comprehensive pedestrian plan or a complete streets ordinance, or proposing a redesign for a central square, park, or thoroughfare. In the second assignment, partners or teams completed a worksheet by developing a comprehensive list of livability stakeholders in their community, then developed a plan for outreach to these stakeholders and a vision for developing a larger coalition following the training. The second assignment included writing a script to use in approaching a new community partner to elicit support for a community action or for collaboration in a citizen-led initiative. When trainees returned from the two-week breaks, they shared reports from their completed assignments. These shared reflections on the activities provided trainees the opportunity to discuss working together and exercising leadership in completing the work, to explore challenges encountered in applying training content to the activity, and to reveal unexpected outcomes.

On the final day of training, local decision makers and policy leaders identified by the trainees were invited to attend a session to discuss livability. Across the six communities, thirty-five leaders attended these sessions. Among leaders participating were mayors and former mayors; directors and program administrators from local community foundations; city planners; parks and recreation directors; United Fund directors; directors of redevelopment, county planning, city planning, or building commissions; clergy members; and housing administrators. The goal was to introduce these organizational leaders to the highly trained cadre of advocates and, through guided discussion, to explore how these advocates and community leaders could work together to make their communities more livable. Trainees also shared their priorities, individual and collective, for achieving greater livability and some specific ideas and plans for moving this forward, even if organizational leaders were not yet ready to take action themselves. Opportunities for collaboration and co-production were explored.

Before officially graduating, trainees formally pledged to take at least two individual actions related to the livability priorities identified earlier in the following six months. Trainees were assisted in developing a rough transition plan for these pledges, that is, how they would operate post-training. This varied by community, but action steps such as establishing a regular meeting date and place, creating a set of priority action items for livability (e.g., apply for a microloan to assist low-income neighborhoods to begin their own sidewalk repairs), selection of a group leader, and development of a Facebook page for communication were among the actions planned. Advocates were also asked to propose at least one livability group action or priority on which to focus. Ensuring a local business adhered to accessibility guidelines and transit stop improvements were among the targets for group action.

Six months following the initial training, follow-up sessions were held to assess knowledge retention, to evaluate activity that the individual trainees and the group had made toward their commitments to action, and to identify needs for additional technical assistance to support trainees' efforts. At the close of the project, the advocates from the six communities attended a combined summit and shared experiences and community activities, and they competed for small grants to incentivize their livability efforts.

Making the Training Accessible

Inclusion in livability initiatives requires making sure that adequate policies and practices are in effect. To ensure that training materials and experiences were accessible for persons with disabilities, the workbook was translated into formats accessible to the blind or visually impaired, and all PowerPoint presentations and handouts were prepared for accessibility and sent electronically to blind or visually impaired trainees two weeks in advance. This allowed trainees to prepare by using screen readers or other software or by having an assistant read the materials to them. Sign interpreters assisted hearing-impaired trainees in all sessions. Personal assistants, family members, and other supportive agents assisted those with intellectual and developmental disabilities as needed to complete written assignments and to engage in group activities or individual presentations.

Outcomes

Formal Evaluation

Evaluation of the project included pre- and post-training assessment surveys to spur interest at the start of the training and to measure change in knowledge, a post-survey assessment of the training delivery and content, and a six-month follow-up survey to assess the extent to which trainees had taken specific advocacy actions in their communities. Progress toward individual action pledges made at the close of the training was assessed alongside the follow-up survey.

As shown in table 2.1, significant positive changes in knowledge and skills were found for all items for the ninety-two trainees completing both the pre- and post-survey.

In the initial survey, trainers also asked participants to state two of their own goals for attending the training. Qualitative analysis of the goals found several themes emerging in both goals 1 and 2. Among the most common goals were the following:

- Improve my community
- Learn how to be an effective advocate
- Learn how to assess my local community for livability

TABLE 2.1. Knowledge and Skills Pre- and Post-Survey (n = 92)

Survey Questions	Z*	Asymp. Sig. (2-tailed)**
I can describe key aspects of a livable community.	-5.325	.000
I know how to use specific tools to measure certain aspects of livability in my community.	-6.648	.000
I can describe some changes in the physical design of my community that would improve mobility for everyone.	-5.621	.000
I understand how zoning and ordinances can be used to improve mobility.	-5.452	.000
I can describe the concept of visitability.	-7.011	.000
I know some ways my community can provide resources to help residents modify their homes so they are safer and more accessible.	-5.835	.000
I understand how the physical design of my community affects my health and the health of others.	-5.224	.000
I can assess my local parks and recreation facilities and determine ways in which they can better serve people of all ages and abilities.	-6.214	.000
I understand how the way my community is built, its transportation options, and other factors affect everyone's ability to get a job, an education, and to volunteer.	-5.220	.000
I can craft an effective message to educate community members about livability.	-6.004	.000
I know how to work together with others to be an effective advocate.	-5.551	.000
I feel confident I can prepare and present effective testimony to community leaders.	-5.829	.000
I understand the comprehensive land use planning process.	-7.055	.000
I understand how I can get involved in land use planning to promote livability.	-6.722	.000
I am prepared to serve on a local commission or board and represent "livable communities" concepts.	-3.047	.002
I can identify new partners in my community to collaborate with to promote livability.	-6.326	.000
I can work effectively with people of different ages and abilities to promote livability.	-4.815	.000

Survey Questions	Z*	Asymp. Sig. (2-tailed)**
I can contact key local leaders to advocate for livable community issues.	-6.107	.000
I can advocate for a more livable community on behalf of everyone, not just for myself.	-6.249	.000
I can help others understand what it means to promote a livable community.	-5.119	.000

*Based on negative ranks.
**Wilcoxon signed ranks tests of significance.

Additional common goals were to "understand livability," "inform others," "identify best contacts in community," and "learn how to reach and work with local leaders." Other goals focused on learning how to help a relative and others like them in the community; improving welcoming, safety, or housing aspects of the community; and collaborating to take action and help consumers take action.

Not all trainees identified two goals in the pre-test or completed the post-assessment query on achievement toward goals. Thus, the number reporting their progress toward goals is lower than for other survey items. As shown in table 2.2, of those reporting, three-quarters indicated they achieved both goals. While fewer indicated they achieved their second goal, the majority of all attendees reported achieving either fully or somewhat the goals they set before attending the sessions.

TABLE 2.2. Trainee Report on Progress toward Goals for Attending Sessions

Goal	Achieved		
	Yes	Somewhat	No
1st Trainee Goal for Attending Training (76 responded)	76 percent	20 percent	4 percent
2nd Trainee Goal for Attending Training (69 responded)	75 percent	17 percent	7 percent*

*Total not equal to 100 percent due to no rounding.

At the end of the five-day sessions, trainees completed an assessment of the training and the trainers. Trainees were asked to rate their level of agreement with a series of statements using a five-point scale of "strongly agree," "agree," "not sure," "disagree," or "strongly disagree." Results shown in table 2.3 indicate a positive overall assessment of all aspects of the training. Those aspects of the training receiving the highest ratings were organization of the sessions, staff well-prepared, staff treatment of all trainees with dignity and respect, and trainee indication they would recommend the sessions to others.

TABLE 2.3. Post-Training Assessment of Training Quality

Survey Questions	N	Mean	Standard Deviation
The training sessions were well organized.	99	4.81	.396
The training sessions included enough time for discussion.	100	4.41	.767
The training sessions included enough time for discussion.	99	4.43	.657
The workbook exercises helped me to think about how to get started in my community.	97	4.39	.715
The visual presentations in the training sessions were clear.	100	4.55	.672
The visual presentations in the training sessions were useful in understanding the topics.	99	4.56	.759
The homework assignments helped to reinforce the topics.	100	4.65	.592
The Advocates training staff was well-prepared.	99	4.86	.350
The Advocates training staff was knowledgeable about the topics.	100	4.84	.368
The Advocates training staff treated all trainees with respect and dignity.	100	4.87	.338
My contributions and questions were treated as valuable by Advocates staff.	100	4.82	.386
The sessions made me think differently about some things.	98	4.74	.461
I have information and contacts to help me become an advocate for livability in the future.	96	4.58	.691
I would recommend Advocates training to others.	97	4.84	.400

During the half-day reunions six months post-training, trainees reported on actions toward their pledges. As a group, they described ways in which they had taken action to promote livability. Outcomes were reported on 114 pledges. Of these, 28 percent were reported as "achieved," and 25 percent were "planned or in progress." The most common action reported was "talking to others." This varied, however, from making presentations to membership organizations, to sharing or discussing with a formal group or community leader, to talking to friends and family. Others reported more specific actions on livability projects. Here are some examples:

- Pledge: Pursue the improvement of streetscape in downtown, including benches and landscaping.
    - Outcome: "Talked to a lot of people; identified group that might achieve it; banners were ordered; still working on benches and landscaping."
- Pledge: Attend city council and advocate for green space/gateway.
    - Outcome: "Spoken to two individual city council members and one candidate re: gateway ideas."
- Pledge: Meet with [city leader] regarding sawed-off metal posts [in the street].
    - Outcome: "Met with mayor, economic development and parks department to discuss action plan."

The follow-up survey provided a list of possible advocacy actions, based on skill areas included in the training, and asked advocates to what extent they had taken these actions. The survey questions were guided by the GPCD, based on similar surveys the organization required for other programs focused on advocacy or leadership development that it funds. As shown in table 2.4, talking to others, whether informally to family and friends or to those in one's sphere of influence (churches, community meetings), were the most frequently reported actions. These results must be interpreted with some caution, as many of the respondents did not complete the survey as designed. That is, some respondents just checked a box by the action rather than providing the number of times the action was taken.

"Other" actions taken included the following:

- "Talked to pollsters about accessibility for early voting."
- "Did research on livable housing."
- "Developed curriculum for groups about the needs, concerns, and livability of persons with disabling conditions."

TABLE 2.4. Follow-Up Survey: Post-Training Actions

Action	Number Reporting an Action (n = 45)		Estimated Number of Actions	# Checked Yes Box Only (n = 19)
	Number	Percent	Number	Number
Testified at public hearing	4	11 percent	4	5
Made presentation to group (club, church, other)	12	27 percent	64*	11
Participated in a local community meeting where you could advocate for livability	21	47 percent	79	7
Served on a committee	20	44 percent	62	6
Made a TV or radio appearance	2	4 percent	3	2
Spoke to friends or family	42	93 percent	230**	17
Took some other action(s): [please describe]	9	20 percent	9	6

*Some actors included a large number in their response, say 15, to indicate they made a group presentation to about 15 people.
**One actor's report is not represented, as it indicated 365 "in a nutshell chats." Another mentioned "probably 400–500 by sharing on Facebook." Adding an option for social media shares would be important in future assessments of actions.

In communication with individual advocate communities following the reunions, the trainers learned of other advocacy actions taken by trainees:

- Expanded Healthy County Coalition to include advocate trainees.
- Worked with colleagues maintaining softball fields to develop a plan to improve accessibility of restrooms and resurface the parking lot for greater accessibility.
- Developed and received grant funding to establish a microloan program for sidewalk repair. Program targets neighborhoods low on the city's priority schedule for repair and allows households (or groups of households) to receive funding for materials if they provide labor for projects.
- Developed a one-day study program on improving accessibility in churches. Program was delivered at two statewide conventions of United Methodist Women in the United States.
- Approached the city Board of Works engineer regarding sidewalk issues and advocated for low-cost improvements such as paint and signage. Explored collaborative materials/labor project.

- Engaged mayor in a tour of a local park, sharing findings from park assessment completed as part of the training that included barriers to accessibility and safety issues.
- Made presentation focused on livability to Healthy County Coalition and discussed specific actions community residents could take to bring about improvements to the town square.
- Brought legal action against a local business to force implementation of accessibility features required by the ADA.

The Summit

On 4 May 2017, the project team convened a summit, which brought together trainees and community partners from the six training sites. The summit included speakers on state highways as community main streets, a common issue for all of the communities and one for which they requested additional assistance to help them take action. A panel of trainees from five communities shared advocacy efforts in their home communities, outcomes made possible from attending the training and challenges to continued advocacy.

Skills of the advocates were also on display during the "5 x 5" competition. In this rapidly paced competition for a $5,000 prize, advocate communities proposed a community livability project to the audience (and judges) in five minutes and using five slides. The first-place winners proposed the development of a downtown pocket park to provide a gathering space for community members of all ages and abilities. In their application, the winners noted an impressive partnership developed to move the project forward, in addition to a comprehensive design plan. Partners included the Animal Welfare League, Purdue Extension, the mayor's office and other city offices, a community foundation, the visitors bureau, Parks and Recreation, the Council on Aging, the public library, and skilled nursing facilities. Members of local sustainability initiatives were also invited to partner.

In a surprise outcome, the competition and project funder (GCPD) found a second entry of such high quality that the proposers of that project too were given a prize of $2,500. This community entry outlined a detailed project to improve information about walking possibilities by identifying park destinations from trolley stops and trolley stop distances from the park. The project would include signage of distances, accessibility, and level of difficulty of walking pathways. The second-place winner presented slides with detailed renderings of routes and design of signage. Both winners will use the funds to move their projects forward.

Beyond these specific actions, many of the training participants reported that the most valuable outcome of attending was an increase in their knowledge and awareness of what is meant by a livable community. They now talk more about livability issues; see the term *livability* being used more often in publications, in the news, and by local organizational leaders; and feel they can more clearly articulate the concepts, including the link between livability and their community's economic health. They feel empowered to take action, such as organizing training for others, serving on a board or commission, writing effective letters to the editor, critiquing initiatives proposed by planners and city leaders, and leading projects they identify. Additionally, building relationships with others, of different ages and abilities, and working together to identify issues and develop strategies for advocacy was a highly valued outcome.

Conclusion

The case example here was designed to develop an age- and ability-friendly community initiative using ideas from urban theory and social change models to uncover what is needed for effective community change. If livability is to become a social movement not just for elites but one that can empower those excluded from these efforts, and if we want to ensure that those not previously engaged have the knowledge and power to make change, we must be creative and build on strategies used by other effective models.

As noted earlier, three questions guiding the training project emerged out of the theory. The first question asked, "Could citizen advocates' determination of what is livable be combined with best practices from age- and ability-friendly initiatives and broader livability concepts to help them identify and prioritize 'livable for all' actions in local settings?" The project found this to be so. Advocate trainees determined what is livable in their respective communities, and after completing the learning course, they developed priorities for action integrating the knowledge and local livability issues. The second question asked, "Could these citizen advocates be given resources, such as access to expertise and effective organization, to move beyond a simple deliberative model of democracy?" Perhaps the best example of an affirmative response shows up in the livability initiatives that advocate trainees proposed at the project summit. In these initiatives, graduate advocates developed quality project ideas, based on best practices in livable community design, and led broad involvement of local policy makers to ensure success. The third question asked, "Could the unique needs and voices of competing groups—in this case, older adults and persons with disabilities—who often advocate for their individual group needs be empowered so they can be heard and act in livable community efforts as a voice both common and distinct?" Through relational capacity building, we believe the project was highly successful in uniting the voices of older adults and adults with disabilities to act on behalf of common livability issues while maintaining respect for group differences. Future projects might explore whether other groups such as teens, young parents, and other community groups, especially those often marginalized from such efforts, can be mutually engaged in age- and ability-friendly initiatives.

The training model and evaluation results also indicate that our approach addressed Fainstein's challenge to go beyond empowering non-elite groups to providing them with resources such as access to expertise. It also provided, to some degree, training in effective organization, but it fell short of addressing the need to ensure that these trained advocates are in structural positions that will allow them genuine influence.

In the context of Foster-Fishman et al.'s model for building collaborative capacity and the IAF framework, the pilot was successful in enhancing relational capacity and in building bridging capital, thus creating cooperative connections across age and ability. It was also successful in implementing a limited model of relational organizing. That is, while the overarching issue of livability came from the trainers, through the training exercises the participants engaged in identifying specific and important issues related to livability in their communities and then engaged in working together to find common ground for action. The training pilot effectively drew on the strengths of the individual group identities but overcame the narrow group outlook, as older adults and people with disabilities became citizen advocates for changes in which not only their needs but those of the community could be met. The training also reflected the IAF approach in not focusing only on the technical but also on using the experiences and stories of trainees as a basis for motivation to action. Reflection on the assignments provided the opportunity for trainees to assess their work and their roles as livability leaders so they could continue to hone their skills.

One key strategy of the IAF framework was missing from our work, and it is critical to the long-term effectiveness of any training model. Knowledge and skills trainings are powerful, and an initial experience of relational organizing is a good start. But without longer-term support for the initial advocate trainees and a system by which they can recruit and develop additional advocates, their impacts will be limited. The discussions at the six-month follow-up reunions highlighted that while many of the trainees had individually engaged in advocacy for livability, only three of the trainee groups remained collectively engaged. Thus, long term, the bridging capital may be lost even if a few individual advocates become skilled and continue their work.

The successes are important. We built an age- and ability-friendly training model firmly rooted in urban theory and in models of effective social change. We have shown that even among a small cohort of trainees, gains can be seen in advocacy actions and in advocates gaining access to positions where their knowledge and skills can be used to move livability forward. We have created a cadre of advocates who can not only engage with planners and decision makers in the language and "culture" of livability but also identify their own livability priorities and develop projects and coalitions to act on them. There is room for many more ideas on how to ensure that livability becomes broadly defined and implemented with extensive engagement of community residents. Next steps should be ensuring that different generations, including youth, as well as persons with disabilities, diverse ethnic groups, and others have access to this kind of knowledge and experience of capacity building as well as "shared vision" building.

In summary, we must move beyond age-friendly or livable community planning by power groups, such as academics, planners, and large-scale funded advocacy groups, and reach deeper to engage a wide range of citizens with a stake in the livability agenda. To create these advocates, we can and should build on urban theories and effective models of social change to provide effective training approaches that empower them to not only advise and collaborate with decision makers, but identify and spearhead projects as well.

Sharon A. Baggett is associate professor of aging studies at the University of Indianapolis. Grounded in urban planning and policy, her research had focused on improving public policies, service delivery, and engaging residents and public service clients in dynamic activism. She has extensive experience in developing and evaluating training and empowerment models and uses the life course lens in her research on community planning and policy implementation. She serves on the Public Policy committee of the Association of Gerontology in Higher Education and is a board member of Health by Design, an Indianapolis-based organization focused on the intersection of health and the built environment.

Notes

I would like to acknowledge everyone involved in this project team, especially Jennie Todd, MS of the Indiana Institute on Disability and Community, Indiana University, who helped in the development of the project training materials, served as an inspiring trainer, and organized many events to make the project a success. My very great appreciation to Dr. Phil Stafford for his valuable and constructive suggestions during the planning and development of this research work. His willingness to give his time and to assist us in securing funding is appreciated. I would also like to thank Deborah Williams for her work in developing and presenting the housing content. Finally, the project was funded with generous support from the Indiana Governor's Council for People with Disabilities, who provided support for the three years of training as well as generous awards to winners of the 5x5 design competition.

1. Throughout this chapter, the term *livability* or *livable communities* implies age- and ability-friendly communities.
2. View video of walkabout reports: http://www.youtube.com/playlist?list=PLAT wzYAMABFa7GGm9LCbnVFdk34aMAz6o.
3. In the United States, recent challenges to the 2012 merger of the federal Administration on Aging, the Administration on Intellectual and Development Disabilities, and the Office on Disability exemplify this these long-standing tensions.
4. Baggett, Sharon, Jennie Todd, Phil Stafford, and Deborah M. Williams, *Advocates for Livable Communities: Working Together for Change*, 2013, http://uindy.edu/documents/LivableCommunityWorkbookCR.pdf.

References

Buffel, Tine, and Chris Phillipson. 2012. "Ageing in Urban Environments: Developing 'Age-Friendly' Cities. *Critical Social Policy* 32(4): 597–617. doi: 10.1177/0261018311430457.

Campbell, Heather, and Robert Marshall. 2006. "Towards Justice in Planning." *European Planning Studies* 14(2): 239–52.

Castells, Manuel. 1977. *The Urban Question: A Marxist Approach*, trans. A. Sheridan. Cambridge, MA: MIT Press.

———. 1983. *The City and the Grassroots: A Cross-Cultural Theory of Urban Social Movements*. London: Edward Arnold.

Everyday Democracy. n.d. http://www.everyday-democracy.org/en/Page.ApproachTo Change.aspx.

Fainstein, Susan S. 2000. "New Directions in Planning Theory." *Urban Affairs Review* 5(4): 451–78.

———. 2010. *The Just City*. New York: Johns Hopkins University Press.

Farber, Nicholas, Douglas Shinkle, Jana Lynott, Wendy Fox-Grage, and Rodney Harrell. 2011. *Aging in Place: A State Survey of Livability Policies and Practices*. Washington, DC: AARP. http://assets.aarp.org/rgcenter/ppi/liv-com/aging-in-place-2011-full.pdf.

Foster-Fishman, Pennie. G., Shelby L. Berkowitz, David W. Lounsbury, Stephanie Jacobson, and Nicole. A. Allen. 2001. "Building Collaborative Capacity in Community Coalitions: A Review and Integrative Framework." *American Journal of Community Psychology* 29(2): 241–61. doi: 10.1023/A:1010378613583.

Friedmann, John. 2002. *The Prospect of Cities*. Minneapolis: University of Minnesota Press.

———. 2008. "The Uses of Planning Theory: A Bibliographic Essay." *Journal of Planning Education and Research* 28(2): 247–57. doi: 10.1177/0739456X08325220.

Ghazaleh, Rana A., Esther Greenhouse, George Homsy, and Mildred Warner. 2011. *Multigenerational Planning: Using Smart Growth and Universal Design to Link the Needs of Children and the Aging Population*. Chicago: American Planning Association.

Greenfield, Emily A., Mia Oberlink, Andrew E. Scharlach, Margaret B. Neal, and Philip B. Stafford. 2015. "Age-Friendly Community Initiatives: Conceptual Issues and Key Questions." *Gerontologist* 55(2): 191–98. doi: 10.1093/geront/gnv005.

Harvey, David. 1973. *Social Justice and the City.* Baltimore: Johns Hopkins University Press.

———. 1992. "Social Justice, Post-modernism and the City." *International Journal of Urban and Regional* 16(4): 588–601.

Healey, Patsy. 2003. "Collaborative Planning in Perspective." *Planning Theory* 2(2): 101–24. doi: 10.1177/14730952030022002.

Henkin, Nancy Z., April Holmes, Benjamin Walter, Barbara R. Greenberg, and Jan Schwarz. 2005. "Communities for All Ages: Planning across Generations." In *Intergenerational Strategies Series.* Baltimore, MD: The Annie E. Casey Foundation. http://www.aecf.org/m/resourcedoc/aecf-CommunitiesforAllAgesPlanningGenerations-2005.pdf

Huxley, Margo and Oren Yiftachel. 2000. "New Paradigm or Old Myopia? Unsettling the Communicative Turn in Planning Theory." *Journal of Planning Education and Research* 19(4): 333–42. doi: 10.1177.0739456X0001900402.

Kennedy, Christine. 2010. "The City of 2050: An Age-friendly, Vibrant, Intergenerational Community." *Generations* 34 (3): 70–75.

Lawson-Remer, Terra. 2011. "#OccupyDemocracy." Accessed 6 March 2018. http://www.possible-futures.org/2011/12/08/occupydemocracy/.

Lehning, Amanda J., and Emily A. Greenfield. 2017. "Research on Age-Friendly Community Initiatives: Taking Stock and Moving Forward." *Journal of Housing for the Elderly* 31(2): 178–92. doi: 10.1080/02763893.2017.1309937.

Lehning, Amanda J., Andrew E. Scharlach, and Jennifer P. Wolf. 2012. "An Emerging Typology of Community Aging Initiatives." *Journal of Community Practice* 20(3): 293–316. doi: 10.1080/10705422.2012.700175.

Mathers, A. R. 2008. "Hidden Voices: The Participation of People with Learning Disabilities in the Experience of Public Open Space." *Learning Environment* 13(6): 515–29. doi: 10.1080/13549830802259912.

Mayer, Margit. 2006. "Manual Castells' *The City and the Grassroots.*" *International Journal of Urban and Regional Research* 30(1): 202–6.

Plouffe, Louise, and Alexandre Kalache. 2010. "Towards Global Age-Friendly Cities: Determining Urban Features That Promote Active Aging." *Journal of Urban Health: Bulletin of the New York Academy of Medicine* 87(5): 733–39. doi:10.1007/s11524-010-9466-0.

Purcell, Mark. 2013. *The Down-Deep Delight of Democracy.* Oxford: Wiley-Blackwell.

Rémillard-Boilard, Samuèle, Tine Buffel, and Chris Phillipson. 2017. "Involving Older Residents in Age-Friendly Developments: From Information to Coproduction Mechanisms." *Journal of Housing for the Elderly* 31(2): 146–59. doi: 10.1080/02763893.2017.1309932.

Research and Training Center on Disability in Rural Communities (RTC). 2012. *Healthy and Livable Rural Communities 1: A Disability Perspective.* Missoula: University of Montana Rural Institute. http://rtc.ruralinstitute.umt.edu/RuEcD/Livable percent 20Communities percent201 percent20read percent20only.pdf.

Sandercock, Leoni. 2004. "Towards a Planning Imagination for the 21st Century." *Journal of the American Planning Association* 70(2): 131–41. doi: 10.1080/01944 360408976368.

Sites, William, Robert J. Chaskin, and Virginia Parks. 2007. "Reframing Community Practice for the 21st Century: Multiple Traditions, Multiple Challenges." *Journal of Urban Affairs* 29(5): 519–41. doi: 10.1111/j.1467-9906.2007.00363.x.

Stafford, Philip. B. 2009. *Elderburbia: Aging with A Sense of Place in America.* Santa Barbara, CA: Praeger.

Vanags, Alise. 2010. *Creating Livable Communities for People with Disabilities.* Hauppauge, NY: Nova Science.

Warren, Mark R. 2001. *Dry Bones Rattling: Community Building to Revitalize American Democracy.* Princeton, NJ: Princeton University Press.

WHO (World Health Organization). 2007. *Global Age-Friendly Cities: A Guide.* Geneva: World Health Organization. http://www.who.int/ageing/publications/age_friendly_cities_guide/en/index.html.

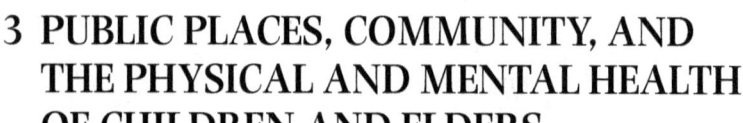

3 PUBLIC PLACES, COMMUNITY, AND THE PHYSICAL AND MENTAL HEALTH OF CHILDREN AND ELDERS

Suzanne H. Crowhurst Lennard

> *The architects must be set the task of . . . building for human contact, building surroundings that invite meeting and centers that shape meeting.*
> —Martin Buber, *Believing Humanism*

Introduction

In this chapter, I look at the problem of social isolation for children and elders and propose how changes to the built environment can prevent social isolation. The first part focuses on how social isolation affects the mental and physical health of children and elders and on the special social needs of these age groups. The second part focuses on how improvements in land use planning, urban design, and transportation planning can bring people together, foster social propinquity, and strengthen social networks.

Health Implications of Social Isolation

Humans are social beings. Contact with family, friends, and social circles is not just pleasurable, it is essential. An individual's very sense of self is shaped and maintained through social life. The quality and quantity of social interaction and sense of belonging strongly influence physical and mental health (House, Landis, and Umberson 1988; Lomas 1998; Cohen 2004).

The intrinsic value of personal social contact consists in the boost to self-esteem, pleasure, and sense of well-being associated with eye contact, being acknowledged and confirmed by another human being, emotional reciprocity, an "authentic" encounter, and knowing others are concerned

FIGURE 3.1. Humans are social beings (photo by author)

and interested in one's well-being (Buber 1965). "The unavowed secret of man," stressed Buber (1967: 95), is that he wants to be confirmed in his being and his existence by his fellow men and that he wishes them to make it possible for him to confirm them."

Harlow (1964) dramatically raised awareness of the effects of social isolation on rhesus monkeys isolated at birth: depression, violence, and self-immolation, "autistic" behavior, hostility, and inability to form adequate social or heterosexual attachments to others when such opportunities are provided (Cross and Harlow 1965). Partial social isolation resulted in blank staring, repetitive circling, and self-mutilation. Their lack of social skills caused them to be shunned or bullied, or they became violent when placed with normally raised monkeys. Human beings suffer from social isolation in similar ways. Indeed, one of the most serious punishments we can inflict is solitary confinement.

The design of the built environment creates contexts that either facilitate or discourage social interaction. "By its very nature, sprawl isolates Americans from one another," observed Morris (2005: 47), and many urbanists before and since confirm this evaluation (Langdon 1994; Kunstler 1998; Montgomery 2013). Leyden (2003: 1546) demonstrated that "persons living in walkable, mixed-use neighborhoods have higher levels of social capital compared with those living in car-oriented suburbs. Respondents living in walkable neighborhoods were more likely to know their neighbors, participate politically, trust others, and be socially engaged." And Mouratidis (2017: 1) finds that "compact urban forms enable residents to maintain larger networks of close relationships, socialize more frequently with friends and family, receive stronger social support, and enjoy increased opportunities to make new acquaintances."

High-rise housing has also been associated with symptoms of social isolation: greater rates of juvenile delinquency (Gillis 1974), greater feelings of alienation (McCarthy and Saegert 1978), and more depression among young mothers (Richman 1974). Gifford (2007) and Evans (2003) provide comprehensive reviews of the literature on the effects of high-rise housing on children, mental health, social behavior, crime, and suicide. As Gifford (2007: 2) summarizes, "The literature suggests that high-rises are less satisfactory than other housing forms for most people, that they are not optimal for children, that social relations are more impersonal and helping behavior is less than in other housing forms, that crime and fear of crime are greater, and that they may independently account for some suicides."

The need for contact with community members of all ages is a universal need:

> In Tokyo, the lack of personal contact with neighbours that results from the development of high-rise buildings is regarded as an age-friendly barrier. In Sherbrooke, older people express concern about the lack of multigenerational spaces for interaction. In Geneva, the lack of contact with younger people in apartment buildings is seen as a disadvantage. In Udaipur, caregivers are concerned that modern flats without front verandas leave no room for community interaction. The importance of design that facilitates community interaction is mentioned in Dundalk as well, where it is suggested that houses should overlook communal facilities to reduce the sense of isolation. (WHO 2007: 34)

Dangers to Elders

Breakdown in community social life has particularly serious health consequences for elders. An increased risk of ill health and death exists "among persons with a low quantity, and sometimes low quality, social relationships" (House et al. 1988: 241). According to Berkman (1995), lack of social ties or social networks predict mortality from almost every cause of death. According to Berkman et al. (2000: 845), "The power of these measures to predict health outcomes is indisputable."

With insufficient or negative social interaction, elders especially are vulnerable to suffer loneliness, low self-esteem, social anxiety, and depression (House et al., 1988; Hawe and Shiell, 2000; Cohen-Mansfield and Parpura-Gill, 2007). Bellah et al. (1985) proposed that without a meaningful sense of connectedness to others, and without a clear involvement in a meaningful social fabric, individuality and life itself lose meaning. As Durkheim (1951) proposed, the underlying reason for suicide is lack of social integration into a supportive group.

In suburban areas, multilane highways designed for speeding traffic and lack of sidewalks put elders and children at risk from traffic and often isolate them in their home. The resultant absence of pedestrians in residential areas fosters a paranoid attitude toward strangers. The suburbs have been designed according to single-use zoning laws, preventing mixed use. Shops, cafés, and services have been placed in separate commercial zones distant from residential areas, making them too difficult to access without a car. This land use planning further isolates elders and children—there is nowhere for them to go, by foot or wheelchair, even if the streets are safe.

Stafford (2009: 143) asks, "What are the characteristics of communities that enable elders to flourish?" He emphasizes that it is not enough to design a physical environment that is easily accessible for the elderly, but most significant is to "promote opportunities for social interaction. Social interaction is abetted by the creation of foils for conversation—elements in the environment that bring people together around a common interest or focus."

Social isolation and neighborhood fragmentation proved an involuntary death sentence for hundreds of elders during the 1999 Chicago heat wave. Klinenberg (2003: 92, 110) found that disproportionately high numbers of elderly deaths occurred in neighborhoods "dominated by boarded or dilapidated buildings, rickety fast-food joints, closed stores with faded signs, and open lots" filled with "tall grass and weeds, broken glass and illegally dumped refuse." In these areas (such as Northlawn), elders lived in isolation, afraid to go onto the street, and far from people or places that could help them survive the heat wave.

In an adjacent, equally poor neighborhood (Southlawn), elders were protected during the heat wave:

> First, the action in and relative security of the local streets pulled older people into public places, where contacts could help them get assistance if they needed it. Second, the array of stores, banks and other commercial centers in the area provided seniors with safe, air-conditioned places where they could get relief from the heat. Seniors felt more comfortable in and are more likely to go to these places, which they visit as part of their regular social routines, than the official cooling centers that the city established during the heatwave. ... The robust public life of the region draws all but the most infirm residents out of their homes, promoting social interaction, network ties, and healthy behavior. (Klinenberg 2003: 110)

Dangers to Children and Youth

For children and youth, the dangers of social isolation are not only emotional ill-health and depression, but also the lack of opportunity to learn and practice essential social skills.

When children lack social contact, they do not learn the social skills needed to maintain health and well-being throughout life and to strengthen resilience in avoiding social pathology. As Bronfenbrenner (1979) observed, all aspects of child development benefit from positive social contexts within which this learning is embedded. If children lack the experience of belonging to a supportive complete community, they will find difficulty in fitting into a community later in life and will therefore not pass this skill on to the next generation.

Tietjen (1989: 406) suggests:

> In Western societies, we have perhaps lost sight of the crucial role of social support in preparing children for their adult roles. Families are often fragmented and socially isolated, relationships transient, and the roles of parents, schools, and other institutions unclear and discontinuous. ... There are many Western children and adolescents for whom the discontinuities are defeating, and who fail to make the transition from childhood to competent adulthood for lack of continuous and coherent social support.

Greenspan (1997: 168, 169) emphasizes that children need "to grow up amid a network of close interactions with adults." Until recently, he observed, "even in cities, families spent their days mostly within the compass of neighborhoods one could easily traverse on foot. ... Ordinary life thus naturally and routinely provided the conditions that the complex human nervous system needs to fulfill its potential."

In the sprawling suburban environments in which most U.S. children are raised, children have fewer friends than ever before. Due to the absence of accessible, lively public places where children can meet, rules forbidding them to play on the street, and strict instructions from parents to stay in the house, teens spend more time alone—3½ hours per day—than with family or friends (Schneider and Stevenson 1999). With long work hours, long commutes, and long drives to run simple errands, parents leave kids "home alone" (Eberstadt 2001).

Most time alone is spent interacting not with a living world, but with technology, where children are exposed to and shaped by the dysfunctional and violent role models presented in the "virtual" world (Bok 1998). Hochschild (1997: 224) reported that "children who were home alone for eleven or more hours a week were three times more likely than other children to abuse alcohol, tobacco or marijuana." Since smartphones have come on the scene, Twenge (2017) reports, the phone has taken the place of drugs, but teens are becoming more socially isolated than ever. "The number of teens who get together with their friends nearly every day dropped by more than 40 percent from 2000 to 2015."

Given a lack of real social networks, it is no surprise that children and adolescents find difficulty in social situations. Shyness is increasingly treated as a medical problem, termed "social anxiety syndrome," for which medications are often prescribed—though these occasionally lead to violence and suicide.

Lynn Henderson (Henderson and Zimbardo, n.d.), director of the Palo Alto Shyness Clinic, maintains "this rise in shyness is accompanied by spreading social isolation within a cultural context of indifference to others and a lowered priority given to being sociable." She proposes this may be "a warning signal of a public health danger that appears to be heading toward epidemic proportions." Lack of real-life social skills may also lead young people desperate for some form of social contact into inappropriate, predatory, or damaging exchanges in technologically mediated social networks.

Loneliness can lead to low self-esteem, separation anxiety, and being bullied (Bullock 1998). In the United States, 8.3 percent of adolescents suffer from depression (Birmaher et al. 1996). Since 2007, noted Twenge (2017), "as teens have started spending less time together, they have become . . . more likely to kill themselves." From 2007 to 2015, suicide rates doubled among teen girls, reaching its highest rate in forty years. The increase among teen boys was more than 30 percent (CDC 2017).

Combative youth lacking social skills may be violent toward others, especially toward those who are different and who lack social skills to defend themselves. School shootings are committed by "adolescent outcasts" (Eberstadt 2001; Newman 2004). Gang warfare provides youth a sense of membership and a feeling that their existence is of significance to others. In 2010, homicide was the second leading cause of death for young people aged ten to twenty-four years old (CDC 2012).

Social Immune System

Positive social interactions, membership in a social support system, and a sense of belonging protect and promote good health. It has been found that social capital protects against negative health outcomes and mortality (House et al. 1988). For people of all ages, physical and mental health is improved by face-to-face interaction and membership in a community (Resnick et al. 1997). It is through frequent informal face-to-face interaction that social ties develop (Greenbaum 1982).

FIGURE 3.2. Building a social immune system (photo by author)

Circles of friends and familiars form a "social immune system" to buffer stress, improve coping, and protect health. Social support prevents isolation and improves psychological well-being through being valued, receiving signs of love, and knowing that help is there if needed. Integration in a social network produces positive psychological states (Cohen, Underwood, and Gottlieb 2000); it fosters self-esteem, self-assurance, sense of security, and well-being (Berkman and Glass 2000). Social circles "maintain, protect, promote and restore health" (Nestmann and Hurrelmann 1994: 5).

Kawachi and Berkman (2001) conceptualized three pathways through which social capital could affect health at the neighborhood level: access to services and amenities, psychosocial processes, and health-related behaviors. The significant psychosocial processes were refined by Berkman et al. (2000) as (a) social and emotional support; (b) social influence, values, and norms; and (c) social engagement in community life.

Frequent meetings and greetings in a neighborhood public realm allow people to become familiar with one another and to "learn one another's stories" (Berry 1990: 154), which builds trust and caring. Higher levels of trust in a community are associated with lower rates of most major causes of death, including heart disease, cancer, infant mortality, and violent deaths, such as homicide (Kawachi et al.1997). Kawachi and Berkman (2001) analyzed the varied mechanisms by which social ties contribute to mental health.

At the neighborhood level, Lochner and colleagues (2003) found that social capital, as measured by reciprocity, trust, and civic participation, was associated with lower neighborhood mortality rates after adjusting for neighborhood material deprivation.

Communities with high collective efficacy, that is, "mutual trust and the willingness to intervene for the common good" (Sampson, Raudenbush, and Earls 1997: 919), generally experience low homicide and violence rates and low levels of physical and social disorder, while neighborhoods with low collective efficacy suffer high rates of violence and significant physical and social disorder (Earls 1998). A functioning neighborhood community in which people take some responsibility for others helps elders to continue to live a normal, healthy life in their community even in neighborhoods with problems of high vandalism and crime (Earls et al 2005).

Social Needs of Children and Youth

Good social skills and the ability to take pleasure in face-to-face social interaction are fundamental to maintaining good health, to all aspects of child development, and to achieving success and well-being later in life. Social skills do not develop automatically. They are learned through interaction in the family and in the community, observing how adults around them behave and reenacting the same behavior (Bandura 1977).

Children must learn trust (Bowlby 1973) and the ability to distinguish between those who are trustworthy and those who are not (Rubin, Fein, and Vandenberg 1983). They must learn the skills of making friends and negotiating and maintaining friendships (Rubin and Rose-Krasnor, 1992).

Children must learn how to interact with people who are very different from themselves. "The more varied and reciprocal these interactions, the richer will be the individual's self-image and the more comprehensive her consciousness" (Greenspan 1997).

Social support helps children develop resilience and successfully cope with stress (Garmezy 1983; Werner and Smith 1982). Children as well as adults need to feel they "belong" within a community (McMillan and Cha-

FIGURE 3.3. Children learn social skills through participation, observation, and reenactment (photo by author)

vis 1986). For adolescents, supportive relationships with adults in the community are particularly valuable in preventing psychological harm from stressful life experiences (Rutter 1983). This is especially true for vulnerable adolescents with few personal assets (Blyth and Leffert 1995). African American youth, especially adolescent girls, who have neighbors who look out for them are less likely to report feeling depressed than adolescents in less supportive neighborhoods (Stevenson 1998). Even in high-risk neighborhoods, if community members take responsibility for others, children are more likely to develop positive social skills (Earls et al. 2005).

Youth in dysfunctional settings who have at least one good relationship are at lower risk of psychiatric disorder (Rutter and Giller 1983). When comparing communities with high rates of healthy youth to communities with low rates, the healthy youth were found to be better connected to a variety of social systems (Blyth and Leffert 1995). Leffert et al. (1998: 226) emphasize that "elements of community life, which include the engagement and participation of multiple community forces, persons, organizations, and sectors, serve as important protective factors across multiple domains of child and adolescent health," and the effects of these interactions are cumulative in preventing adolescent risk behavior.

Children must also develop independence, but they are not permitted independence in neighborhoods that lack strong community bonds. In examining social and environmental factors that facilitated children's independence, Russell (2010) found a strong correlation between neighborhoods with strong community networks and increased children's independence.

Social Needs of Adults and Elders

For elders, walking in the neighborhood is an important activity to maintain physical health. When the walking environment improves, so does physical health (Kerr, Rosenberg, and Frank 2012)

The opportunity for social interaction, companionship, people-watching, and a "friendly neighborhood" were reported as reasons why adults chose to walk in their neighborhood, whether to shop, run errands, recreate, or simply to get exercise (Ball et al. 2001; Giles-Corti and Donovan 2002; Booth et al. 2000; Humpel, Owen, and Leslie 2002). Indeed, as Ståhl et al. (2001: 7) reported in a study of adults across six countries, "The social environment was the strongest predictor of being physically active."

As one interviewee recorded by Altschuler, Somkin, and Adler (2004: 1226) reported, "I feel that my neighborhood contribute(s) to my health, and it does so in many ways. (If) something, an accident happens and I break my leg in my house I know my neighbors will come to my aid. (But) I think that over time even a greater impact is having a sense of belonging and a sense of neighbors that I trust around me helps reduce anxiety and it's good for my mental well being."

FIGURE 3.4. Elders walk if this offers social interaction (photo by author)

Importance of an Intergenerational Community

Peter Benson (2006: 1, 104), president of the Search Institute, observed, "Instead of embedding our children in webs of sustained relationships, we segregate them from the wisdom and experience of adults, raising them in neighborhoods, institutions, and communities where few know their names. Instead of celebrating them as gifts of energy, passion, and hope, we view them with suspicion in public places and places of commerce and deny them meaningful roles in community and civic life."

He recognized that the key problem that thwarts these efforts is that our physical environment does not support community and adds, "If there were only one thing we could do to alter the course of socialization for American youth, it would be to reconstruct our towns and cities as intergenerational communities. Cross-generational contacts would be frequent and natural."

"Designing a community that works for people across the lifespan," asserts Stafford (2009: 141) "is not simply the work of architects and urban planners. While the built environment is critically important to the quality of life for citizens, so too is the social environment in which daily activities are embedded." The challenge, then, is to reshape the built environment so as to foster positive social interaction and a multigenerational community.

A Built Environment to Facilitate Social Interaction

Independent Mobility for All

An essential factor in facilitating social life is that streets must be safe and hospitable for all pedestrians; children and elders must be able to leave their home and move around in the public realm without fear of traffic and in a safe social environment. The first priority is to provide safe, continuous pedestrian networks throughout residential neighborhoods and to essential destinations—school, shops, gathering places, parks, and services (AAP, 2009; Kerr et al. 2012).

European cities have found that the most effective way to facilitate social interaction in streets that support the busiest pedestrian traffic (at the city center or neighborhood shopping street) is to close the street to traffic for part of every day (usually 10:30 a.m. to midnight). This allows vehicle access for delivery in the morning (and always for emergency vehicles) and transforms the street into a safe pedestrian environment that fosters social interaction during the afternoon and evening. While complete networks of pedestrian streets are common in Europe, pedestrian streets in the United States so far are "islands."

Tentative steps in the United States to make streets safer and more hospitable include the emphasis on designing porches facing the street and enlarging sidewalks to allow space for outdoor cafés and restaurants. In many cities, "parklets" and "street seats" are being created out of parking areas.

In streets that carry vehicles, traffic must be calmed to reduce danger in case of accidents. Traffic-calming devices increase independent mobility and encourage residents to use their street as living space (Engwicht 1992). In a "living street" (*Wohnstrasse* in Germany), all pedestrians have equal right to the full width of the street, and traffic is required to move at walking speed. In traffic-calmed streets and arterial roads, vehicle speed is reduced by the street design—narrower lane widths, jogged lanes, plantings, and roundabouts. Where pedestrian routes cross traffic, the pedestrian must be given priority, with raised crosswalks and medians (Untermann 1984). To improve the public realm, main traffic arteries may be redesigned as "complete streets," suitable for pedestrians, bikes, and public transit—all modes that facilitate social interaction, as opposed to the automobile, which encapsulates and isolates the individual.

Temporary closing for two or three hours after school of residential streets where children live, turning them into "play streets," encourages play activity and social interaction. Studies in the United Kingdom demonstrate that children play longer, are more active, and engage in more social interaction when they play in safe streets near home than when they play on playgrounds (Mahdjoubi 2015).

Safe mobility for old and young also requires safe routes for bicyclists. The safest designs are "buffered" bike lanes, separated from pedestrians by the sidewalk curb and protected from vehicular traffic by a physical barrier and a buffer zone, as in Long Beach, California. "These cycle tracks had a 28 percent lower injury rate" (NACTO 2012: 46). For long distances, public transportation needs to be the most convenient, comfortable, economical, efficient, and appealing transportation mode for people of all ages and in all walks of life.

Healthy Urban Fabric to Support Social Propinquity

To enable people of all ages and income groups to live within walking distance of each other and in such a way that their normal everyday lives overlap in the public realm requires a compact mixed-use urban fabric at the heart of each suburban neighborhood characteristic of traditional towns. Here, people's paths cross in multiple situations—on the way to work or school, at the market or running errands, at a "third place" (Oldenburg 1991), or relaxing—and in different social contexts—alone, with family members, friends, or business associates. Meetings may lead to introductions that expand social networks. This promotes a multifaceted appreciation of each person's life and a resilient community network system.

To achieve this, a large city needs to be structured along principles of "true urbanism" (Crowhurst Lennard and Lennard 2004), as a "city of short distances" or "Stadt der kurzen Wege" (Feldtkeller 2001), composed of "urban villages" (Aldous 1992) where all resources needed to support everyday life can be found in a mixed-use core within a ten-minute walking radius.

The principles that Jane Jacobs (1961) identified—"eyes on the street," mixed-use, corner grocery stores, human-scale buildings, and wide sidewalks—have been shown in research studies to be essential in fostering social interaction. A significantly greater sense of community is found in mixed-use neighborhoods (Nasar and Julian 1995; Leyden 2003; Lund 2002). The availability of local shops and restaurants is seen by residents to be health promoting. "The provision of decent housing, safe playing areas, transport, green spaces, street lighting, street cleaning, schools, shops, banks, etc. impacts upon participation in that their presence facilitates social interaction and a 'feel good' sense about a place" (Baum and Palmer 2002: 353). Mehta (2007) emphasized additional factors supportive of social interaction, such as hospitable commercial streets, mixed-use streets with shops and restaurants, wide sidewalks, and a personalized public realm. As Cozens and Hillier (2008) stressed, it requires a great many more

FIGURE 3.5. Mixed-use human-scale urban fabric fosters social life (photo by author)

factors than simple street layout to create a neighborhood that fosters social interaction.

Frank et al. (2004) showed that the greater the degree of land use mix, the less time adults spent in cars and the lower the rate of obesity. Small city blocks, street connectivity, mixed land uses, and proximity of shops are associated with an increase of walking (Cervero and Duncan 2003; Duncan and Mummery 2004; Frank et al. 2005).

Dangerous settings discourage individuals from building social ties (Evans 2006). Public places must be designed to feel safe as well as to prevent criminal activity. This is achieved by encouraging a sense of ownership, ensuring eyes on the street, maintaining active use of the space and surrounding buildings, controlling access (Crowe 2000), and making it possible for people to communicate between the public and private realm.

Even a courtyard in an apartment building can provide some support for a significantly greater development of community among residents than exists in an apartment building without a courtyard (Nasar and Julian 1995).

Style of housing and land use patterns have been found to affect social networks (Cattell, 2001) and health (Macintyre, Maciver, Sooman 1993). Their data showed a strong link between social interactions and "local opportunity structures"—"socially constructed and socially patterned features of the physical and social environment which may promote or damage health either directly or indirectly through the possibilities they provide for people to live healthy lives" (Macintyre and Ellaway 2000: 343).

Williams and Pocock (2010) emphasize that the more informal "third places" there are in a neighborhood, the greater the opportunity for serendipitous social interaction that can lead to caring relationships and social capital. Some third places, such as cafés and bars, cater to specific population groups (adult drinkers and those who can afford to eat there), and some exclude children, so attention must be paid to exactly which social networks are facilitated by each third place.

Design of Public Places to Support Social Interaction

Fleming, Baum, and Singer (1985) found that public places are important venues for casual social contact in a neighborhood. Pendola and Gen (2008) demonstrated that neighborhoods with main streets have a significantly higher sense of community than that which exists in high-density suburban style neighborhoods without a main street. Of still greater value for community social life that includes children and elders are central public plazas open to all. As Kuo et al. (1998: 823) observed, "The formation of neighborhood social ties (NSTs) may substantially depend on the informal social contact which occurs in neighborhood common spaces." Greenbaum (1982) observed that relations among neighbors grow primarily in the course of repeated visual contacts and through short-duration outdoor talks and greetings. Thus, the frequency of face-to-face contacts is a strong predictor of the development of social ties and development of friendships (Ebbesen, Kjos, and Konecni 1976).

The European tradition of a multifunctional agora, forum, or marketplace served to generate social interaction and democratic dialogue at the city center (Crowhurst Lennard and Lennard 2008). When well located, surrounded by appropriate mixed use, and hospitably designed, neighborhood plazas facilitate face-to-face social networks and strengthen community.

Social interaction is tied to physical elements in the public realm. Analysis of social life on public plazas (Whyte 1980; Gehl 2010) revealed patterns of behavior: small groups clustered to talk at the entrance or in the middle of the pedestrian flow; people-watching took place along pathways; movable tables and chairs allowed individuals to sit alone and groups to sit together, in sun or shade; ledges and steps were popular sitting places; the presence of hot dog stands and food vendors attracted people at lunchtime; sun, trees, and water attracted people.

In a more ethnographic study, Low (2000) showed detailed patterns of behavior tied to physical elements of the space, their cultural significance, and spatial relationships. Low also emphasized the important role a plaza can play in facilitating community engagement and democratic dialogue.

A comparison of European squares that support social life and community (Crowhurst Lennard and Lennard 2008) highlights elements that time and again are present in the liveliest squares and that enhance social interaction. Successful plazas are multifunctional places people need to visit or pass through on a frequent basis to go shopping, to go to the market, or to go to work. Intense level of use by a substantial residential population within walking distance can generate the high frequency of social encounters required to develop inclusive community ties.

To ensure frequent use of the square, shops serving daily needs are located there; many surrounding buildings are surmounted by a residential population overlooking the square. To encourage civic engagement, one building on the square (library or community hall) may contain meeting rooms available to the community.

To encourage people to spend time on the square, facilitating opportunities for encounters, restaurants and cafés serve out of doors in fine weather. Being less expensive, cafés attract a more inclusive clientele. A large square often contains several restaurants catering to the full range of tastes and pocketbooks.

FIGURE 3.6. Community social life is generated in multifunctional neighborhood squares (photo by author)

To bring community members on a regular basis from a wider radius, a weekly farmers market selling fresh local produce may be held on the square. Local community festivals take place there, and entertainers such as musicians and clowns perform.

To be successful in building community, the square must have the proportions and ambience of a community hall or living room. To convey a sense of place and group membership, entrances to the square are designed as subtle thresholds, accentuating the experience of entering the community's gathering place. Once inside the space, the visitor is encouraged to stay by the clear sense of being in a hospitable enclosed space; while there may be many exits, these are not obvious (Kidder Smith 1954).

The hospitality of the space encourages people to linger. There is a choice of shade or sun, protection from the elements, ample formal seating (chairs and benches with backrests suitable for elders) as well as informal seating (ledges, walls, and steps suitable for young people). There is a focal point, a fountain or work of art that attracts old and young and stimulates "triangulation," that is, conversation among strangers (Whyte 1980). And the square captures the heart of community members by its abundance of beauty—in architectural facades, details, skyline, paving, or natural elements, flowers, and trees (Coley, Sullivan, and Kuo 1997).

Fundamental to the success of a community square is freedom from traffic, which enables children to safely play and facilitates conversation for all (not only the hearing impaired). Freedom from the noise and potential dangers of traffic opens all the senses, making it possible for people to pay more attention to other human beings and subtle social cues (Cohen and Lezak 1977) and to appreciate the ambience of the place.

When designed according to these principles and well located at the heart of a mixed-use neighborhood, squares are powerful catalysts in building community and social support systems that protect health. Ideally, every neighborhood would have a hospitable small square or plaza at its heart, accessible within a ten-minute walk, just as in many European cities (Crowhurst Lennard 2017).

Conclusion

In the Netherlands, where declining health levels were linked to decrease in social contacts, social science researchers called for a more developed and detailed governmental policy to promote community (De Vos 2003). Dutch authorities recognized that while involving city planning professionals is essential, it is difficult to achieve: "For the reduction of health inequalities, intersectoral collaboration between the public health sector and ... physical policy sectors (e.g. housing, spatial planning) is essential, but in local practice difficult to realize" (Storm et al. 2016: 1).

In Norway, particularly for the most disadvantaged, it has been observed that "public health strategies that strengthen people's social networks ... may have considerable potentials for health improvement" (Gele and Harsløf 2010). Swedish authorities noted, "Reducing social differences in health is a key public-health objective. ... The foremost method is to improve children's and adolescents' living conditions" (Swedish National Institute of Public Health 2011: 28–29). In the United Kingdom, well-being of the population, significantly influenced by having strong social networks, is already used by the government as a measure of a successful health policy (Barton et al. 2017).

If we want to improve physical and mental health for people of all ages, reduce social pathology, and strengthen "social immune systems" in North America, we need a governmental policy that acknowledges that "health promotion rests on the shoulders not only of individuals but also of their families and communities" (Berkman 1995: 245). This will lead us to reshape sprawling suburbs and inner-city neighborhoods so that they support the development of face-to-face interaction and community. The time-tested principles of true urbanism will help to make our neighborhoods and cities safe and lively, which will increase a sense of well-being and help people of all ages to live healthier lives.

Suzanne H. Crowhurst Lennard is co-founder and director of International Making Cities Livable (http://www.livablecities.org). She authored or co-authored eight books including *Genius of the European Square*, *The Forgotten Child*, and *Livable Cities Observed*, has published widely in professional journals (e.g., *Planning, Urban Land, Western Planner*), and speaks and consults internationally. Her interdisciplinary work pays special attention to effects of the built environment on children's health, well-being, and development; designing public urban places; and equitable city planning guidelines to improve health and well-being for all—old and young, poor and well-to-do.

References

AAP Committee on Environmental Health. 2009. "The Built Environment: Designing Communities to Promote Physical Activity in Children." *Pediatrics* 123 (6 June): 6. Accessed 30 June 2009. http://pediatrics.aappublications.org/content/123/6/1591.

Aldous, Tony. 1992. *Urban Villages: A Concept for Creating Mixed-Use Urban Developments on a Sustainable Scale*. London: Urban Villages Group.

Altschuler, Andrea, Carol P. Somkin, and Nancy E. Adler. 2004. "Local Services and Amenities, Neighborhood Social Capital, and Health." *Social Science and Medicine* 59(6): 1219–29.

Ball, Kylie, Adrian Bauman, Eva Leslie, and Neville Owen. 2001. "Perceived Environmental Aesthetics and Convenience and Company Are Associated with Walking for Exercise among Australian Adults." *Preventive Medicine* 33(5): 434–40.

Bandura, Albert. 1977. *Social Learning Theory*. New York: Prentice Hall.

Barton, Hugh, Susan Thompson, Sarah Burgess, Marcus Grant, eds. 2017. *The Routledge Handbook of Planning for Health and Well-Being*. Abingdon and New York: Routledge.

Baum, Fran, and Catherine Palmer. 2002. "'Opportunity Structures': Urban Landscape, Social Capital and Health Promotion in Australia." *Health Promotion International* 17(4): 351–61.

Bellah, Robert N., Richard Madsen, William M. Sullivan, Ann Swidler, and Steven M. Tipton. 1985. *Habits of the Heart: Individualism and Commitment in American Life*. Berkeley: University of California Press.

Benson, Peter L. 2006. *All Kids Are Our Kids*. San Francisco: Jossey-Bass.

Berkman, Lisa F. 1995. "The Role of Social Relations in Health Promotion." *Psychosomatic Medicine* 57: 245–54.

Berkman, Lisa F., and Thomas Glass. 2000. "Social Integration, Social Networks, Social Support, and Health." In *Social Epidemiology*, ed. Lisa F. Berkman and Ichiro Kawachi, 137–73. Oxford: Oxford University Press.

Berkman, Lisa F., Thomas Glass, Ian Brissette, and Teresa E. Seeman. 2000. "From Social Integration to Health: Durkheim in the New Millennium." *Social Science and Medicine* 51: 843–57.

Berry, Wendell. 1990. *What Are People For?* San Francisco: North Point Press.

Birmaher, Boris, Neal D. Ryan, Douglas E. Williamson, David A. Brent, Joan Kaufman, Ronald E. Dahl, James Perel, and Beverly Nelson. 1996. "Childhood and Adolescent Depression: A Review of the Past 10 Years; Part I." *Journal of the American Academy of Child and Adolescent Psychiatry* 35(11): 1427–39.

Blyth, Dale A., and Nancy Leffert. 1995. "Communities as Contexts for Adolescent Development: An Empirical Analysis." *Journal of Adolescent Research* 10: 64–87.

Bok, Sissela. 1998. *Mayhem: Violence as Public Entertainment*. Reading, MA: Perseus Books.

Booth, Frank W., Scott E. Gordon, Christian J. Carlson, and Marc T. Hamilton. 2000. "Waging War on Modern Chronic Diseases: Primary Prevention through Exercise Biology." *Journal of Applied Physiology* 88(2): 774–87.

Bowlby, John. 1973. *Attachment and Loss: Separation, Anxiety, and Anger*. New York: Basic Books.

Bronfenbrenner, Urie. 1979. *The Ecology of Human Development: Experiments by Nature and Design*. Cambridge, MA: Harvard University Press.

Buber, Martin. 1965. *Between Man and Man*. New York: Collier Books.

———. 1967. *A Believing Humanism*. New York: Simon & Schuster.

Bullock, Janis R. 1998. "Loneliness in Young Children." ERIC Clearinghouse on Elementary and Early Childhood Education. Accessed 29 July 2014. http://athealth.com/topics/loneliness-in-young-children-3/.

Cattell, Vicky. 2001. "Poor People, Poor Places, and Poor Health: The Mediating Role of Social Networks and Social Capital." *Social Science and Medicine* 52: 1501–16.

CDC (Centers for Disease Control and Prevention). 2018. "Overweight and Obesity: Causes and Consequences." CDC, 5 March 2018. Accessed 29 July 2014. http://www.cdc.gov/obesity/adult/causes/index.html.

———. 2012. "Youth Violence: Facts at a Glance 2012." Accessed 29 July 2014. http://www.cdc.gov/ViolencePrevention/pdf/yv-datasheet-a.pdf.

Cervero, Robert, and Michael Duncan. 2003. "Walking, Bicycling and Urban Landscapes: Evidence from the San Francisco Bay Area." *American Journal of Public Health* 93(9): 1478–83.

Cohen, S. 2004. "Social Relationships and Health." *American Psychologist*, November 2004, 676–84.

Cohen, Sheldon, and Anne Lezak. 1977. "Noise and Inattentiveness to Social Cues." *Environment and Behavior* 9: 559–72.

Cohen, Sheldon, Lynn G. Underwood, and Benjamin H. Gottlieb, eds. 2000. *Social Support Measurement and Intervention: A Guide for Health and Social Scientists*. Oxford: Oxford University Press.

Cohen-Mansfield, Jiska, and Aleksandra Parpura-Gill. 2007. "Loneliness in Older Persons: A Theoretical Model and Empirical Findings." *International Psychogeriatrics* 19(2): 279–94.

Coley, Rebekah Levine, William C. Sullivan, and Francis E. Kuo. 1997. "Where Does Community Grow? The Social Context Created by Nature in Urban Public Housing." *Environment and Behavior* 29: 468–92.

Cozens, Paul, and David Hillier. 2008. "The Shape of Things to Come: New Urbanism, the Grid and the Cul-de-Sac." *International Planning Studies* 13(1): 51–73.

Cross, Henry A., and Harry F. Harlow. 1965. "Prolonged and Progressive Effects of Partial Isolation on the Behaviour of Macaque Monkeys." *Journal of Experimental Research in Personality* 1: 39–49.

Crowe, Timothy D. 2000. *Crime Prevention through Environmental Design: Applications of Architectural Design and Space Management Concepts.* Woburn, MA: Butterworth-Heinemann.

Crowhurst Lennard, Suzanne. 2017. "Planning a Neighborhood Square." *Western Planner,* 21 November 2017. Accessed 13 January 2018. https://www.westernplan ner.org/urban-design-articles/2017/11/21/planning-a-neighborhood-square.

Crowhurst Lennard, Suzanne, and Henry L. Lennard. 2004. "Principles of True Urbanism." International Making Cities Livable. Accessed 29 July 2014. http://www .livablecities.org/articles/principles-true-urbanism.

———. 2008. *Genius of the European Square: How Europe's Traditional Multi-functional Squares Support Social Life and Civic Engagement.* Carmel, CA: Gondolier Press.

De Vos, Henk. 2003. "Geld en 'de rest': Over uitzwerming, teloorgang van gemeenschap en de noodzaak van gemeenschapsbeleid" [Money and "the rest": About sprawl, decline of community and the necessity of community policy]. *Sociologische gids* 50(3): 285–311.

Duncan, Mitch, and Kerry Mummery. 2004. "Psychosocial and Environmental Factors Associated with Physical Activity among City Dwellers in Regional Queensland." *Preventive Medicine* 40: 363–72.

Durkheim, Emile. 1951. *Suicide: A Study in Sociology.* Glencoe, IL: Free Press.

Earls, Felton. 1998. "Linking Community Factors and Individual Development: Summary of Presentation by Felton Earls." *National Institute of Justice Research Preview,* September. Accessed 1 July 2018. https://www.ncjrs.gov/pdffiles/fs000230.pdf.

Earls, Felton J., Stephen W. Raudenbush, Albert J. Reiss, Jr., and Robert J. Sampson. 2005. *Project on Human Development in Chicago Neighborhoods (PHDCN): Systematic Social Observation, 1995.* Ann Arbor, MI. Accessed 1 July 2018. https://www.icpsr .umich.edu/icpsrweb/PHDCN/instruments.jsp#systematic.

Ebbesen, Ebbe B., Glenn L. Kjos, and Vladimir J. Konečni. 1976. "Spatial Ecology: Its Effects on the Choice of Friends and Enemies." *Journal of Experimental Social Psychology* 12: 505–18.

Eberstadt, Mary. 2001. "Home-Alone America." *Hoover Institution Policy Review.* Accessed 29 July 2014. http://www.hoover.org/research/home-alone-america.

Engwicht, David. 1992. *Towards an Eco-City: Calming the Traffic.* Sydney, NSW: Envirobook.

Evans, Gary W. 2003. "Housing and Mental Health: A Review of the Evidence and a Methodological and Conceptual Critique." *Journal of Social Issues.* 59(3): 475–500.

———. 2006. "Child Development and the Physical Environment." *Annual Review of Psychology* 57: 423–51.

Feldtkeller, Andreas. 2001. *Städtebau: Vielfalt und Integration. Neue Konzepte für den Umgang mit Stadtbrachen.* Frankfurt: Campus Verlag.

Fleming, Raymond, Andrew Baum, and Jerome E. Singer. 1985. "Social Support and the Physical Environment." In *Social Support and Health,* ed. Sheldon Cohen and S. Leonard Syme, 327–345. Orlando, FL: Academic Press.

Frank, Lawrence D., Martin A. Andresen, and Thomas L. Schmid. 2004. "Obesity Relationships with Community Design, Physical Activity, and Time Spent in Cars." *American Journal of Preventive Medicine* 27(2): 87–96.

Frank, Lawrence D., Thomas L. Schmid, James F. Sallis, James Chapman, and Brian E. Saelens. 2005. "Linking Objectively Measured Physical Activity with Objectively

Measured Urban Form—Findings from SMARTRAQ." *American Journal of Preventive Medicine* 28(2S2): 117–25.
Garmezy, Norman. 1983. "Stressors of Childhood." In *Stress, Coping, and Development in Children*, ed. Norman Garmezy and Michael Rutter, 43–85. New York: McGraw Hill.
Gehl, Jan. 2010. *Cities for People*. Washington, DC: Island Press.
Gele, Abdi A., and Ivan Harsløf. 2010. *International Journal of Equity Health* 9: 8. Accessed 1 July 2018. http://www.ncbi.nlm.nih.gov/pmc/articles/PMC2848659/.
Gifford, Robert. 2007. "The Consequences of Living in High-Rise Buildings." *Architectural Science Review* 50(1): 2–17.
Giles-Corti, Billie, and Robert J. Donovan. 2002. "The Relative Influence of Individual, Social, and Physical Environment Determinants of Physical Activity." *Social Science and Medicine* 54(12): 1793–1812.
Gillis, A. R. 1974. "Population Density and Social Pathology: The Case of Building Type, Social Allowance and Juvenile Delinquency." *Social Forces* 53: 306–15.
Greenbaum, Susan D. 1982. "Bridging Ties at the Neighborhood Level." *Social Networks* 4: 367–84.
Greenspan, Stanley I. 1997. *The Growth of the Mind*. Cambridge, MA: Perseus Books.
Harlow, Harry. 1964. "Early Social Deprivation and Later Behavior in the Monkey." In *Unfinished Tasks in the Behavioral Sciences*, ed. Arnold Abrams, Harry H. Garner, and James E. P. Toman, 154–73. Baltimore: Williams and Wilkie.
Hawe, Penelope, and Alan Shiell. 2000. "Social Capital and Health Promotion: A Review." *Social Science and Medicine* 51(6): 871–85.
Henderson, Lynne, and Philip Zimbardo. n.d. "Shyness and Culture." In *Encyclopedia of Mental Health*. Accessed 29 July 2014. http://www.shyness.com/encyclopedia.html#VI.
Hochschild, Arlie. 1997. *The Time Bind*. New York: Holt.
House, James S., Karl R. Landis, and Debra Umberson. 1988. "Social Relationships and Health." *Science* 241(4865): 540–45.
Humpel, Nancy, Neville Owen, and Eva Leslie. 2002. "Environmental Factors Associated with Adults' Participation in Physical Activity." *American Journal of Preventive Medicine* 22(3): 188–99.
Jackson, Richard J. 2008. "Environment Shapes Health, Including Children's Mental Health." *Journal of the American Academy of Child & Adolescent Psychiatry* 47(2): 129–31.
Jacobs, Jane. 1961. *The Death and Life of Great American Cities*. New York: Random House.
Kawachi, Ichiro, and Lisa F. Berkman. 2001. "Social Ties and Mental Health." *Journal of Urban Health* 78(3): 458–67.
Kawachi, Ichiro, Bruce P. Kennedy, Kimberly Lochner, and Deborah Prothrow-Stith. 1997. "Social Capital, Income Inequality, and Mortality." *American Journal of Public Health* 87:1491–98.
Kerr, J., D. Rosenberg, and L. Frank. 2012. The Role of the Built Environment in Healthy Aging: Community Design, Physical Activity, and Health among Older Adults. *Journal of Planning Literature* 27(1): 43–60.
Kidder Smith, George Everard. 1954. *Italy Builds*. New York: Reinhold.
Klinenberg, Eric. 2003. *Heat Wave: A Social Autopsy of Disaster in Chicago*. Chicago: University of Chicago Press.

Kunstler, James Howard. 1998. *Home from Nowhere.* New York: Touchstone.
Kuo, Frances E., William C. Sullivan, Rebekah Levine Coley, and Liesette Brunson. 1998. "Fertile Ground for Community: Inner-City Neighborhood Common Spaces." *American Journal of Community Psychology* 26(6): 823–51.
Langdon, Philip. 1994. *A Better Place to Live: Reshaping the American Suburb.* Amherst: University of Massachusetts Press.
Leffert, Nancy, Peter L. Benson, Peter C. Scales, Anu R. Sharma, Dyanne R. Drake, and Dale A. Blyth. 1998. "Developmental Assets: Measurement and Prediction of Risk Behaviors Among Adolescents." *Applied Developmental Science* 2(4): 209–30.
Lennard, Henry L., and Suzanne H. Crowhurst Lennard, 2000. *The Forgotten Child: Cities for the Well-Being of Children.* Carmel, CA: Gondolier Press.
Leyden, Kevin M. 2003. "Social Capital and the Built Environment: The Importance of Walkable Neighborhoods." *American Journal of Public Health* 93(9): 1546–51.
Lochner, Kimberly A., Ichiro Kawachi, Robert T. Brennan, and Stephen L. Buka. 2003. "Social Capital and Neighborhood Mortality Rates in Chicago." *Social Science and Medicine* 56(8): 1797–1805.
Lomas, Jonathan. 1998. "Social Capital and Health: Implications for Public Health and Epidemiology." *Social Science and Medicine* 47(9): 1181–88.
Low, Setha M. 2000. *On the Plaza: The Politics of Public Space and Culture.* Austin: University of Texas Press.
Lund, Hollie. 2002. "Pedestrian Environments and Sense of Community." *Journal of Planning Education and Research* 21(3): 301–12.
Macintyre, Sally, and Anne Ellaway. 2000. "Ecological Approaches: Rediscovering the Role of the Physical and Social Environment." In *Social Epidemiology,* ed. Lisa F. Berkman and Ichiro Kawachi. Oxford: Oxford University Press. Accessed January 2018. https://www.researchgate.net/publication/246003474_Ecological_Approaches_Rediscovering_the_Role_of_the_Physical_and_Social_Environment.
Macintyre, Sally, Sheila Maciver, and Anne Sooman. 1993. "Area, Class and Health: Should We Be Focusing on Places or People?" *Journal of Social Policy* 22: 213–14.
Mahdjoubi, Lamine. 2015. *Healthy Streets for Children.* Accessed January 2018. https://www.youtube.com/watch?v=Dfata461q0g.
McCarthy, Dennis, and Susan Saegert. 1978. "Residential Density, Social Overload and Social Withdrawal." *Human Ecology* 6(3): 253–71.
McMillan, David W., and David M. Chavis. 1986. "Sense of Community: A Definition and a Theory." *Journal of Community Psychology* 14: 6–23.
McPherson, Miller, Lynn Smith-Lovin, and Matthew E. Brashears. 2006. "Social Isolation in America: Changes in Core Discussion Networks over Two Decades." *American Sociological Review* 71: 353–75.
Mehta, Vikas. 2007. "Lively Streets: Determining Environmental Characteristics to Support Social Behavior." *Journal of Planning Education and Research* 27(2): 165–87.
Montgomery, Charles. 2013. *Happy City: Transforming Our Lives through Urban Design.* New York: Farrar, Straus & Giroux.
Morris, Douglas. 2005. *It's a Sprawl World After All.* Gabriola Island, BC: New Society.
Mouratidis, Kostas. 2017. "Built Environment and Social Well-Being: How Does Urban Form Affect Social Life and Personal Relationships?" *Cities,* 10.020. Accessed 13 January 2018. http://dx.doi.org/10.1016/j.cities.2017.10.020.
NACTO (National Association of City Transportation Officials). 2012. *Urban Bikeway Design Guide.* New York: NACTO.

Nasar, Jack, and David A. Julian. 1995. "The Psychological Sense of Community in the Neighborhood." *Journal of the American Planning Association* 61(2):178–84.

Nestmann, Frank, and Klaus Hurrelmann, eds. 1994. *Social Networks and Social Support in Childhood and Adolescence*. Berlin and New York: De Gruyter.

Newman, Katherine S., Cybelle Fox, Wendy Roth, Jal Mehta, and David Harding. 2004. *Rampage: The Social Roots of School Shootings*. New York: Basic Books.

Oldenburg, Ray. 1991. *The Great Good Place*. New York: Paragon House.

Pendola, Rocco, and Sheldon Gen. 2008. "Does 'Main Street' Promote Sense of Community? A Comparison of San Francisco Neighborhoods." *Environment and Behavior* 40(4): 545–74.

Putnam, Robert. 2000. *Bowling Alone*. New York: Simon & Schuster.

Resnick, Michael D., Peter S. Bearman, Robert W. Blum, Karl E. Bauman, Kathleen M. Harris, Jo Jones, Joyce Tabor, et al. 1997. "Protecting Adolescents from Harm: Findings from the National Longitudinal Study on Adolescent Health." *Journal of the American Medical Association* 278: 823–32.

Richman, N. 1974. "The Effects of Housing on Pre-school Children and Their Mothers." *Developmental Medicine & Child Neurology* 16: 53–58.

Rubin, K. H., G. Fein, and B. Vandenberg. 1983. "Play." In *Handbook of Child Psychology*, vol. 4, *Socialization, Personality, and Social Development*. New York: Wiley.

Rubin, Kenneth H., and Linda Rose-Krasnor. 1992. "Interpersonal Problem-Solving and Social Competence in Children." In *Handbook of Social Development: A Lifespan Perspective*, ed. V. B. van Hasselt and M. Hersen. New York: Plenum.

Russell, Anna. 2010. "Free Range Kids: Independence and the Urban Child." PLAN7122 Planning Project, University of New South Wales. Accessed 29 July 2014. http://www.be.unsw.edu.au/sites/default/files/upload/pdf/cf/hbep/research/Theses/Russell_thesis.pdf.

Rutter, Michael. 1983. "Stress, Coping and Development: Some Issues and Some Questions." In *Stress, Coping, and Development in Children*, ed. Norman Garmezy and Michael Rutter, 1–43. New York: McGraw-Hill.

Rutter, Michael, and Henri Giller. 1983. *Juvenile Delinquency: Trends and Perspectives*. New York: Guilford Press.

Sampson, Robert J., Stephen W. Raudenbush, and Felton Earls. 1997. "Neighborhoods and Violent Crime: A Multilevel Study of Collective Efficacy." *Science* 277: 1–7.

Schneider, Barbara, and David Stevenson. 1999. *The Ambitious Generation: America's Teenagers; Motivated but Directionless*. New Haven, CT: Yale University Press.

Stafford, Philip B. 2009. *Elderburbia: Aging with a Sense of Place in America*. Santa Barbara, CA: Praeger.

Ståhl, T., A., D. Rütten, A. Nutbeam, L. Bauman, T. Kannas, G. Abel, D. Lüschen, J. Rodriquez, and J. van der Zee Vinck. 2001. "The Importance of the Social Environment for Physically Active Lifestyle—Results from an International Study." *Social Science and Medicine* 52: 1–10.

Stevenson, Howard C. 1998. "Raising Safe Villages: Cultural-Ecological Factors That Influence the Emotional Adjustment of Adolescents." *Journal of Black Psychology* 24(1): 44–59.

Storm, Ilse, Frank den Hertog, Hans van Oers, and Albertine J. Schuit. 2016. "How to Improve Collaboration between the Public Health Sector and Other Policy Sectors to Reduce Health Inequalities?—A Study in Sixteen Municipalities in the Nether-

lands" *International Journal of Equity Health* 15: 97. Accessed 13 January 2018. https://www.ncbi.nlm.nih.gov/pmc/articles/PMC4918104/.
Swedish National Institute of Public Health, 2011. *Social Health Inequalities in Swedish Children and Adolescents—A Systematic Review.* 2nd ed. Accessed 4 June 2017. https://www.folkhalsomyndigheten.se/pagefiles/12698/A2011-11-Social-health-inequalities-in-swedish-children-and-adolescents.pdf.
Tietjen, A. M. 1989. "The Ecology of Children's Social Support Networks." In *Social Networks and Social Support in Childhood and Adolescence*, eds. F. Nestmann and K. Hurrelmann, 395–407. New York: Wiley.
Twenge, Jean. 2017. "Have Smartphones Destroyed a Generation?" *Atlantic*, 3 August 2017. Accessed 12 January 2018. https://www.theatlantic.com/amp/article/534198/.
Untermann, Richard K. 1984. *Accommodating the Pedestrian: Adapting Towns and Neighborhoods for Walking and Biking.* New York: Van Nostrand Reinhold.
Werner, Emmy E., and Ruth S. Smith. 1982. *Vulnerable but Invincible: A Longitudinal Study of Resilient Children and Youth.* New York: McGraw-Hill.
WHO (World Health Organization). 2007. *Global Age-Friendly Cities: A Guide.* Geneva: World Health Organization. Accessed 29 July 2014. http://www.who.int/ageing/publications/Global_age_friendly_cities_Guide_English.pdf.
Whyte, William H. 1980. *The Social Life of Small Urban Spaces.* Washington, DC: Conservation Foundation.
Williams, Philippa, and Barbara Pocock. 2010. "Building 'Community' for Different Stages of Life: Physical and Social Infrastructure in Master Planned Communities." *Community, Work and Family* 13(1): 71–87.

4 THE INTERSECTION BETWEEN SUSTAINABLE AND AGE-FRIENDLY DEVELOPMENT

Alan DeLaTorre

Introduction

PORTLAND, OREGON, HAS BEEN A leader in sustainable development as government agencies, nonprofit organizations, and businesses have been considered innovators in policy making and practice aimed at creating a more sustainable city and region. Despite the established public and private push toward sustainable development, little is known about how, or whether, urban planners, policy makers, and the development community have considered population aging and older adults in those efforts. In 2006, researchers at Portland State University (PSU) conducted an age-friendly research project in the city, in collaboration with the World Health Organization (WHO). This project aimed to identify barriers, opportunities, and suggestions for creating a Portland that addresses the needs—and utilizes the assets—of communities of all ages. The project has grown into a translational research project considered to be a university-city-community partnership that has become part of the wider community push to make Portland more sustainable, equitable, and resilient to demographic, social, and economic change over time.

This chapter explores the intersection between sustainable development and the age-friendly project in Portland by detailing a case study of factors that affected the planning and development of sustainable, affordable housing for older adults in Portland. The findings detail extant policies and practices that have affected planning and development in Portland and offer a new definition for sustainable development—one that incorporates a life course perspective—and a set of guiding principles for sustainable development for an aging society. Additionally, the Portland age-friendly movement will be placed within the context of efforts surrounding sustainable development, in an attempt to understand how the two approaches to development have intersected in the city.

Sustainable Development

The term *sustainability* is derived from the word *sustain*, which means "to endure without giving way or yielding . . . to keep up or keep going, as an action or process" (Costello 1992: 1347). Aguirre (2002: 102) explained that "the scientific practice of sustainability antedates the recent collective surge centered on the idea of sustainable development," and Wheeler (2000: 436) noted that "the birth of the sustainability concept in the 1970s can be seen as the logical outgrowth of a new consciousness about global problems related to the environment and development, fueled in part by 1960s environmentalism." Aguirre (2002) opined that the term *sustainability* had always referred to matters of the natural environment; however, Choguill (2007) suggested that the concept of sustainable development was initially conceived as a term most relevant to economic development.

An Internet search for the terms *sustainability* or *sustainable development* yields millions of results, ranging from urban planning and design to food systems and recycling. The wide range in the use of the terms makes it important to provide sufficient context when discussing them in this chapter. For example, the *Oregon Sustainability Act* (State of Oregon 2001: 1) defined *sustainability* as "using, developing and protecting resources in a manner that enables people to meet current needs and provides that future generations can also meet future needs, from the joint perspective of environmental, economic and community objectives."

Oregon's definition has a distinct similarity to the best-known and most commonly embraced origin of the concept of sustainable development (Williams and Millington 2004) that emerged from the *Report of the World Commission on Environment and Development* (United Nations 1987: 16), commonly referred to as the "Brundtland Report"; the report stated that "humanity has the ability to make development sustainable to ensure that it meets the needs of the present without compromising the ability of future generations to meet their own needs." The United Nation's Commission attempted to identify the essential components of a sustainable future, summarized as the need to balance, "the three E's" of environment, (social) equity, and economy (Berke 2002: 30). According to Meadowcroft (2000), the Brundtland Report helped legitimize the concept of sustainable development, which was formally endorsed by political leaders in 1992 at the United Nation's Rio Earth Summit in Brazil.

It was not until the 1990s that the concept of sustainable development moved beyond environmental and economic applications and into the areas of human settlements, urban areas, and housing (Choguill 1999). It has been suggested that social equity issues within sustainability studies and practice were largely peripheral issues compared to economic and environmental concerns; however, they are now becoming mainstream due to the necessity of community involvement and the realization that "social sustainability is the only bedrock on which meaningful environmental sustainability can be grounded" (Dillard, Dujon, and King 2009: 1). Although many variations of the terms *sustainability* and *sustainable development* permeate political, academic, professional, and popular culture, we must remember that the theory and practice exist as a part of human systems as they exist in the natural world.

We can turn to Wheeler (2000) to gain an understanding of elements of sustainable urban development that are useful for academics, practitioners, and community stakeholders. His nine elements include (1) compact, efficient land use; (2) less automobile use, better access; (3) efficient resource use, less pollution and waste; (4) restoration of natural systems; (5) good housing and living environments; (6) a healthy social ecology; (7) sustainable economics; (8) community participation and involvement; and (9) preservation of local culture and wisdom.

Returning to Portland, many of the elements described by Wheeler can be found in extant policies and approaches. It is not surprising that Portland was an early adopter in pushing to become the nation's "sustainability capital" (Giegerich 2008: 1). The city has been lauded as a "paradigmatic sustainable city," although it should be noted that criticisms exist regarding whether sustainability fixes (i.e., green investment in the city's core) have aided gentrification and other social inequities (Goodling, Green, and McClintock 2015: 9). In 2009, the City of Portland integrated its Bureau of Planning and Office of Sustainable Development into the Bureau of Planning and Sustainability to better align the complementary efforts of the agencies and to improve sustainable practices and public engagement (City of Portland 2009).

Population Aging and Age-Friendly Development

The introduction to this book has detailed the massive demographic change that is global population aging. Moving forward, Portland, like the United States and the world, will face the unprecedented aging of populations and the need to address the challenges and opportunities that accompany this unprecedented demographic shift (He, Goodkind, and Kowal 2016). The

WHO's *Global Age-Friendly Cities* guide stated that in order to create "sustainable communities [cities must provide] structures and services to support their residents' wellbeing" and that "older people in particular require supportive and enabling living environments" in order to compensate for changes—both physical and social—that are associated with aging (WHO 2007: 4).

A call to action has been issued by U.S. policy experts to urban and regional planners and policy makers that highlights the growing need to prepare for population aging through thoughtful, intentional planning and development of housing that is affordable, well-designed, close in proximity to essential services and infrastructure, and intended to integrate a diversifying population while fostering social well-being (Farber et al. 2011). In *Planning for an Aging Society* (Howe, Chapman, and Baggett 1994: 6), it is suggested that a community's ability to effectively respond to the needs of an aging society depends on how well they are addressed in planning and public education efforts; the authors argued that "creativity in defining opportunities to make improvements will maximize the use of both public and private resources." There is also a need for research that addresses how the development community responds to aging-specific issues such as accessibility and mobility and also how the public sector plans for and encourages age-appropriate development (Giuliano 2004).

For more than a decade there has been a substantial growth in efforts aimed at improving housing and environments—both physical and social—in anticipation of the aging of the population, including the focus by AARP on livable communities (AARP 2000, 2005, 2015) and the WHO's more recent focus on age-friendly cities and communities (WHO 2007, 2014). The active aging framework from the WHO (2002) has been foundational to the age-friendly movement, as it has encouraged policy changes and refinement of services and programs to better meet the needs of older adults; in doing so, environments are expected to benefit a wide range of users, including younger generations, families with children, people with disabilities, and others across the age and ability spectra. This active aging framework is particularly valuable, as it urges planners and policy makers to look beyond needs-based, deficiency-oriented approaches often associated with aging, instead urging for the consideration of available opportunities—and assets—that may result from our changing age structure.

The Portland Region's Age-Friendly Efforts

Before Portland's age-friendly efforts are detailed, it should be noted that myriad services and programs have existed to address older adults' day-today needs and activities prior to the age-friendly efforts (e.g., transit and para-transit services, area agencies on aging operations, urban and regional planning efforts; the vast majority of age-related services are critically important and highly successful and operate independently of the age-friendly project). Additionally, in 2006, Portland's regional government, Metro, funded a multidisciplinary project by PSU's College of Urban and Public Affairs to examine age-related shifts in housing and transportation demand (Neal et al. 2006); that project aided PSU's gerontologists in preparing to undertake future age-friendly research activities.

In late 2006, PSU's Institute on Aging was invited by the WHO to participate in a research project assessing Portland's age-friendly features and barriers as part of the WHO's Global Age-Friendly Cities project. Portland was the only U.S. city involved in the original global project, which consisted of thirty-three cities in twenty-two countries.

Since that project, the WHO has initiated its Global Network of Age-Friendly Cities and Communities, AARP began coordinating the U.S. Network of Age-Friendly Communities (AARP 2014), and Portland has continued to advance its age-friendliness as a member of the global and U.S. networks. As of this writing the Age-Friendly Portland Advisory Council, coordinated by the Institute on Aging (IOA) at PSU, advises the initiative. In October 2013, the Action Plan for an Age-Friendly Portland (Age-Friendly Portland Advisory Council 2013) was unanimously approved by City Council resolution, and implementation efforts are under way. In 2014, Multnomah County—Portland is the county seat for Multnomah County—joined the WHO and AARP Networks under the coordination of the Advisory Council for an Age-Friendly Portland and Multnomah County (Age-Friendly Portland and Multnomah County 2018); in 2016, Multnomah County approved its own action plan (Multnomah County 2016), sharing three broad environmental domains with Portland's action plan (i.e., physical, service, and social environments).

Concurrent Efforts: Age-Friendly, Livable Communities and Sustainable Development

AARP's focus on livable communities and Portland's age-friendly research were under way at the same time that jurisdictional and private sector efforts have been aiming to further sustainable development in Portland and Oregon. The findings from the initial age-friendly Portland study (Neal and DeLaTorre 2007a, 2007b) shed light on aspects of sustainable development, albeit under the auspices of age-friendly environments. First, every participant group from the initial study—older adults, caregivers, and providers of service—identified a lack of affordable housing for an aging society. Second, housing that was available was seen as disconnected from important services and infrastructure that was needed by older adults to maintain independence and quality of life, and suggestions were made to make improvements for future generations. Third, housing was not planned for and developed in a way that met the needs of aging individuals. Finally, suggestions for improving housing and environments for the burgeoning numbers of older adults were offered, including changes in planning policies and development practices.

However, those concurrent attempts to plan for and develop housing and environments that were sustainable and those that were age-friendly were not linked; both undertakings required forward-looking approaches, but no researchers or practitioners in the city or region were looking at the efforts in an integrated fashion. Although it seems logical to assume that the rapid aging of society would be integral to sustainable development based solely on the temporal component of sustainability—providing opportunities for current and future generations—scant attention was being paid to the incorporation of population aging into sustainable development research, policies, and practices. In order to address this disconnect, a case study was conducted that aimed to understand the factors that affect the planning and development of sustainable, affordable housing for older adults in Portland (DeLaTorre 2013).

Description of the Case Study

Housing for older adults that is considered sustainable and affordable[1] exists in Portland and other cities. However, the factors that influence the planning and development of such housing have yet to be studied in depth. In order to better understand those factors, a qualitative case study was carried out to learn about the phenomenon of sustainable, affordable housing for those aged fifty-five and older in Portland.

The primary data collected and analyzed for the study was gathered from thirty-one interviews of key informants in public, for-profit, and nonprofit organizations who were identified using a snowball sampling technique. A review of documents pertaining to six Portland-area developments identified as sustainable and affordable for those aged fifty-five and older was also conducted to provide context for the study.[2] Based on these data, the meaning of sustainable, affordable housing for older adults was explored, as well as policies that affected the development of this housing type in order to identify those that have had positive impacts, those that need changes, and policy recommendations for consideration in the future. The findings were used to create guiding principles for understanding what constitutes sustainable development for an aging society.

Limitations of the Research

The ability to make generalizations based on this qualitative case study is constrained by several aspects of the research design. First, some of the findings are limited geographically and temporally based on the unique set of policies, practices, and developments that exists in the City of Portland, the greater metropolitan region, and the state of Oregon.

Second, the findings are not fully triangulated, as they are based on two sources: existing literature and key-informant interviews. As a result, these findings are limited to expanding theoretical understanding rather than generalizing to populations (Yin 2003).

Third, the nature of qualitative research is such that these findings may be questioned by those who may not value or understand this line of inquiry. Although every methodological precaution has been taken to ensure both the reliability and the validity of the data, there is still room for error.

Fourth, the researcher has attempted to conduct a valid and reliable study while also undertaking social, civic, and academic activities with the aim of studying and creating better environments. These activities have heightened the researcher's understanding of what constitutes sustainable, affordable housing for older adults but could be seen as leading to bias and/or a loss of objectivity. However, as Christians (2003: 234) posited, a historical overview of theory and practice in qualitative research has pointed to the need for "an entirely new model of research ethics in which human action and conceptions of the good are interactive." This study is an example of that type of research as it involved, simultaneously, ongoing human action (e.g., civic and social activities), recalculations of what was considered good housing and environments for older adults (e.g., policy suggestions to local government and the development of guidelines for future development), and data collection and analysis.

The research design was informed by the ecological perspectives based in gerontology and public health. In gerontology, the ecology of aging (Lawton 1986; Lawton and Nahemow 1973) has considered the importance of many factors in the health and well-being of older adults, including aspects of the social and built environment: (1) personal environments; (2) group environments; (3) suprapersonal environments (e.g., characteristics of the aggregate of individuals in proximity to an individual such as average age, income, and/or race); (4) social environments (e.g., social and political movements, economic cycles, traditions, and values); and (5) physical environments. These environmental factors extend beyond an individual's home to include aspects of the neighborhood, as well as the policies and programs that have had an impact on older adults. The field of public health has also utilized an ecological model in an attempt to guide the building of healthy communities, including application in the fields of gerontology (Satariano 2006) and urban planning (WHO 2010). Public health practitioners have applied the ecological model when seeking to achieve health promotion through five areas of influence: (1) intrapersonal; (2) interpersonal; (3) institutional; (4) community; and (5) public policy (National Institutes of Health 2005).

The ecological models in both gerontology and public health have sought to explain the behavior of individuals and what Altman (1975: 206) described as a social-systems perspective that emphasized the "design of flexible, changing environments that can be manipulated, shaped, and altered." Similarly, the WHO (2002) provided an active aging policy framework positing that active aging depends on determinants ranging from individual attributes to social, physical, economic, and service environments. The WHO's suggested policy response was the creation of a framework that suggested action based on three pillars: health, participation, and security.

The ecological perspective informed the research design by calling to question various aspects of sociocultural, institutional, and policy environments. According to Stake (1995: 46), data gathering for qualitative research often begins before there is a commitment to the study, and a considerable proportion of data is impressionistic: "Many of these early impressions will later be refined or replaced, but the pool of data includes the earliest of observations." The impressions that have shaped this research design can be seen as having been influenced by the author's engagement in past research, advocacy, and civic engagement activities related to environments for older adults and people with disabilities since 2002.

The Meaning of Sustainable Development as It Pertains to Aging

Sustainable development and sustainability have become ubiquitous concepts often understood through the use of language similar to the Brundtland Report: development that meets the needs of the present generation without compromising the ability of future generations to meet their own needs (United Nations 1987). The three areas often discussed in conjunction with this definition are distinct, yet interconnected: the environment (or planet), the economy (or profit), and social equity (or people), also known as "the three E's" (Berke 2002; Elkington 2004).

It was clear that respondents, in general, did not clearly associate the meaning of sustainable development with the phenomenon of population aging. Introducing the topic of aging into the discourse of sustainable development ultimately led to a more robust understanding of its meaning during the interviews. At the beginning of each key-informant interview, respondents were asked to react to two descriptions that were provided by the researcher. The first was the City of Portland's definition of sustainable development (City of Portland 2001)—development that seeks to balance human development, growth, and equity with ecological stewardship—and the second was a modified description of the WHO's definition of an age-friendly city (WHO 2007)—sustainable housing and environments for older adults that encourage active aging by optimizing opportunities for health, participation, and security in order to enhance quality of life as people age. Using the descriptions allowed the researcher to uncover perceptions held with regard to the language used in current research and practice settings.

The findings revealed several insights. First, the social equity component of sustainable development was often minimized with respect to both the environmental and economic components; this reinforces the findings in previous research (Dillard et al. 2009). Second, even though the terms *future generations* and *human development* were articulated in descriptions of sustainable housing and environments for older adults, respondents felt that little, if any, attention was paid to aging-related demographic trends. Finally, respondents felt that the prevailing concept of sustainable development should better address the future needs of society—especially population aging—and go beyond the identification of needs toward opportunities that society should be striving to maximize (e.g., optimizing health, enhancing quality of life).

Taken together, these findings indicated that it is possible to shape a more robust, hybrid description of sustainable development that maintains the commonly used and understood definition and also addresses the dynamic changes that humans face throughout the life course, including those encountered by older adults. The researcher proposes that the following description of sustainable development is more appropriate in describing the challenges and opportunities of future generations:

> Sustainable development seeks to meet human needs while cultivating opportunities for human development across the life course, cultures, and geographies. Such development must address the current generations' ability to sustain their quality of life and well-being while maintaining the ability for future generations to do the same. Furthermore, human development must be integrated into evolving ecological systems by balancing aspects of the natural, built, and social environments. Growth patterns, services, and underlying economic systems must foster social equity in a manner that leads to the health of people, places and systems, both now and in the future.

Five Elements of Sustainable Housing for an Aging Society

Housing and environments for older adults have long been of interest in the field of gerontology. Physical environments that older adults use on a day-to-day basis are critical to their independence and are a key component of the ability of individuals to function. Recently, sustainable development and green building principles have become commonplace in affordable housing developments, including affordable housing developed for older adults, and have led to buildings that save energy and expenses for the resident and contribute to better environmental outcomes (e.g., greater air quality, fewer pollutants). During this study, respondents identified five aspects of sustainable housing and environments that were specific to older adults.

The first element, physical accessibility, was described by respondents as being critical for meeting the functional needs of older adults. Interviewees described the importance of going beyond the minimum requirements currently in place (e.g., Americans with Disabilities Act [ADA] guidelines, building codes) in an attempt to create environments that not only comply with accessibility standards, but more importantly, are able to be used by the widest possible set of individuals in society. Two specific design approaches were identified as appropriate for incorporating into the planning and development of sustainable housing for older adults. The first, universal design, is the design of products and environments to be usable by all people, to the greatest extent possible without the need for adaptation or specialized design (Center for Universal Design 2006). The second, visitable housing, is housing that requires at least three criteria: one zero-step entrance, wide doorways with thirty-two inches of passage, and a half-bathroom on the main floor that can be accessed by a person in a wheelchair (AARP 2008; National Council on Independent Living 2018). These two approaches were seen by respondents as having the ability to foster opportunities for people of all ages and abilities (e.g., frail older adults, people using wheelchairs and walkers, parents with baby strollers, able-bodied people) to be independent and better integrated into day-to-day activities in the community.

The second and third elements identified by respondents were closely related: the first was proximity to community services, and the second was infrastructure that connected housing with services. Regarding the first area, proximity of housing for older adults to commercial and public services was seen as vitally important, especially as functional mobility declines. Certain patterns of development (e.g., automobile-oriented urban sprawl, separation of land uses) were seen as leading to social isolation, and the need to bring housing and services closer together was evident. Furthermore, some key informants reported that bringing housing and critical services (e.g., supermarkets, government services, public transit) together is especially important with respect to affordable housing options, for social equity reasons. Regarding infrastructure connections, quality pedestrian facilities and transportation services were noted as important if housing was to be considered sustainable. If a person lived near important services but could not overcome barriers to mobility (e.g., lack of contiguous sidewalks or streets, no transportation options), proximity was rendered irrelevant. If transportation and pedestrian infrastructure afforded housing residents direct access to community services, this was seen as enabling older adults to better address their personal needs, to maintain community engagement, and to age in their homes and communities, if they desired and it was appropriate.

The fourth element of sustainable housing for older adults pertained to healthy living environments. In particular, the adoption of green building principles was seen as facilitating healthier housing (e.g., reducing the use of toxic materials, better thermal comfort). Respondents also noted that healthy housing for an aging society should be designed to take into account changes in human function that occur with age (e.g., reduced vision, greater risk of falls). Examples of sustainable, healthy housing included that which has good air quality, is well lit, and has residential units with individually controlled thermostats to ensure comfortable indoor temperature. Additionally, some respondents felt that current green building principles do not encompass adequate design features that are of particular benefit to older adults; in fact, only one of the six sustainable housing developments for older adults in Portland hired an aging expert to address the needs of the future residents aged fifty-five and older. Overall, green building practices in Portland have improved the health of housing for residents of all ages. However, additional design is needed to address the specific health needs of older adults (e.g., allowing more daylight into units, durable and glare-free flooring, accessible design features).

The fifth element of sustainable housing for older adults is the inclusion of social spaces in and near housing developments. Participants explained that a balance was needed between personal privacy and access to social activities. Finding the right balance of privacy and access to opportunities for social participation was seen as vital in facilitating both independence and interdependence as people age. One suggestion for achieving such design outcomes was through the inclusion of future residents and/or knowledgeable older adults in the housing design processes. Specific attention to social spaces within a housing development (e.g., community rooms and libraries, seating spaces, smoking areas, consultation rooms) was seen as important. Also identified was access to social spaces located outside of the walls of the housing unit, considered to be an external feature available to the residents of the development (e.g., parks, plazas, street furniture), as well as private spaces that serve public functions (e.g., cafés, businesses with seating).

The Relationship between Sustainable Housing and Affordability

Affordable housing in Portland is required to include green building features as part of Portland's push to become more sustainable. The city's *Green Building Resolution* (City of Portland 2005) and the Portland Development Commission's (2005) guidelines for green building have ensured that government-subsidized affordable housing is built in a manner that preserves environmental resources and creates better living environments for its residents. These policies have been influenced by the Enterprise Foundation, an early national trendsetter, and have led to changes in development practices in the public, nonprofit, and for-profit sectors (U.S. Department of Housing and Urban Development 2010).

Defining how affordability and sustainability related to one another was not straightforward. Although many respondents felt that a housing development could be environmentally sustainable without being affordable, others commented that the social equity component of sustainable development required addressing the needs of lower-income groups through the provision of affordable housing. This is consistent with the literature that has suggested that sustainable development must include policies and programs that result in affordable housing, including housing for an aging population (Altman and Shactman 2002; Commission on Affordable Housing and Health Facility Needs for Seniors in the 21st Century 2002; Perl 2010).

With respect to quantifying sustainable development and affordability, there was no clear determination of affordability criteria (i.e., rent levels) that was considered equitable or sustainable. Several respondents, who worked in public and nonprofit organizations serving the needs of lower-income older adults, suggested that paying 30 percent of one's income toward rent was the most appropriate housing affordability criterion. However, housing programs offer vastly different affordability levels based on funding streams[3] and organizational missions. Looking collectively at the responses offered for this study, it was clear that the varied understanding and usage of affordability criteria obscured the relationship between sustainable housing and affordability; nonetheless, a clear need for well-designed, healthy, affordable housing for older adults was confirmed by respondents.

Advancing the Meaning of Sustainable, Affordable Housing for Older Adults

Based on the findings from this study, it is clear that the meaning of sustainable development must continue to include aspects of social equity, including the growing needs and assets that are inherent in an aging society. The growing number and proportion of older adults and the population's increasing diversity require considerations of cultural, economic, environmental, and social impacts as we plan for the future. The development of housing and environments must be broadened to improve the well-being of future generations, which will require a concerted effort to create enabling, affordable, healthy, and interdependent cities and communities. Regardless of whether the concept is labeled sustainable development, livable, age-friendly, or another term (e.g., resilient), the core components of the concept should continue to survive and evolve in an effort to plan for and meet the needs of current and future generations.

Public Sector Policies Impacting Sustainable, Affordable Housing for Older Adults

As was described by the respondents, the public sector has focused on addressing the needs of the population it serves through the development of policies and programs that must be adhered to by those sectors carrying out planning and developing activities (e.g., determination of housing needs, accessible development). Respondents reported that housing development in Portland was influenced by many levels of policy making, including federal funding guidelines and legislation, state-level agencies that administer federal funding and Oregon-specific programs, and government bodies at the regional and local levels.

Oregon, in particular, has a system in place that requires local jurisdictions to create comprehensive plans that guide growth and development. In the greater Portland region, the regional government, Metro, sets the planning framework for the three counties and more than twenty cities in its jurisdiction; this regional planning leads to local comprehensive plans such as the one created by the City of Portland. Citywide comprehensive plans work within the constraints of larger plans (e.g., a growth plan to the year 2040 and defined urban growth boundary) to plan for housing, transportation, and land uses that affect the housing and environments used by older adults and all others who live within a given jurisdiction.

Portland's government consists of many bureaus, offices, and commissions that carry out the City of Portland's day-to-day operations and, ultimately, affect housing development opportunities for both the for-profit and nonprofit sectors. The Portland Housing Bureau, the Bureau of Planning and Sustainability, and the Portland Development Commission were all viewed as critical agencies in the identification of the needs of the city's population and the application of processes that lead to the funding, planning for and designing, and building of housing for older adults. Many respondents felt that housing for an aging society has not been seen by the city as a top priority, but that it appeared to be slowly growing in importance, as new efforts were under way (e.g., a revised comprehensive plan).

Policies at every level of government were seen as having a positive impact on the planning and development of housing that is considered sustainable and affordable for older adults. Federally, a number of acts (i.e., Fair Housing, ADA, and the Architectural Barriers Act), programs (i.e., Sections 8, 202, 811, 236, and 232), grants (i.e., the Neighborhood Stabilization Program and Community Development Block Grant program), and requirements (i.e., Section 504 compliance) were identified as fostering the funding, design, and development of needed housing for an aging society.

At the state level, Oregon's planning goals (maintained by the Department of Land Conservation and Development), guidelines for housing development, a document recording fee that funds affordable housing, and a statewide visitability policy—Oregon Revised Statute 456.510 (State of Oregon 2011)—were all seen as positively affecting such housing. Regionally, Multnomah County's weatherization program, regional transportation efforts, and regional planning efforts were identified as leading to positive outcomes.

In Portland, a number of policies and programs have contributed to better environments for older adults, including a climate action plan; specific policies pertaining to homelessness, workforce housing, and green building; housing policy requirements for long-term affordability of new development and building material durability; goals for meeting specific levels of affordable housing; specific development agreements between public and for-profit sectors; and public initiatives to preserve affordable housing subsidies that were expiring.

Needed Policy Changes Related to Sustainable, Affordable Housing for Older Adults

Respondents felt that several changes were needed in policy at the federal level to improve the outcome of housing development, including broadening the scope of the ADA, expanding Housing and Urban Development program funding and scope, improving health-related policies (e.g., Medicaid,

Medicare), and attempting to improve the insufficient funding of affordable housing. In Oregon, respondents identified the need for the tax system to be altered to allow for better revenue streams for government; additionally, home- and community-based services were seen as insufficient for meeting the needs of aging Oregonians. Regionally, planning efforts were identified as needing to strive for better social equity outcomes, as well as a more even geographic distribution of affordable housing. At the local level, building and zoning codes were identified as insufficient in producing enough accessible housing and urban planning strategies, and policies were seen as underserving older adults and people with disabilities.

A number of new policies were suggested by respondents that were seen as having the potential to positively affect the planning and development of sustainable, affordable housing for older adults. Federally, increased funding of the National Housing Trust Fund was noted as needed in order to improve the availability of affordable housing, as well as the suggestion that national green building standards would improve housing quality and tenant health. Statewide, health-care and public health policies were suggested as needing to be better aligned with urban planning and development practices. One barrier to affordable housing was the ban on jurisdictions being able to implement inclusionary zoning practices—that is, the creation of affordable housing that requires developers to set aside a percentage of housing units in new developments to low- and moderate-income households (Hickey 2013).

In Portland, respondents suggested several specific policy opportunities, including creating tax incentives and/or abatement programs for accessible, accessory dwelling units and accessibility retrofits in homes; locating accessible housing close to transit and services; and creating the first municipal policy aimed at addressing the housing needs of aging Portlanders.

Policies that have an impact on the quantity and quality of sustainable, affordable housing for an aging society exist at every level of government, even if they do not explicitly address older adults. Based on the interviews in this study, it is clear that some of this policy is good, some can be improved, and opportunities exist for new policies and programs to be created. Of utmost importance is the need for explicit policies on housing for an aging population; the absence of such policy leaves Portland vulnerable to the rapidly changing demographics that will increase demands on local governments at a time when resources are increasingly scarce. Without proactively addressing this issue, Portland may not be able to adequately address the needs of future generations, a key component of sustainable development. To aid in the creation of informed, sustainable policies that help to meet the needs of future generations, the following section proposes guiding principles of sustainable development for an aging society.

Proposed Guiding Principles of Sustainable Development for an Aging Society

Many of the principles of sustainable development have been integrated into Portland's development-related policies, practices, and culture. More recently, researchers and practitioners have expanded the concept of sustainable development to include social equity, and there is strong and growing attention paid to age-related planning and development. However, our window for preparing for the demographic imperative continues to shrink, and a set of guiding principles of sustainable development for an aging society will be useful in informing future policy, research, and practice.

The formation of these guiding principles has drawn from the ecological models of environmental gerontology and public health, explored previously in this chapter. Additionally, we must consider the WHO's active aging framework (WHO 2002), as it has served as the theoretic base for the domains of age-friendly cities and communities (WHO 2007). The WHO established the following determinants of active aging: (1) physical environments; (2) social environments; (3) economic resources; (4) services; (5) population determinants; and (6) individual determinants. By combining the core aspects of the social ecological models in public health and gerontology with the WHO's active aging framework and domains of age-friendly cities and communities, the following seven factors have been identified as contributing to the health and well-being of older adults in cities and communities: (1) individual factors; (2) social factors; (3) aggregated population characteristics; (4) physical environments; (5) institutional and service environments; (6) economic factors; and (7) public policy.

Additionally, this study sought to answer a call for needed research. Giuliano (2004) and Howe et al. (1994) detailed the need for investigation into developers' focus on older adults, city-led efforts to appropriately locate housing for older adults, new initiatives related to planning for an aging society, and innovative solutions used in planning for older adults. Furthermore, Laws (1995: 17) called for "attention to the interaction of population aging, elderly people, and environmental problems" and stated the need for planning and policy making that is sensitive to local histories and geographies, research on the vulnerability of older adults to environment change, research on older adults' roles in environmental issues and solution, and research concerning the distribution of resources according to the needs of competing groups.

By taking the ecological models, factors contributing to health and well-being of older adults, elements of sustainable urban development, and the need for research and inquiry into consideration, ten guiding principles of sustainable development for an aging society have been developed (see table 4.1), which should have utility for research, practitioners, and policy makers who are concerned with creating quality communities for older adults.

In the development of housing policies and programs, we can look to these guiding principles to incorporate a comprehensive collection of considerations that should be made, including involving older adults in decision-making and goal setting; engaging stakeholders and advocacy groups that represent communities of color, low-income groups, and other vulnerable populations; establishing policies that protect against the ebbs and flows of the economy, including sustained funding sources for affordable

TABLE 4.1. Proposed Guiding Principles of Sustainable Development for an Aging Society

1. Enable meaningful processes, participation, and partnerships across sectors, organizations, and community stakeholders in an attempt to achieve informed decision-making and to bolster community development efforts.
2. Value culture, wisdom, and other assets that exist throughout the life course.
3. Consider social equity implications when creating and/or refining policies and programs in order to provide an appropriate collective response that addresses the identified needs of vulnerable populations and protected classes of people.
4. Create viable and sustainable economic resources that utilize the assets of people of all ages and abilities.
5. Provide appropriate community and health services that focus on enhancing independence and well-being in an affordable and efficient manner.
6. Expand environmental sustainability and green building principles to better address the planning and development of healthy housing and communities that are appropriately and accessibly designed.
7. Refine codes, regulations, plans, and strategies to better align the proximity of and connections among accessible housing, transportation, and land uses in order to create efficient infrastructure systems and appropriate levels of density for an aging society.
8. Foster the creation of accessible and useful places for social interaction and civic activities within, and in close proximity to, housing for older adults.
9. Integrate research efforts in gerontology, urban planning, public health, and related fields in an attempt to inform practice and improve the implementation of housing and community development policies and programs.
10. Share best practices among municipalities that pertain to sustainable housing and communities for an aging society, and adopt or adapt those in an effort to best serve local and regional needs and abilities.

housing; aligning housing and services, including access to health care; expanding green building principles to improve healthy housing for older adults; refining zoning and building codes that address the need for accessible and affordable environments and the proximity of housing to transportation and services; creating social spaces that promote engagement with other people; and making concerted efforts to advance practice through translational research efforts and the incorporation of best practices.

Conclusion

The term *sustainable development* gained traction with the Brundtland Report in the late 1980s and became ubiquitous in the environment, planning, and development fields in the 1990s and 2000s. Government agencies in Portland have taken this approach to development through policies and programs that have sought to meet existing and future needs without explicit consideration for the future composition of the population. In Portland in the 2000s, the push for livable and age-friendly communities emerged, in many ways parallel to the push for sustainable development; however, a structural lag occurred that delayed the intersection of the two efforts and the opportunities for synergy. Nonetheless, there is growing evidence that members of the government, for-profit, nonprofit, and academic communities in Portland have integrated the efforts and are now preparing for the future aging of the city and region.

In part, this collaboration has occurred with the assistance of academics in PSU's College of Urban and Public Affairs and in line with the university's motto, "Let knowledge serve the city." Faculty from the university's Schools of Public Health, Government, and Urban Studies and Planning (including the Institute on Aging) have served as experts by informing public processes including, but not limited to, visioning, advocacy, and policy making. As far back as 1994, PSU faculty published *Planning for an Aging Society* (Howe et al. 1994) for the American Planning Association; the faculty who authored that report have enabled the current generation of scholars to become "translators" who "speak" research, gerontology, public policy, and urban planning and development. Within this milieu, urban gerontology has emerged as part of an action-based research agenda, beginning around 2006, including early collaborations with Metro, the regional government, the WHO, and AARP Oregon. Since those initial projects, the university-city-community partnership focused on age-friendly development has continued to grow and strengthen over time.

In 2007, global and local findings informed the launching of the WHO Age-Friendly Cities project in London, Geneva, and other projects sites throughout the world. In Portland, the research report from the original baseline assessment (Neal and DeLaTorre 2007a) was rewritten to provide a set of findings and resources that were more accessible for the community at large; this was funded by AARP Oregon and written by researchers at the Institute on Aging (Neal and DeLaTorre 2007b). Those findings piqued the interest of PSU and facilitated the offering of a service-learning course in 2009 titled "Livable Communities for an Aging Society," which partnered the Institute with the Bureau of Planning (later the Bureau of Planning and Sustainability), Multnomah County Aging and Disability Services (the area agency on aging that covers the City of Portland's geography), Elders in Action, and AARP Oregon.

Around this time three important opportunities emerged: Portland joined the WHO Global Network of Age-Friendly Cities and Communities; the author, an Institute on Aging researcher, joined the newly formed Portland Commission on Disability (PCOD); and Portland's mayor appointed two IOA researchers (including the author) to the Portland Plan Advisory Group (PPAG), the mayor's advisory body to the Portland Plan, considered a "once in a generation" long-range visioning process for the city (City of Portland 2012).

Once appointed to PPAG and PCOD, IOA researchers became more involved in the Portland policy-making system, first attending a variety of meetings and attempting to integrate aging and disability into the discussions and planning processes whenever possible. One critical task was, and continues to be, offering public opinion in verbal and written form, including comments on the draft Portland Plan. A line-by-line review of concerns about the plan's shortcomings with respect to aging and disability was given to Bureau of Planning and Sustainability staff. Oral testimony was then provided at a public meeting at which aging and disability advocates placed paper grocery bags over their heads to demonstrate that even after engaging proactively in set public participation processes they "remained an invisible community" based on the omission of written comments in the draft plan. Bureau staff eventually arranged a special meeting with aging and disability stakeholders that led to a modification of the Portland Plan's final version, approved by the Portland City Council in 2012, including a section titled "Portland Is a Place for All Generations," which contained ten specific five-year policy action items designed to "make Portland a more physically accessible and age-friendly city" (City of Portland 2012: 25). These actions were the first age-friendly policies created under the guidance of the Bureau of Planning and Sustainability.

Currently, PCOD operates the Accessibility in the Built Environment Committee, which includes a focus on accessible housing; the commission was also instrumental in the creation of the city's Office of Equity and Human Rights, where disability and race (but not aging) have been established as a priority. Commission members work with the community to review the design of citywide projects and policy proposals to ensure that Portland is a place that is accessible for all ages and abilities.

The Age-Friendly Portland Advisory Council has continued to operate and advance the initiative over time. With the passage of the Action Plan for an Age-Friendly Portland in 2013 and the corresponding Multnomah County Age-Friendly Action Plan in 2016, age-friendly policies have been established by local government. These plans have created age-friendly policies that overlap between sustainability domains (see table 4.2). To date, five committees have been established that seek to advance efforts pertaining to housing, transportation, health, employment and economy, and civic engagement. Additional ad hoc workgroups have focused on the development of a website to enhance communication, align age-friendly and municipal priorities, and advance age equity within the initiative. Perhaps the strongest evidence of success is the financial support from the City of Portland and in-kind staff time dedicated from Multnomah County that is intended to implement the action plans.

Portland and now Multnomah County have substantial work remaining with respect to achieving sustainable and age-friendly development. Collaborators of the age-friendly initiative must be persistent in shaping policy and programs (e.g., implementing aspects of the Portland Plan and Comprehensive Plan); the initiative must learn how to navigate multiple municipal bodies such as the City of Portland, Multnomah County, and Metro (the regional government); and secure funding for a backbone or-

TABLE 4.2. Corresponding Elements of Sustainable Development and Portland's Age-Friendly Communities

Sustainability Domains	Age-Friendly Domains
Environmental equity	• Housing • Transportation • Outdoor spaces and buildings
Social equity	• Respect and social inclusion • Social participation • Civic participation and volunteering • Communication and information • Community services • Health services
Economic equity	• Employment • Economic development

ganization will go a long way to maintaining and furthering the long-term and wide-reaching goals of the initiative.

The definition of sustainable development and the guiding principles of planning for an aging society offered here can assist in guiding continued collaboration, engagement, planning, and education. They may also elucidate aging and older adulthood in a positive, asset-based manner, rather the ubiquitous needs- and deficit-based perspective that is common in society. Finally, it is critically important that sustainable development is understood with respect to temporal and equitable outcomes—that is, providing opportunities for the various groups that compose current and future generations, including those who will be part of tomorrow's markedly older population—as well as considering the inextricable connection between human and natural systems. Although it is clear that sustainable and age-friendly development have intersected in Portland, the need for planning and development that utilizes an aging lens will continue to grow as our population ages.

Alan DeLaTorre is a research associate at Portland State University's Institute on Aging, where he coordinates the Senior Adult Learning Center and co-coordinates the Age-Friendly Portland and Multnomah County initiative. Dr. DeLaTorre serves as the chair of the Age-Friendly Design Committee of the Association for Gerontology in Higher Education and as treasurer and past president of the Oregon Gerontological Association. He is passionate about using research to inform and advance community planning and livability and feels strongly that housing and environments should be more inclusive and enabling for all.

Notes

1. Criteria for what constitutes sustainable, affordable housing for older adults include housing developments that are (1) "sustainable" (i.e., described as sustainable, having identified "green" elements, or having had an approach that was environmentally friendly); (2) "affordable" (i.e., the majority of the units are available to residents who have incomes at or below the threshold of 80 percent of the area's median family income; and (3) specifically for "older adults" (i.e., housing exclusively for adults aged fifty-five and older).
2. An Internet search was conducted using terms such as *senior housing, green building, LEED, affordable, low income,* and *sustainable.* Additionally, phone calls were placed to public and nonprofit agencies that were knowledgeable about sustainable, affordable, and/or age-specific housing in Portland. Based on the aforementioned criteria, six housing development projects were identified, ranging in size from 51 to 176 units that had been completed from 2001 to 2008 through part-

nerships that involved community development corporations and City of Portland agencies. They also incorporated Portland's for-profit sector design and construction industries.
3. Affordable housing developments were funded by federal programs (sections 8 and 202; low-income housing tax credits), allocated at the state level, that enabled rents to be made more affordable, depending on income qualifications.

References

AARP. 2000. *Fixing to Stay: A National Survey on Housing and Home Modification Issues.* Accessed March 2018. https://assets.aarp.org/rgcenter/il/home_mod.pdf.
———. 2005. *Livable Communities: An Evaluation Guide.* Accessed July 2018. https://assets.aarp.org/rgcenter/il/d18311_communities.pdf.
———. 2008. *Increasing Home Access: Designing for Visitability.* Accessed July 2018. https://assets.aarp.org/rgcenter/il/2008_14_access.pdf.
———. 2014. "The AARP Network of Age-Friendly Communities: An Introduction." AARP. Accessed July 2018. www.aarp.org/livable-communities/network-age-friendly-communities/info-2014/an-introduction.html.
———. 2015. "AARP Livability Index." AARP. Accessed March 2018. https://livabilityindex.aarp.org/.
Age-Friendly Portland and Multnomah County. 2018. "About: Advisory Council." Age-Friendly Portland & Multnomah County. Accessed July 2018. http://agefriendlyportland.org/about/advisory-council.
Age-Friendly Portland Advisory Council. 2013. *Action Plan for an Age-Friendly Portland.* Age-Friendly Portland & Multnomah County. Accessed July 2018. http://agefriendlyportland.org/our-work/action-plan.
Altman, David I., and Stuart A. Shactman. 2002. *Policies for an Aging Society.* Baltimore: Johns Hopkins University Press.
Altman, Irwin. 1975. *The Environment and Social Behavior: Privacy, Personal Space, Territory, Crowding.* Monterey, CA: Brooks-Cole.
Berke, Philip R. 2002. "Does Sustainable Development Offer a New Direction for Planning? Challenges for the Twenty-First Century." *Journal of Planning Literature* 17(1): 21–36.
Center for Universal Design. 2006. *Universal Design in Housing.* Accessed July 2018. projects.ncsu.edu/design/cud/pubs_p/docs/UDinHousing.pdf.
Choguill, Charles L. 1999. "Sustainable Human Settlements: Some Second Thoughts." In *Sustainable Cities in the 21st Century,* ed. A. F. Foo and B. Yuen, 131–144. Singapore: Singapore University Press.
———. 2007. "The Search for Policies to Support Sustainable Housing." *Habitat International* 31(1): 143–49.
Christians, Clifford G. (2003). "Ethics and Politics in Qualitative Research." In *The Landscape of Qualitative Research: Theories and Issues,* 2nd ed., ed. Norman K. Denzin and Yvonna S. Lincoln, 208–244. Thousand Oaks, CA: Sage.
City of Portland. 2001. *Green Building Policy (Binding City Policy BCP-ENB-9.01).* Portland: Office of the Auditor. Accessed July 2018. https://www.portlandoregon.gov/citycode/article/54355.

———. 2005. *Green Building Resolution*. Portland: Office of the Auditor. Accessed March 2018. www.portlandoregon.gov/bps/article/112681.

———. 2009. *Bureau of Planning Merges with Office of Sustainable Development*. Accessed March 2018. www.portlandonline.com/portlandplan/index.cfm?a=225850&c=50730.

———. 2012. *The Portland Plan*. Accessed March 2018. www.portlandonline.com/portlandplan/.

Commission on Affordable Housing and Health Facility Needs for Seniors in the 21st Century. 2002. *A Quiet Crisis in America: A Report to the United States Congress*. Accessed July 2018. https://govinfo.library.unt.edu/seniorscommission/pages/final_report/finalreport.pdf.

Costello, Robert B. 1992. *Random House Webster's College Dictionary*. New York: Random House.

DeLaTorre, Alan. 2013. "Sustainable, Affordable Housing for Older Adults: A Case Study of Factors That Affect Development in Portland, Oregon." Ph.D. dissertation, Portland State University. Accessed March 2018. https://pdxscholar.library.pdx.edu/open_access_etds/714/.

Dillard, Jesse F., Veronica Dujon, and Mary C. King. 2009. Introduction to *Understanding the Social Dimension of Sustainability*, ed. Jesse F. Dillard, Veronica Dujon, and Mary C. King, 1–14. New York: Routledge.

Elkington, John. 2004. "Enter the Triple Bottom Line." In *The Triple Bottom Line, Does It All Add Up? Assessing the Sustainability of Business and CSR*, ed. Adrian Henriques and Julie Richardson, 1–16. Sterling: Earthscan.

Farber, Nicholas, Douglas Shinkle, Jana Lynott, Wendy Fox-Grage, and Rodney Harrell. 2011. *Aging in Place: A State Survey of Livability Policies and Practices*. Accessed July 2018. https://assets.aarp.org/rgcenter/ppi/liv-com/aging-in-place-2011-full.pdf.

Giegerich, Andy. 2008. "World Class Sustainability." *Portland Business Journal*, April 27. Accessed March 2018. www.bizjournals.com/portland/stories/2008/04/28/story1.html.

Giuliano, Genevieve. 2004. "Land Use and Travel Patterns among the Elderly." In *Transportation in an Aging Society: A Decade of Experience*. Conference 27 proceedings—Transportation Research Board, 192–210. Accessed July 2018. https://onlinepubs.trb.org/onlinepubs/conf/reports/cp_27.pdf.

Goodling, Erin, Jamaal Green, and Nathan McClintock. 2015. *Uneven Development of the Sustainable City: Shifting Capital in Portland, Oregon*. Urban Studies and Planning Faculty Publications and Presentations. Paper 107. Accessed July 2018. https://pdxscholar.library.pdx.edu/usp_fac/107/.

He, Wan, Daniel Goodkind, and Paul Kowal. 2016. *An Aging World: 2015*. U.S. Census Bureau. Accessed July 2018. https://www.census.gov/library/publications/2016/demo/P95-16-1.html.

Hickey, Robert. 2013. *After the Downturn: New Challenges and Opportunities for Inclusionary Housing*. Center for Housing Policy. Accessed July 2018. https://www.nhc.org/publication/after-the-downturn-new-challenges-and-opportunities-for-inclusionary-housing/.

Howe, Deborah. A., Nancy J. Chapman, and Sharon A. Baggett. 1994. *Planning for an Aging Society*. Planning Advisory Service Report no. 451—American Planning Association.

Laws, Glenda. 1995. "Elderly People and the Environment." In *An Aging Population, an Aging Planet, and a Sustainable Future,* ed. Stanley R. Ingman, Xiaomei Pei, Carl D. Ekstrom, Hiram J. Friedsam, and Kristy R. Bartlett, 1–21. Denton: University of North Texas Press.

Lawton, M. Powell. 1986. *Environment and Aging.* Albany: Center for Study of Aging.

Lawton, M. Powell, and Lucille Nahemow. 1973. "Ecology and the Aging Process." In *The Psychology of Adult Development and Aging,* ed. Carl Eisdorfer, and M. Powell Lawton, 619–674. Washington, DC: American Psychological Association.

Meadowcroft, James. 2000. "Sustainable Development: A New(ish) Idea for a New Century?" *Political Studies* 48: 370–97.

Multnomah County. 2016. *Multnomah County: Age-Friendly Action Plan.* Accessed July 2018. http://agefriendlyportland.org/sites/afp.tumblehome.com/files/docs/AFMC_ActionPlan_April2016.pdf.

National Council on Independent Living. 2018. *Visitability: Basic Access to Homes.* Accessed March 2018. https://visitability.org/.

National Institutes of Health. 2005. *Theory at a Glance: A Guide for Health Promotion Practice.* U.S. Department of Health & Human Services, NIH publication no. 05-3896. Washington, DC: Create Space Independent Publishing Platform.

Neal, Margaret B., Nancy Chapman, Jennifer Dill, Irina Sharkova, Alan DeLaTorre, Kathleen Sullivan, Tomoko Kanai, and Shelia Martin. 2006. *Age-Related Shifts in Housing and Transportation Demand: A Multidisciplinary Study Conducted for Metro by Portland State University's College of Urban and Public Affairs.* Portland State University. Accessed July 2018. https://pdxscholar.library.pdx.edu/usp_fac/63/.

Neal, Margaret B., and Alan DeLaTorre. 2007a. *The World Health Organization's Age-Friendly Cities Project in Portland, Oregon: Final Report.* Portland State University. Accessed July 2018. pdxscholar.library.pdx.edu/cgi/viewcontent.cgi?article=1001&context=aging_pub.

———. 2007b. *The World Health Organization's Age-Friendly Cities Project in Portland, Oregon: Summary of Findings.* Portland State University and AARP Oregon. Accessed July 2018. pdxscholar.library.pdx.edu/aging_pub/2/.

Perl, Libby. 2010. *Section 202 and Other HUD Rental Housing Programs for Low-Income Elderly Residents.* Congressional Research Service Report for Congress 7-7806. Accessed July 2018. chapa.org/sites/default/files/202CRSreportonS118(2).pdf.

Portland Development Commission. 2005. *Green Building Policy Program Guidelines: Resolution No. 6262.* Accessed March 2018. www.portlandonline.com/shared/cfm/ image.cfm?id=112680.

Satariano, William A. 2006. *Epidemiology of Aging: An Ecological Approach.* Sudbury, MA: Jones and Bartlett.

Stake, Robert E. 1995. *The Art of Case Study Research.* Thousand Oaks, CA: Sage.

State of Oregon. 2001. *Oregon Sustainability Act: Oregon Revised Statute 184.421.*

———. 2011. *Visitability Requirements: Oregon Revised Statute 456.510.*

United Nations. 1987. *Report of the World Commission on Environment and Development.* United Nations General Assembly. Accessed July 2018. http://www.un-documents.net/our-common-future.pdf.

U.S. Department of Housing and Urban Development. 2010. *Strategy of the Month: Green Affordable Housing Policy Toolkit.* Accessed March 2018. http://archives.huduser.org/rbc/ archives/strategy/vol7.html.

Wheeler, Stephen. 2000. "Planning Sustainable and Livable Cities." In *The City Reader*, 2nd ed., ed. Richard T. LeGates and Frederic Stout, 434–445. New York: Routledge.

WHO (World Health Organization). 2002. *Active Ageing: A Policy Framework.* Accessed July 2018. apps.who.int/iris/bitstream/10665/67215/1/WHO_NMH_NPH_02.8.pdf.

———. 2007. *Global Age-Friendly Cities: A Guide.* Geneva: World Health Organization. Accessed July 2018. www.who.int/ageing/publications/Global_age_friendly_cities_Guide_English.pdf.

———. 2010. *Urban Planning Essential for Public Health.* Accessed July 2018. www.who.int/mediacentre/news/releases/2010/urban_health_20100407.

———. 2014. *WHO Global Network of Age-Friendly Cities and Communities.* Accessed July 2018. www.who.int/ageing/age_friendly_cities_network.

Williams, Colin C., and Andrew C. Millington. 2004. "The Diverse and Contested Meanings of Sustainable Development." *Geographic Journal* 170(2): 99–104.

Yin, Robert K. 2003. *Case Study Research: Design and Methods.* 3rd ed. Applied Social Research Methods Series 5. Thousand Oaks, CA: Sage.

PART II
Age-Friendly Neighborhoods

PART II PROVIDES TWO CASE studies that take age-friendly community development to the locale. In offering one of the most important messages of this volume, Birgit Wolter (chapter 5) notes that "a strong, lively neighborhood forms an important basis for healthy aging." She illustrates the importance of attention to locale by noting how older adults who leave the workforce (the workaday world) and deal with changing physical capacities become more dependent on and only active in their particular quarters (neighborhoods). She describes an intervention organized to improve the lives of elders in such a quarter—a large housing estate in Berlin (thirty-six thousand residents, 21 percent of whom are over age sixty-five). While the orientation is place-based, she notes how service networks of various kinds are layered over the place, and with this realization, the intervention began with the formation of a formal, extensive, and dedicated network of service providers. An ethnographic knowledge of the setting helped her team better understand the internal segregation of certain segments of the population and the attendant tensions between long-standing German residents and incoming older migrants from Russia, Turkey, and Poland. In line with the recommendations regarding public space in chapter 3, Wolter notes the importance of the commercial center as a social gathering point, along with the more informal points of interaction such as mailboxes, benches, and waste disposal stations (the last having been removed, with unfortunate social consequences). Chapter 5 concludes with an illustration that demonstrates how building collaboration across the service networks and promoting resident participation in change led to positive impacts in health and knowledge. This suggests that service providers are necessary but not sufficient stakeholders in age-friendly community development.

Mia R. Oberlink and Barbara S. Davis (chapter 6) describe a neighborhood-based approach that also cites the importance of working with service organizations while focusing primarily on consumer expressions of need and strength. Here the mechanism for obtaining consumer voice is not ethnography but a powerful randomized survey developed by the Center for Home Care Policy and Research. The survey has been employed in over sixty U.S. communities through the AdvantAge Initiative. As in the Berlin project, a major effort to organize service-providing organizations helped cement their ownership over the data and their commitment to respond collectively to the voiced needs and opinions of the residents being served in a large urban, seniors-only housing project.

5 ACCESSIBILITY, PARTICIPATION, NETWORKING
The Impact of a Local Network on the Environment and the Life Relationship of Older People

Birgit Wolter

Introduction

AS PEOPLE GROW OLDER, THEIR neighborhood and immediate residential setting often become increasingly important. Although "old age" is a life phase of great heterogeneity and diversity, and lifestyles continue to differentiate, most older people find themselves confronted with health-related restrictions and/or diminishing resources. As spheres of activity shrink and everyday journeys shorten, the relative importance of local services and activities increases. Socially disadvantaged older people in particular are frequently dependent on infrastructure close to the home for coping with everyday life, as they are unable to compensate mobility or health restrictions by deploying additional (economic) resources. Quarters with substandard infrastructure, socially troubled neighborhoods, and residential areas with environmental problems thus exacerbate the difficulties of older socially disadvantaged people. As well as the absolute provision of services, social participation, and support, their accessibility and visibility to groups with limited physical, economic, cultural, and/or social resources are also significant. By involving target groups in their design, services can be configured to respond directly to existing needs. Participation in local development and neighborhood processes—especially by marginalized older people—represents an ongoing challenge for civil society and political structures at all levels. Developing quarters into productive and supportive environments for older people requires cooperation between numerous actors at the spatial, social, structural, and political levels. This contribution describes the Network for Better Life in Old Age,[1] established in a large housing estate in Berlin in order to improve local living conditions, in particular for resource-poor older people. The Network's impacts on the community, the target group, and the actors themselves were evaluated in a research project (2007–10, funded by the German Federal Ministry of Education and Research). On the basis of the findings, strategies to improve the work of the Network were prepared jointly with the Network actors and representatives of the target group.

Residential Setting, Neighborhood, Age

Most older people live in their own home and wish to live out their lives there (BMVBS 2011). As people grow older, their residential quarter in particular becomes increasingly central—alongside the home—as the immediate spatial reference. Changes in everyday routines associated with aging and mobility restrictions, such as the transition to retirement or giving up hobbies and activities, often mean that everyday routines and social exchange become increasingly concentrated in the neighborhood (Kreuzer 2006; Saup 1999). The spatial qualities, infrastructure, and services of the quarter are thus important factors influencing quality of life in old age. Supportive activities and services and stimulating design of the sociospatial residential setting can foster and promote coping with everyday life, social participation, and health of older people, whereas physical and psychological barriers considerably impair the same (Buffel, Phillipson, and Scharf 2012; Garvin, Nykiforuk, and Johnson 2012).

Without a supportive environment, aging can lead to a retreat from public life and ultimately to isolation and loneliness: "When one is confined to the home it becomes a place of isolation and invisibility" (Anne-Marie Seguin 2008, quoted in Burns 2012: 9). This initiates a temporal and spatial withdrawal that leads to older people becoming less present and less visible in public space. Their needs and requirements concerning the quarter becoming increasingly invisible (Buffel et al. 2012; Burns 2012). At the same time the obstacles to mobile and active participation in the everyday life of the community grow, and it becomes increasingly difficult to adapt to and accept changes in the quarter. The outside world becomes foreign, friendships are no longer maintained, and self-confidence evaporates (Wolter 2011). Information and support become more difficult to access, while opportunities to appropriate new spaces diminish, even more so possibilities to participate in shaping the local development. More broadly, "invisibility" in public space leads to the loss of social ties, as networks virtually cease to be maintained. Socially disadvantaged older people are especially affected by such developments, because they frequently suffer multiple mutually reinforcing impairments but at the same time are less able to draw on financial, social, or cultural resources of their own to compensate for individual restrictions. Resource-poor older people are especially reliant on services, social contacts, and support in an easily accessible quarter with a minimum of barriers. After the end of the employment phase and with declining health and mobility, the sphere of activity concentrates largely on the quarter (Friedrich 2001: 155ff.; Marbach 2005: 515ff.). Sustainable support strategies therefore relate increasingly to the quarter as the sphere of intervention.

The World Health Organization's Ottawa Charter of 1986 points to the importance of the living situation for health: "Health is created and lived by people within the settings of their everyday life; where they learn, work, play, and love" (WHO 1986). The setting approach calls for sustainable health promotion measures to influence not only the behavior of the target group, but simultaneously to improve the conditions under which people live. Health risks are exacerbated by difficult living situations. The widely demonstrated empirical connections between poverty and health are frequently intensified by additional restrictions and burdens as people grow older (Knesebeck 2006; Kümpers 2008; Maschewsky 2005). In every phase of life, it is not only a shortage of economic capital (financial income and wealth), but often also a lack of the education and knowledge (cultural capital) required to locate, classify, and utilize relevant information that makes it more difficult to live healthily. Among disadvantaged groups there is frequently also a lack of social capital in the sense of supportive social relationships capable of compensating for other deficits (Mielck 2005). Resource poverty in each of these three areas tends to be mutually reinforcing and tends to cumulate with age-related health problems as people grow older. Effective local support for older people therefore draws on existing resources and establishes new ones.

The demographic transformation is generating change in the housing situation. Declining populations in many places create demand-led housing markets and create pressures for housing providers to adapt. At the same time, numerous major cities, including Berlin, are experiencing great pressure on their inner-city housing markets, with lower-income households increasingly being displaced to the outskirts and to large (often high-rise) housing estates (Senatsverwaltung für Stadtentwicklung und Umwelt 2014). Germany's large postwar social housing developments are currently in the throes of an incisive transformation process, influenced not least by the public image of many estates as socially troubled. Surveys of the kind conducted regularly for the Berlin Social Structure Atlas reveal overwhelmingly negative social data and prognoses for large public housing schemes (Senatsverwaltung für Stadtentwicklung und Umwelt 2013) and confirm the theory that such developments are especially affected by phenomena of exclusion and poverty. One prominent proponent of that view was Hartmut Häußermann, who predicted that the concentration of social housing in new-build estates on the outskirts of the major cities would create a risk of twenty-first-century ghetto formation (Häußermann, Kronauer, and Siebel 2004: 32). According to Bernt and Kabisch, this negative scenario (for western Germany) is relativized by examination of the eastern German comparison. Studies conducted in the large prefab estates there show a contradictory picture characterized by both depopulation and segregation, as well as well-rooted stability (Bernt and Kabisch 2006: 7). In this connection, however, Bernt and Kabisch also point to significant internal segregation within these housing schemes, which demands a differentiated and detailed examination.

In a research project funded by the German Federal Ministry of Education and Research, the Institute for Gerontological Research investigated the impacts of the voluntary Network "Netzwerk Märkisches Viertel e.V." on the lives of older people in the large social housing complex in the Märkisches Viertel district in Berlin. The setting of a large social housing estate offers various possibilities for drawing on the resources of the older people and those of the setting. Cooperation between different local professionals facilitates the identification of needs and gaps in provision and enables effective interface management. In this way activities can be better coordinated and the targets of supportive measures more easily reached. Cooperation and communication among the different actors and with local residents can strengthen the resources available for shaping healthy everyday routines.

Against that background the Network faces the task of improving the spectrum of services in the quarter to promote independent living, especially for resource-poor older people. This contribution presents the findings of the investigation and discusses Network activity as a possible community-based strategy for improving living conditions for older people.

Methods

The investigation focused on the following questions:

- How this locally operating network arose and developed
- Whether such a network generates health-promoting local impacts
- Whether such a network strengthens the resources of older people
- Which population groups the network reaches
- Whether the model is transferable to other quarters

A mix of methods was used to answer the research questions, with the research divided into three distinct phases.

Phase 1: Focus Network—Origins and Development

The heart of the first research phase was to evaluate the Network itself with respect to relevant indicators such as communication, openness, cooperative structures, organization, goal setting, and planning (Spieckermann 2005: 188ff.). Network documents (statutes, minutes, press releases, etc.) were assessed and documented (Flick 2005). The Network's internal communication was recorded using techniques of participant observation, formal and informal hierarchies were analyzed, and the workings of the Network's various organs were documented. The motives, expectations, and experiences of about twenty Network members were elucidated in structured interviews.

Phase 2: Focus Population Sixty-Plus and Setting

The objective of the second phase was to gather information about the living situations of older people in Märkisches Viertel and about the effects of the Network's activities on the setting and the target group. First a socio-spatial analysis of the Märkisches Viertel quarter was conducted. The local services and spatial infrastructure of the quarter were recorded and mapped by means of field surveys augmented by analysis of information and advertising material (including newspapers, brochures, internet). This made it possible to contextualize statements made by Network partners about service deficits and the activities and needs of local older people.

In order to investigate the impact of the Network's activities on socially disadvantaged older people and enrich the analysis with data about their living situations, focus groups were conducted with members of these groups. The focus-group method was selected because it is known that socially disadvantaged individuals and (older) members of migrant communities tend to be underrepresented in conventional "representative" surveys. The definition of "social disadvantage" was based on the criteria used by the Bundeszentrale für gesundheitliche Aufklärung (Federal Center for Health Education), which include low income, low employment status, and lack of formal education (BZgA 2007). On this basis, taking into account the local population structure, focus groups were held with a total of fourteen socially disadvantaged older Germans, ten older ethnic Germans from the former Soviet Union, and fifteen older Turkish people. In the focus groups, participants discussed their everyday lives, experiences, and problems in Märkisches Viertel. Two participative methods were selected. Participants collectively defined spheres of activity and evaluated the residential area of Märkisches Viertel using the "needle method" to identify and document personally significant places (Franzen 2005; Ortmann 1999). Map-based visualization of the data stimulated discussion about the characteristics of the quarter and individual use patterns within it.

The focus groups were also presented with a discussion-provoking scenario. The ensuing discussion examined the positive and negative aspects of the area and the problems and needs of the participants. The results of the discussion were represented using the "balloons and stones method" (Kumar 2006) in order to give an overview of the named aspects (see figure 5.1).[2]

Finally, the focus group participants completed a sociodemographic questionnaire. After the focus groups had been conducted, a written representative survey of the sixty-plus population was undertaken. The questionnaire was posted to one thousand individuals from this age group officially registered as living in Märkisches Viertel. The random sample was generated from the official population register. The return rate was approximately 25 percent.

Phase 3: Focus Evaluation and Development of the Network

In the third phase, the findings were discussed with representatives of the Network to develop and trial methods for qualitative development and ongoing evaluation of the Network and for involving the target group in the Network.

FIGURE 5.1. Focus group using balloons and stones method (source: IGF)

Practice Example: Netzwerk Märkisches Viertel e.V.

The Setting: Märkisches Viertel Housing Estate

The Märkisches Viertel housing scheme was built between 1960 and 1974 on the outskirts of what was then West Berlin. The development comprises approximately seventeen thousand apartments, which are largely run by the city-owned GESOBAU housing association. The development consists largely of meandering eight- to twelve-story blocks separated by large expanses of green space (see figure 5.2). At the center of the estate there is a park, on the margins of which social agencies, education facilities, and an old people's home with a geriatric clinic are located. Until 2008 most of the apartments were subsidized under the social housing program, but after the city-state government terminated the subsidy program, the number of subsidized units fell rapidly to a minimum.

The heart of the Märkisches Viertel quarter is a large shopping center serving a wider catchment area. The same location also has a building containing council offices and a community center, the offices of the housing company, several churches, three old people's homes, a health center, a care support point, the Network office, and a neighborhood drop-in center. The extensive estate is served by a number of bus lines, which connect it with nearby light rail and underground stations.

FIGURE 5.2. Märkisches Viertel (source: IGF)

According to the latest Berlin Social Structure Atlas, Märkisches Viertel is one of the areas of Berlin with the highest proportion of pensioners receiving only the minimum pension (Hilfe zum Lebensunterhalt; Senatsverwaltung für Stadtentwicklung und Umwelt 2013). Although Germany has conducted no full census since 1987, the city-state of Berlin provides a certain amount of socioeconomic data for "lifeworld-orientated spaces" with average populations of about eight thousand. Märkisches Viertel comprises six such units, which permit a coarse examination of the local data. The social ranking of geographical units, based on indicators such as unemployment and benefits, clearly reflects the problems of large-scale social housing. Whereas the areas of owner-occupied housing on the margins of Märkisches Viertel achieve a mid-level position on the status index, the immediately adjoining estate scores "very low." This finding points to a "spatialization of social inequality" (Dangschat and Hamedinger 2007: 2ff.) at a very small scale. At the same time, differences within the estate suggest internal segregation and social inequality.

About one-fifth of the roughly thirty-six thousand people living in Märkisches Viertel are sixty-five or older (21 percent), slightly more than the Berlin average of about 19 percent. Whereas more than 50 percent of the children and adolescents in the quarter have a "migrant background" (at least one parent born outside Germany or born in Germany as a noncitizen), the same applies to only about 10 percent of older people (Amt für Statistik Berlin-Brandenburg, as of 31 December 2011). The latter proportion is steadily increasing, however, because many migrants regard Märkisches Viertel as their home and wish to grow old there. Most of the older members of migrant communities originate either from Turkey or were ethnic German immigrants from the former Soviet Union and Poland. Many of the longer-established older residents have lived on the estate since it was built and identify strongly with it. To some extent this group adopts a negative stance toward new incoming migrant families.

Current developments in the setting are characterized by an aging population that is in part low-income, generational conflicts that intersect with intercultural conflicts, unlet properties, and increasingly, new tenants forced to move there by changes in the benefits rules (which no longer cover higher rents in more desirable parts of the city). In response to these trends, various projects aiming directly to improve the quarter have been initiated in recent years, including a comprehensive renovation of the housing stock and improvements to infrastructure and public spaces through the national government's Stadtumbau West program. These strategies aim primarily to enhance built structures rather than to improve services in the community. Netzwerk Märkisches Viertel, with its motto "I want to stay here," on the other hand, explicitly seeks to adapt the service structure to the needs of the older population, to enable older people to live independently in their own homes for as long as possible and thus contribute by that route to longer-term stabilization of the quarter.

In terms of its built structures the quarter actually offers positive conditions for older people: small apartments, barrier-free access, short distances to shops and services, and good infrastructure. But, especially for older people and those with restricted financial resources, life in a large housing scheme can also mean loneliness and a lack of social support, which in turn have a direct and negative influence on perceived health (Kroll and Lampert 2007). This raises the question of which resources different population groups can access and what potentials for improvement can be opened up by the Network. That means clarifying what opportunities for participation and health promotion already exist for older people, which are perceived or overlooked, and which groups are reached or missed and for what reasons.

It was the problems experienced by many older people, with which they were confronted in their various fields of work, that motivated the Network's initiators to get together on a voluntary basis. The Network deserves closer examination for several reasons: (1) it includes service providers from the fields of medicine and nursing, as well as other local actors; (2) in addition to improving nursing services, it aims more broadly to enhance the everyday lives of local older people; and (3) it therefore possesses great potential for influencing the development of the setting.

Findings of Phase 1: Focus Network—Origins and Development

Netzwerk Märkisches Viertel was set up in 2003 at the initiative of staff of the Reinickendorf care support point Koordinierungsstelle Rund ums Alter (now: Pflegestützpunkt Reinickendorf), the borough council, and the housing association GESOBAU. From the outset the question of how older people in a large housing estate can be enabled to live independently in their own homes for as long as they would like was central to the Network. Initially as an informal cooperation, since 2008 as a registered association, the Network can now look back at eleven years of successful networking.

The Network today has about twenty-five paid-up voting members; alongside GESOBAU and the Pflegestützpunkt Reinickendorf, these include small businesses (painting and decorating and plumbing), a pharmacy, nursing agencies, nonprofit organizations, and various private-sector service providers. Reinickendorf borough council, a number of church bodies, and a local secondary school also cooperate with the Network as associated partners.

The Network's overarching goal is to enhance the everyday lives of older people in Märkisches Viertel, through advice, education, and prevention activities designed to strengthen individual resources and enable participation. More broadly, intense inter-sectoral networking allows deficits in service provision to be identified at an early stage, enables gaps to be closed, encourages members to learn from one another, and generates synergy effects through interdisciplinary cooperation.

Through their annual contributions (currently €300 per organization) and other funding, the members of the Network fund an office that coordinates the Network's programs and activities and at the same time functions as a drop-in center for local residents. The Network office organizes the regular Network meetings, at which all important decisions are made by consensus. The conferences are chaired by the four-member executive committee. The Network meetings are responsible for admitting new members and setting up working groups and project committees.

In addition to residence in Märkisches Viertel, a willingness to participate actively in working groups or project committees is a precondition for membership. Some of the working groups are permanent, such as those dealing with "older living," public relations, and qualification measures, the latter of which organizes training events for Network partners. Other groups are temporary—for example, to organize a seminar. The Network training events are directed at the Network partners themselves, who profit from the expertise of other members and can improve their own qualifications or those of their workforce. The Network's publicity work also enhances the public presence of the individual partners and opens up new channels for acquiring business.

Alongside activities for partners, the Network also offers activities aimed at residents. Projects run by working groups have included setting up an age-friendly show apartment and staging an exhibition on careers in nursing. Other activities organized by the Network include free computer courses and a volunteer visiting service for lonely older people. To conduct such activities, the Network also seeks external cooperation partners and regularly applies for funding.

One important element of the Network's activities is the annual neighborhood fete (see figure 5.3), which permits the Network to present itself and its activities to the public. For Network members, this also offers an opportunity to advertise their businesses and to come into discussion with local older people and learn about their needs and concerns. This type of low-threshold contact—"over beer and sausages"—at least in the case of older people who are mobile and fluent in German, is considerably more effective than publicity through leaflets and press releases.

The research project followed the activities of the Network with numerous interviews and participant observation and elucidated the various motivations and expectations of the different partners. The members of the

FIGURE 5.3. Neighborhood fete in Märkisches Viertel (source: IGF)

Network come from a range of fields with different organizational cultures, and their motivations for participation and commitment are correspondingly heterogeneous. The time and financial resources invested by the participants depend above all on the size of the organization and the priority afforded to the Network. Whereas certain Network partners, especially the self-employed, participate outside their working hours, the institutions and voluntary-sector organizations send staff on working time. Many of the private-sector partners are therefore keen to keep the time required for Network activities within limits. They are also guided by economic interests and keep an eye on the economic "added value" of the Network activities for their business. The official and voluntary-sector social organizations in the Network, on the other hand, are primarily interested in improving the range and quality of social services in the quarter. Local networking is one of the tasks of their staff, who pursue this within the scope of their regular working hours.

The housing association fulfills an important mediating function in this context. Although it is itself a business, it has an explicit (also economic) interest in stabilizing the quarter and its tenant population. In that context it devotes financial, structural, and personnel resources to the Network, and as an attractive partner it is also in a good position to bind smaller businesses to the Network. The Network also benefits from the publicity platforms available through the housing association.

Alongside the housing association, the local care support point also plays a decisive role in the Network. Its routine counseling work for older people in need of care and their relatives grants the care support point a good overview of problematic living situations and care deficits experienced by local people with health difficulties. Because the care support point also refers clients to local providers, it maintains a good overview of local provision and deficits in the areas of nursing and health services as well as with respect to social support. This has enabled it to impress upon other Network partners the growing importance of "older people" as clients and customers.

A third and central partner in the Network is Reinickendorf borough council. Although financial constraints have led it to scale back its membership to an associated partnership without voting rights, its participation nonetheless continues to offer the possibility of political backing for Network activities. Especially the patronage of the mayor and councilors delivers an important public message. Furthermore, the Network's discussions, strategies, and activities can be communicated in local authority committees and influence political and administrative decisions there.

Findings of Phase 2: Focus Population Sixty-Plus and Setting

The living situation of the older population of Märkisches Viertel was investigated through a comprehensive socio-spatial analysis, a representative questionnaire survey of the sixty-plus population in the quarter, interviews, and focus groups. The principal questions were how the socio-spatial circumstances influence the target group's ability to cope with everyday life, where older people find everyday support, and what role Netzwerk Märkisches Viertel plays in this.

Regardless of age, gender, health, and socioeconomic indicators, the survey respondents mostly expressed satisfaction with Märkisches Viertel as a residential environment. The relative lack of barriers inside the apartments, elsewhere within the blocks, and in public space and buildings is especially helpful for mobility and independent living. The local public space is conducive to daily walks and thus contributes meaningfully to everyday activity. The shopping center and adjacent infrastructure facilities represent a service structure that is both functionally and socially important and easily accessible for most of the older people.

However, the older people living at the margins of the estate are reliant on car, bicycle, or bus to reach the center for everyday errands, as there is little in the way of shops and services on the outskirts. This makes doing one's own shopping a problem, especially for the old and frail: few of the buses are barrier-free or easy to use with a walker. Some of the surveyed older people prefer only to travel by bus during quieter times of day, avoiding periods when the buses are crowded with school students, which leaves them restricted to particular time slots. A further restriction to mobility, and thus indirectly also to social participation, arises through avoidance of out-of-home activities in the evening. The settlement structure of scattered blocks and large green areas creates "spaces of fear" that considerably restrict the mobility of older residents after dark. Most respondents (regardless of gender) said that they tried to avoid being out and about in the quarter after dark, citing fear of falls due to inadequate street lighting and fear of assault by the adolescents who gather in public spaces. This considerably narrows the temporal frame, especially during winter.

It fits with these findings that the most popular "public" place for older people in Märkisches Viertel is a semipublic space in the shopping center (see figure 5.4). The unroofed plaza has benches, trees, and a fountain,

FIGURE 5.4. Shopping center plaza (Brunnenplatz) (source: IGF)

and the nearby shops in the shopping center orientate their displays to the plaza. The shopping center operator owns the plaza, and its security staff has the right to control what happens there, but the space and seating can be used without spending money. The older people who participated in the survey perceive the plaza as safe and lively. They go there to participate in public life but also to meet with friends.

Märkisches Viertel possesses a very diverse social infrastructure, with numerous social and church organizations offering support, advice, and activities, frequently in cooperation with the housing association. However, the surveys reveal that the target group is only vaguely aware of many of these possibilities. Socially disadvantaged older people are especially likely to be unaware of useful local support and services.

Most of the respondents receive everyday support from relatives, and for many of them family members represent the most important resource for mastering the challenges of everyday life. While the younger old people (aged sixty to seventy) frequently themselves play an important support role in their extended family, by caring for their grandchildren or assisting their children in emergencies, the family support relationship inverts as they grow older. The support structures did not differ meaningfully between the different focus groups, although the older members of migrant communities more often lived in close proximity to their relatives than the German participants did. In some cases, the families of older people from the Soviet Union still lived there, leading to a lack of important informal support structures.

Almost all interview and focus group participants were well connected within their neighborhood and/or ethnic group and possess numerous contacts that they maintain in regular neighborhood meet-ups. Support within the neighborhood is frequently based on reciprocity: "We help each other. If one person asks for help . . . it all gets moving." Well-informed neighbors are multipliers, who themselves possess better resources (in other words better health, a driving license, better education, or language fluency) and are named as the first place to go when assistance or advice is needed: "They [female neighbors] will surely be able to tell me where the doctors are here" (Herr H., approximately seventy years old).

According to the respondents, such informal networks are largely well-developed, resilient, and regularly maintained in everyday life. The neighborhood multipliers are frequently the central—and sometimes the only—source of information about local support and services. Older members of migrant communities with poor knowledge of German rely particularly heavily on the recommendations of well-informed peers. This means that access to support will frequently depend directly on the knowledge and networks of these multipliers, which makes them important partners for service providers and for the Network. Multipliers often shape a neighborhood's culture, communication, and access to external resources. Long residence, education, fluency in German (for older members of migrant communities), and frequently strong social commitment and sociability predestine individuals for a central position in the neighborhood. Yet, their role within the quarter is certainly ambivalent. They occupy a crucial position for low-threshold communication of information (for example, about health) and may control access to difficult-to-reach target groups.

On the other hand, stable neighborly relations frequently develop between individuals who are from the same milieu and often also the same gender and age. The limitations of such neighbor networks often lead to a situation where the quality and scope of knowledge and information and the accessibility of additional resources depend on single individuals who belong to a similar milieu: "If I hadn't had the ladies here who tell me about everything that goes on in the building, I would have had no idea at all" (Herr H., approximately seventy years old). Herr H.'s knowledge depends directly on the knowledge of his neighbors and is shaped by their level of information and experiences—and by their prejudices and subjective assessments. The more homogeneous a neighborhood, the greater the danger that knowledge and social capital will be limited and that such limitations will be exacerbated by the role of local multipliers.

Although there is great uncertainty about certain topics, additional information is rarely sought, and there is often a lack of knowledge about public advice centers. Nonetheless, participants from migrant communities frequently expressed a desire for local native-language advice services. Presently, if they need advice, many of them are strongly dependent on children and grandchildren serving as their interpreters.

At the time of the study, few of the older people knew of the Netzwerk Märkisches Viertel. Even activities that had been initiated by the Network, such as the computer courses and the Network Day, were not always associated with the Network. As a result of the Network's reserved publicity work, its office was also not frequented to the extent it could have been.

The findings reveal the needs and requirements of the older residents concerning their quarter and neighborhood, as well as local conflicts and potentials. They show clearly that neighborly relations, especially within the very large blocks whose entrances serve up to one hundred apartments, represent an important everyday social resource for most: "In such a big building you are lost if you don't have one or two friends you get on well with" (Frau H., approximately sixty years old).

The focus groups also revealed the difficulties with which relationship building must contend in a context of different cultural backgrounds. The German participants in one group discussion, Frau K. (approximately fifty-five years old) and Frau Mi. (approximately eighty-one years old), said: "The Russians here speak Russian so that we can't understand what they are saying"; "They really reject us. Even if you say hello, you don't get so much as a thank-you." In a parallel group discussion, on the other hand, older Russian-Germans reported that they felt unwelcome in a drop-in center at the local old people's home and therefore preferred to keep to themselves. The strains on neighborly relations created by broader, sometimes historically conditioned influences are clearly identifiable: "I know that some women in this block hate everything about Russia because when the [second world] war was over the Russian soldiers came . . ." (Frau Ma., approximately sixty years old).

It was found that neighbor networks are often ethnically homogeneous. The focus group with older people from Turkey discussed the reasons for this. The participants believed that cohesion was greater among migrants than among older Germans. Herr A., sixty-one years old, pointed in this connection to a shared migration history as a basis for neighbor networks: "If the Germans had gone to Turkey as guest workers, they might have organized themselves better, being a minority. Here it's the Turkish people who are guest workers, from a foreign country, and they look after each other."

The experience of Frau Ma., the Russian-German from the former Soviet Union quoted above, illustrates how overcoming cultural barriers to get to know one another and initiate neighborly exchange can lead to lasting and positive relationships: "If you get to know each other, then you don't have any trouble. In my old block I have very many friends, acquaintances, to this day, when we meet we say hello, ask how it's going, and so on." Distance between individual groups is frequently based on prejudices and ignorance. Low-threshold opportunities to meet within the quarter are a helpful precondition for establishing relationships between initially distant neighbors. But overcoming cultural and milieu-specific barriers may sometimes require additional help from multipliers and/or professional social workers.

As the quote from Frau Ma. suggests, intercultural neighborly relations can certainly form, if "you get to know each other." As well as suitable occasions, that also requires appropriate places that are accessible in social as well as physical terms. This could be a neighborhood center or meeting place dedicated explicitly to the purpose. But access to and use of such venues is generally subject to temporal and functional restrictions. "We still have the old clubs, we still run them. Guests are always welcome on Wednesdays" (Frau H., eighty-three years old). The occupation of such venues by neighborhood subgroups on the basis of habit or custom can lead to them no longer being open to all residents or to individuals feeling that they do not belong: "I don't know anybody there. They excluded you, no doubt about it" (Frau S., approximately seventy years old).

In this context a quite different type of place plays an important role in initiating and maintaining neighborly relations: the everyday places in the quarter where people meet one another more by chance. The possibility to talk to one another exists, but contact is discretionary. In Märkisches Viertel, such encounters with immediate neighbors had frequently occurred at the waste disposal chutes on each floor of the tower blocks, and the removal of the chutes in the course of a general overhaul was therefore experienced as a significant loss of more than just convenience. Letter boxes, benches beside the entrances to blocks, shared laundry facilities, and green courtyard spaces serve a similar function for the neighborhood. Local public spaces are also suited for everyday encounters between neighbors. Herr T., eighty years old, reported that he liked to spend time in the nearby shopping center, where he found sufficient opportunities to sit down, and "I always meet someone to chat to." (On the significance of public places for social exchange, see chapter 12).

What these places share in common is their neutrality and accessibility as social spaces. They are visited and used in the everyday life of the area without any particular social activity being expected. Their use is open to all neighbors regardless of which groups they belong to. These "everyday spaces" thus represent an important spatial level for the formation and maintenance of neighborhood networks, and one that is often afforded too little attention in the planning of housing developments. At the same time these are the places where information is passed on and target groups can be reached.

The findings of the first two phases of the investigation were discussed with the Network actors. A participatory third phase trialed and evaluated measures to improve communication between the Network and the target group and possibilities for qualitative improvement of Network activities.

Phase 3: Focus Evaluation and Development of the Network

One central outcome of the research project was identifying the importance of strengthening participation by older people in developing the Network's activities. To that end the Network established an advisory committee composed of representatives of the target group. The first members of the advisory committee were recruited from among the focus group participants. In order to facilitate access to difficult-to-reach older people with the help of multipliers, the first advisory committee includes, along with an older German woman, an older Turkish woman and an older Russian-German woman. The advisory committee participates in Network meetings, where its members have unrestricted speaking rights, although no voting rights. Entrenching the advisory committee in the longer term and legitimation of its members are tasks that remain unresolved.

Various smaller projects also seek to encourage older people to participate in the development of the Märkisches Viertel quarter and to improve communication between the Network and the target group. The Network produced a street map of Märkisches Viertel showing the locations of Network partners, health services, and services and activities for older people and distributed it free of charge in the area. In 2011 the Network staged its first competition for the most senior-friendly business in the quarter. Questionnaires were distributed at public places in Märkisches Viertel, asking older people to nominate their favorites. In a public ceremony, the winner, a supermarket, was ceremoniously presented with a certificate by the responsible borough councilors.

These activities enhance public awareness and perceptions of the Network. The Network addresses older people as local partners and as actors and at the same time offers the target group opportunities to acquire information, to become engaged, and to a restricted extent to shape the development of the quarter. Does this also improve the chances of social participation? Can a network of actors operating in this way influence the social participation of the older people in the quarter?

The availability of appropriate opportunities and venues is an important precondition for social participation. The corresponding activities should be located in the residential setting or quarter. In the research project it became clear that, above all, difficult-to-reach older people, in this case members of migrant communities and low-income groups, find little access to public services and information. What is needed is therefore assertive advertising, a presence in public space, and very low-threshold access to opportunities for social participation and cooperation with multipliers. Frequently the mere identification of these individuals will tell us a great deal about the quarter. Multipliers should, as important protagonists, be integrated into the process of strengthening and promoting a quarter. At the same time their skills should be developed and their resources increased. This can supply stimulation to neighbor networks, which under favorable conditions will multiply.

In the participatory development of the Network's activities, different paths and instruments were tested to explore the possibilities for social participation in the quarter for all older people. Cooperation between the different Network partners is helpful for developing diverse and interdisciplinary approaches for promoting participation and for facilitating the use of different access points to the various target groups. Communication between actors and target group, a genuine will to enable real involvement, and perseverance are always crucial to establishing lasting participatory structures.

Conclusions

A strong, lively neighborhood forms an important basis for healthy aging (Wahl et al. 2009; Evans, Kantrowitz, and Eshelman 2002). Promoting neighborly relations can generate useful support structures, especially for older people. One significant precondition is the existence of places and occasions for encounters that are integrated into the everyday life of the quarter. Networking of different actors involved in different fields of support and services for older people should start at this level. Achieving good access to the target group and identifying local support requirements demands a presence in the neighborhoods and places of everyday life, as well as treating older people as equals.

People's perceptions of their neighborhood vary with characteristics such as age, gender, and milieu (Phillipson et al. 1999; Scharf and Jong Gierveld 2008). People use and maintain their neighbor networks and operate within their neighborhoods in different ways and with different outcomes. Target-group-specific promotion of neighbor networks and relations—at both the social and spatial levels—can strengthen the neighborhood as a whole, enhance resources for everyday coping, have a preventative effect on loneliness, and thus impact positively on the health of older people. Gender- and milieu-specific aspects of neighborhood networking should therefore be taken into consideration, intervening if necessary with encouragement (for men) or language interpretation (for migrants). The substantive planning of services in the quarter, meeting places in the residential setting, and forms of access are aspects that need to be designed for the specific target group. Cooperation with multipliers should be considered in terms of which target groups they are actually supposed to represent or reach.

Socially disadvantaged neighborhoods represent a special problem in this connection. As well as representing spatial concentrations of people who possess limited resources, these are often themselves disadvantageous spatial/social settings where services are inadequate and health-promoting living conditions absent (Mielck 2005). The daily struggle with difficult everyday circumstances can, in combination with declining health, become a serious threat in old age. Ultimately, the individual's limited resources can become largely depleted.

Professional organization of neighborhood support—for example, through neighborhood associations or social workers—is therefore of particular importance in disadvantaged neighborhoods. While it cannot in itself generate neighbor networking, it can give it a boost. Transferring resources and social capital ("bridging social capital") from other quarters can also serve to strengthen local resources (Richter and Wächter 2009: 20). An exchange of skills and knowledge can be promoted by meetings between residents of different quarters, as can the reduction of prejudices.

But it is imperative that encounters are characterized by mutual respect and interest. Here a network of actors can assume a key mediating and initiating role. The participation of the older people themselves in the ongoing work and development of a network is of great importance.

This chapter describes various dimensions of neighborly relations and socio-spatial living conditions and outlines their influence on the lives of older people. It shows how networking of actors can positively influence circumstances in a residential quarter if the target group is included. Accessibility of spaces and services, participation in local development, and networking of actors represent conducive conditions for enabling older people with more and less resources to live well in the quarter.

Birgit Wolter is senior research associate and member of the executive committee at Institute for Gerontological Research (IGF) in Berlin, Germany. She was trained in architecture, and her particular focus at the IGF is on developing solutions for self-determined living in old age, exploring patterns of usage of urban spaces by older people, and investigating dimensions of inclusion and exclusion of older people, especially of socially disadvantaged older people. Since 2016 she is member of the management committee of the network "Reducing Old-Age Social Exclusion" (ROSEnet), COST Action.

Notes

1. The Network is a self-organized, neighborhood-based association of stakeholders, old people, and professionals from care services.
2. The balloons and stones method is used in the group discussion to identify and visualize aspects that influence a situation positively (balloons) or negatively (stones). Ideas for future improvements are noted on clouds. The participants' statements are noted and attached above or below a central line symbolizing a balanced state of the situation of interest. The method promotes reflection within a group by permitting visualization of helpful and obstructive factors during the course of a discussion (see figure 5.1).

References

Bernt, Matthias, and Sigrun Kabisch. 2006. "Ostdeutsche Großwohnsiedlungen zwischen Stabilisierung und Niedergang." *DisP—The Planning Review* 164(1): 5–15.
BMVBS—Bundesministerium für Verkehr, Bauen und Stadtentwicklung, ed. 2011. *Wohnen im Alter.* Forschungen 147. Berlin: BMVBS.
Buffel, Tine, Chris Phillipson, and Tom Scharf. 2012. "Ageing in Urban Environments: Developing 'Age-Friendly' Communities." *Critical Social Policy* 32(4): 597–617. Accessed 4 July 2018. https://doi.org/10.1177/0261018311430457.

Burns, Victoria, Jean-Pierre Lacoie, and Damiens Rose. 2012. "Revisiting the Role of Neighbourhood Change on Social Exclusion and Inclusion of Older People." *Journal of Aging Research*. Accessed 4 July 2018. http://dx.doi.org/10.1155/2012/148287.

BZgA (Bundeszentrale für gesundheitliche Aufklärung). 2007. *Kriterien guter Praxis in der Gesundheitsförderung bei sozial Benachteiligten*. Cologne: BZgA.

Dangschat, Jens S., and Alexander Hamedinger. 2007. "Lebensstile, soziale Lagen und Siedlungsstrukturen—Einführung." In *Lebensstile, soziale Lagen und Siedlungsstrukturen*, ed. Jens S. Dangschat and Alexander Hamedinger, Forschungs- und Sitzungsberichte 230, 2–21. Hannover: Akademie für Raumforschung und Landesplanung.

Evans, Gary, Elyse Kantrowitz, and Paul Eshelman. 2002. "Housing Quality and Psychological Well-Being among the Elderly Population." *Journal of Gerontology* 57B(4): 381–83.

Fischer, Claude S. 1982. *To Dwell among Friends: Personal Networks in Towns and Cities*. Chicago: University of Chicago Press.

Flick, Uwe. 2005. *Qualitative Sozialforschung*. Reinbek bei Hamburg: Rowohlt.

Franzen, Dominik. 2005. "Erkundung von Sozialräumen in Köln-Kalk." In *Sozialraumanalyse*, ed. Marlo Riege and Herbert Schubert, 299–312. Wiesbaden: VS Verlag für Sozialwissenschaften.

Friedrich, Klaus. 2001. "Altengerechte Wohnumgebungen." In *Mobilität älterer Menschen*, ed. Antje Flade, Maria Limbourg, and Bernhard Schlag, 155–69. Opladen: Leske und Budrich.

Garvin, Theresa, Candace I. J. Nykiforuk, and Sherrill Johnson. 2012. "Can We Get Old Here? Seniors' Perceptions of Seasonal Constraints of Neighbourhood Built Environments in a Northern, Winter City." *Geografiska Annaler*, series B, *Human Geography* 94(4): 369–89.

Häußermann, Hartmut Martin Kronauer, and Walter Siebel, eds. 2004. *An den Rändern der Städte: Armut und Ausgrenzung*. Frankfurt am Main: Suhrkamp.

Heusinger, Josefine, Kerstin Kammerer, and Birgit Wolter. 2012. "Netzwerk Märkisches Viertel e.V.: Eine Akteursvernetzung zur Verbesserung der Lebens- und Wohnbedingungen von SeniorInnen im Quartier." *Public Health Forum* 20(74): 16–17.

Heusinger, Josefine, Kerstin Kammerer, Birgit Wolter, and Maja Schuster. 2013. "Quartiersstrukturen für Gesundheit und Selbstbestimmung im höheren Lebensalter verbessern: Improving Structures for Healthy and Self-Determined Ageing in an Urban District." *Das Gesundheitswesen*. DOI: 10.1055/s-0033-1334937.

Knesebeck, Olaf von dem, and Ingmar Schäfer. 2006. "Gesundheitliche Ungleichheit im höheren Lebensalter." In *Gesundheitliche Ungleichheit*, ed. Matthias Richter and Klaus Hurrelmann, 241–55. Wiesbaden: VS Verlag für Sozialwissenschaften.

Kreuzer, Volker. 2006. *Altengerechte Wohnquartiere*. Dortmunder Beiträge zur Raumplanung 125. Dortmund: Universität Dortmund.

Kroll, Lars E., and Thomas Lampert. 2007. "Sozialkapital und Gesundheit in Deutschland." *Das Gesundheitswesen* 69(3):120–27.

Kumar, Somesh. 2006. *Methods for Community Participation: A Complete Guide for Practitioners*. Bourton-on-Dunsmore: ITDG.

Kümpers, Susanne. 2008. "Altern und gesundheitliche Ungleichheit: Ausgangspunkte für sozialraumbezogene Primärprävention." WZB discussion paper, Berlin.

Marbach, Jan H. 2005. "Der Aktionsraum im höheren Lebensalter und Optionen der Netzwerkhilfe: Theoretische Konzepte und empirische Befunde." In *Mit Netzwer-*

ken professionell zusammenarbeiten, ed. Ulrich Otto and Petra Bauer, vol. 1, 515–51. Tübingen: Dgvt Verlag.
Maschewsky, Werner. 2005. "Sozialräumliche Verteilung gesundheitsschädlicher Umwelteinflüsse." In *Netzwerke für eine lebenswerte Umgebung: Gesundheitsförderung in benachteiligten Stadtquartieren*, ed. Rolf-Peter Löhr, 7–14. Berlin: Landesarbeitsgemeinschaft für Gesundheitsförderung.
Mielck, Andreas. 2005. *Soziale Ungleichheit und Gesundheit*. Bern: Verlag Huber.
Ortmann, Norbert. 1999. "Die Stadtteilerkundung mit Schlüsselpersonen; Nadelmethode; Jugendkulturenkataster; Leitfaden-Interview mit Schlüsselpersonen." In *Sozialräumliche Jugendarbeit: Eine praxisbezogene Anleitung zur Konzeptentwicklung in der Offenen Kinder- und Jugendarbeit*, ed. Ulrich Deinet, 74–84. Opladen: Leske und Budrich.
Phillipson, Chris, Miriam Bernard, Judith Phillips, and Jim Ogg. 1999. "Older People's Experiences of Community Life: Patterns of Neighbouring in Three Urban Areas." *Sociological Review* 47(4): 715–43.
Richter, Antje, and Marcus Wächter. 2009. *Zum Zusammenhang zwischen Nachbarschaft und Gesundheit*. Forschung und Praxis der Gesundheitsförderung 36. Köln: Bundeszentrale für Gesundheitliche Aufklärun.
Saup, Winfried. 1999. "Alte Menschen in ihrer Wohnung." In *Alte Menschen in ihrer Umwelt*, ed. Hans-Werner Wahl, Heidrun Mollenkopf, and Frank Oswald, 43–52. Opladen and Wiesbaden: Westdeutscher Verlag.
Scharf, Tom, and Jenny de Jong Gierveld. 2008. "Loneliness in Urban Neighbourhoods: An Anglo-Dutch Comparison." *European Journal of Ageing* 5(2): 103–15.
Senatsverwaltung für Stadtentwicklung und Umwelt Berlin. 2013. *Monitoring Soziale Stadtentwicklung Berlin*. Berlin: Senatsverwaltung für Stadtentwicklung und Umwelt Berlin.
———. 2014. *Berlin Strategie: Stadtentwicklungskonzept 2030: Entwurf.* Accessed 4 July 2018. https://www.stadtentwicklung.berlin.de/planen/stadtentwicklungsko nzept/download/strategie/BerlinStrategie_de_PDF.pdf.
Spieckermann, Holger. 2005. "Zur Evaluation von Netzwerken und Kooperationsmanagement." In *Institutionelle Netzwerke in Steuerungs- und Kooperationsperspektive*, vol. 2 of *Mit Netzwerken professionell zusammenarbeiten*, ed. Petra Bauer, and Ulrich Otto, 181–98. Tübingen: Dgvt Verlag.
Wahl, Hans-Werner, Oliver Schilling, Frank Oswald, and Susanne Iwarsson. 2009. "The Home Environment and Quality of Life-Related Outcomes in Advanced Old Age: Findings of the ENABLE-AGE Project." *European Journal of Ageing* 6: 101–11.
WHO (World Health Organization). 1986. *Ottawa Charter for Health Promotion*. First International Conference on Health Promotion, Ottawa, 21 November 1986. WHO/HPR/HEP/95.1.
Wolter, Birgit. 2010. "Altwerden in der Großwohnsiedlung: Unterstützung durch ein Akteursnetzwerk." *Raumforschung und Raumordnung* 68(3): 207–17.
———. 2011. "Aneignung und Verlust des städtischen Raumes im Alter." In *Eigensinnige Geographien*, ed. Malte Bergmann and Bastian Lange, 195–211. Wiesbaden: VS Verlag.
———. 2013. "Nachbarschaft: förderliche und hinderliche Effekte auf die Gesundheit älterer Menschen." *Jahrbuch für Kritische Medizin und Gesundheitswissenschaften* 48:71–87.

6 ASSESSING THE AGING-FRIENDLINESS OF TWO NEW YORK CITY NEIGHBORHOODS
A Case Study

Mia R. Oberlink and Barbara S. Davis

Introduction

AS THE "AGE-FRIENDLY COMMUNITY" CONCEPT has grown in popularity in the United States over the past ten to fifteen years, researchers and others have sought to categorize age-friendly community initiatives that have been implemented in various parts of the country, not only for research purposes but also to elucidate models that communities could learn from and replicate (GIA 2013; Lehning, Scharlach, and Wolf 2012; Greenfield et al. 2015). Some of these models have been developed by major organizations, such as the World Health Organization and AARP (WHO 2007; AARP 2014) and include materials to help stakeholders develop age-friendly initiatives in their own communities. These materials typically include guides for beginning and sustaining age-friendly community initiatives; tools such as conceptual frameworks, survey questionnaires, and focus group guides used to collect data from various community stakeholders; and practical information on forming coalitions, designing advocacy campaigns, developing collaborations, and engaging community volunteers (Greenfield et al. 2015).

Some years before WHO and AARP developed their models, the Center for Home Care Policy and Research (CHCPR) at the Visiting Nurse Service of New York (VNSNY), the oldest and largest home health care organization in the U.S., developed the AdvantAge Initiative (AI), a practical method that a wide array of organizations can use to "listen" to the voices of older adults in their communities; measure their communities' aging-friendliness; identify and prioritize aging-related issues; develop data-driven solutions to address these issues; and engage a variety of stakeholders throughout the community to make the proposed solutions a reality.

This chapter describes the development of the AI, its framework and tools, and how one community-based organization used the framework and tools to learn how the population they serve—older adults in the performing arts—are faring in two Manhattan neighborhoods in New York City; how the organization can better serve these older adults; and just as importantly, how to make the community safer and more livable for people of all ages.

Developing the AdvantAge Initiative Framework and Indicators

The AI team, consisting of CHCPR staff and several outside consultants, conducted qualitative research to help define the key features of an aging-friendly community (Feldman and Oberlink 2003). A total of fourteen focus groups were conducted with older adults (sixty to seventy-five-plus), younger people (thirty-five to fifty-nine), and community leaders, in Chicago, Illinois; Allentown, Pennsylvania; Asheville, North Carolina; and Long Beach, California. In the focus groups, participants were asked to describe the ideal community for adults who wish to age in place. Participants identified the following factors as being necessary for successful aging in place: (1) financial security; (2) access to high-quality health care; (3) social connections; (4) affordable housing and access to supportive services; (5) access to transportation; and (6) personal and community safety.

Participants' comments were very similar across the four focus group sites and were organized into a set of four domains, each with three or four dimensions. These domains and dimensions became the working definition of an age-friendly community and serve as the AI framework (see figure 6.1).

Next, a set of thirty-three indicators corresponding to the domains and dimensions were developed to assist users in measuring how well their communities were doing in each domain. These indicators had to be actionable, because communities have limited jurisdiction over some of the dimensions within the domains, like financial security and some aspects of personal health. Because the AI team postulated that the ultimate judges of community aging-friendliness were older residents themselves (the "end users," so to speak), we developed a wide-ranging survey questionnaire to provide organizations with a tool to gather information from older residents of the community. Survey findings are then reported using the AI indicators. This consumer-derived information provides community stakeholders an opportunity to (1) "hear" the voices of older people and learn about their experiences in and perceptions of their communities; (2) identify and prioritize aging issues in the community; (3) bring stakeholders together

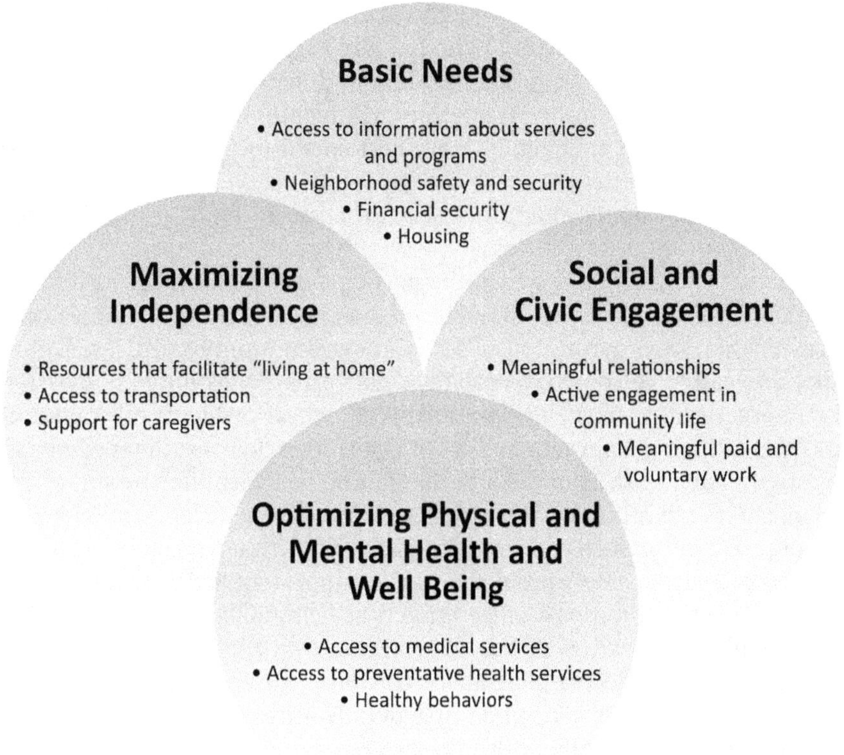

Basic Needs

- Access to information about services and programs
- Neighborhood safety and security
- Financial security
- Housing

Maximizing Independence

- Resources that facilitate "living at home"
- Access to transportation
- Support for caregivers

Social and Civic Engagement

- Meaningful relationships
- Active engagement in community life
- Meaningful paid and voluntary work

Optimizing Physical and Mental Health and Well Being

- Access to medical services
- Access to preventative health services
- Healthy behaviors

FIGURE 6.1. The four domains of an age-friendly community (source: VNSNY)

and provide them with a "common language" (i.e., the survey findings) to discuss aging and other community issues; (4) generate enthusiasm and momentum around potential interventions; and (5) stimulate thought and discussion about the effectiveness of current community programs.

Pilot Testing the AdvantAge Initiative Tools and Processes

The AI team recruited organizations from ten diverse communities to pilot test the survey questionnaire and AI process. Most of these organizations were aging services providers located in various parts of the country. A randomized telephone survey was conducted with over five hundred older adults in each community by a well-known national survey research company. Once the survey findings were made available, the group of ten participant organizations followed a systematic process led by the AI team to understand the survey data and turn it into actionable information for planning purposes. Each of the ten participants engaged community stakeholders in (1) interpreting the data and identifying and prioritizing aging-related issues in the community; (2) identifying which sectors, organizations, and/or individuals were best suited to address those issues; (3) planning for action; and (4) developing messaging strategies to communicate with their communities about the survey findings and planned action steps.

The survey findings provided the participant organizations with information derived from older adults in the community that sometimes confirmed what the organizations already knew, but also revealed issues that they may not have known were seniors' concerns. For example, one participant organization in the Pacific Northwest, where residents rely on automobiles as their primary means of transportation, learned that pedestrian safety was one of the top neighborhood problems identified by survey respondents, suggesting that dependence on personal vehicles creates its own set of problems. In focus groups with older adults that were held to further discuss pedestrian safety problems, participants identified crosswalks near a senior center and a post office branch as being difficult to navigate for older adults. The leaders of the AI project in that community alerted the city public works department about this problem and collaborated with that department to develop and implement features to improve pedestrian safety (Hanson and Emlet 2006).

Since the inception of AI, the team has worked with organizations in sixty communities nationwide to make those communities more aging-friendly. The following case study is an example of how the AI survey and process helped The Actors Fund, a New York City–based organization, identify the needs of older adults who worked or currently work in the performing arts industry and develop supports to help them age in place, while also improving the livability of the neighborhood where they reside.

The Actors Fund AdvantAge Initiative Survey in Two New York City Neighborhoods

Several years after the pilot testing of the AI survey and tools, the AI team developed an online survey option in order to make the survey process more affordable to organizations with limited resources. With many more older adults using computers now than in the early 2000s, and the prediction that even more older adults will be online in the coming years, the AI team felt that it was time to try out this option, and with a generous grant from the Fan Fox and Leslie R. Samuels Foundation, we collaborated with

The Actors Fund to pilot test it. The AI team also provided a paper questionnaire for older adults who did not have access to computers or who were not comfortable filling out the survey online.

The Actors Fund, founded in 1882, is a national human services organization that assists all professionals in the performing arts and entertainment. It is a safety net, providing programs and services for those who are in need, crisis, or transition. Headquartered in New York City's Time Square, The Actors Fund has regional offices in Los Angeles and Chicago. It also operates the Lillian Booth Actors' Home, a 124-bed assisted living and skilled nursing home in Englewood, New Jersey, and three affordable and supportive housing residences. The Fund helps more than seventeen thousand people per year in four key areas: social services and financial assistance; health services and health insurance resources; employment and training; and housing.

The Actors Fund recognized the need to expand its programs and services to support the growing number of seniors, made serving seniors a priority in its strategic planning, and decided to conduct an assessment of seniors' social service and health-care needs, as well as the availability of community supports and services. The Fund decided to engage the AI team to survey adults aged sixty and older in two Manhattan neighborhoods, Chelsea and Clinton/Hell's Kitchen, which have historically been home to many professionals in the arts and entertainment industry because of their close proximity to the theater district. Another factor in this choice of area is the presence of Manhattan Plaza, an affordable housing complex in the Clinton/Hell's Kitchen neighborhood, which opened in 1977 with 70 percent of units designated for performing arts professionals, 15 percent for seniors living in the area, and 15 percent for non-seniors who also live in the area. For decades, Chelsea and Clinton/Hell's Kitchen were considered affordable neighborhoods in which to live. But more recently they have been undergoing major transformations, like many other New York City neighborhoods that have seen widespread gentrification. The availability and affordability of housing are in question; the neighborhoods are more crowded, which has made it more difficult for older pedestrians to navigate the streets; and affordable local stores are closing due to higher rents.

With the assistance of community-based organizations, unions, elected officials, housing providers, and The Actors Fund's staff and its extensive advisory committee, information about the launch of the survey and its importance was quickly and widely disseminated throughout the two neighborhoods. The target audiences for the survey were older adults in the performing arts as well as other older adults in the neighborhoods who were not performing arts professionals. After three months in the field, we received 1,212 completed surveys, 616 online and 604 on paper. While the survey used a convenience sample, the demographics of the sample closely reflected the demographics of the two communities, as reported by the 2010 census.

The AI team analyzed the survey results and shared the findings with The Actors Fund's staff members and the advisory committee. The advisory committee was then divided into four subcommittees, one for each of the four AI domains, and committee members were asked to examine the data related to their assigned domain, identify key needs or issues, and brainstorm recommendations for addressing them.

Key Survey Findings

Survey findings included quantitative data derived from close-ended questions in the survey questionnaire and qualitative data from open-ended questions. These findings offered insight into the everyday lives of older people in the two neighborhoods and provided useful information to propose recommendations for new or retooled policies, programs, and services.

Among the very many survey findings, the responses to questions related to the "Optimizes Physical and Mental Health" and "Basic Needs" domains in the AI framework caught the attention of Actors Fund staff and advisory committee members:

1. Many responses to the open-ended questions on The Actors Fund's questionnaire indicated that even in a resource-rich city like New York, the existing service network may be insufficient to help older adults in certain cases or may not be deployed in an optimal manner in others. One respondent, for example, told a story about trying to help a sick older neighbor and concluded, "It seems there are plenty of services available for the healthy elderly who have the gumption to find it. But for the truly frail and vulnerable, there is nothing." In response to the question "If you were the leader of this community, what changes would you want to make to improve conditions for older persons living here?" a respondent replied, "At [my apartment building], I would bring in services that seniors normally have to seek outside." Still another brought up the need for more active outreach to seniors: "Make more extensive provision for keeping closer in touch with seniors living alone." Having easy access to information was a related recommendation: "Use different ways and means to publish available information to seniors regarding events, social occurrences, help resources, advisory sources of help, and any other

service seniors can avail themselves of, or possibly be of service to, that may be in their area."
2. One of the questions related to the Basic Needs domain asked respondents to rank order a list of typical problems that are found in various neighborhoods. Survey respondents said that heavy traffic was the most pressing problem in their neighborhood. But the magnitude and specificity of the problem, as well as its impact on older residents, only became apparent in the many comments respondents wrote about traffic dangers. For example, one respondent said, "In my neighborhood (Hell's Kitchen) Ninth Avenue is a major crossing for me to get to the stores, gym, community garden, etc., and at no time of the day or night does it feel safe to do so: heavy traffic of all kinds including large trucks and busses are impatient to get to the tunnel; and cyclists RARELY stop for light and sometimes cannot be seen. . . . I would highlight this problem as one that particularly affect[s] seniors." Many other respondents wrote about other mobility issues in the Hell's Kitchen neighborhood as well, and the fact that several traffic fatalities occurred in the area underscored the magnitude of the problem.

Discussion

The Actors Fund AI survey had the overarching goal of gathering information to help The Actors Fund better plan and expand their programming for seniors in Manhattan Plaza and the Chelsea and Clinton/Hell's Kitchen neighborhoods. The Fund was drawn to the idea of expanding and locating services where many of their clients live (e.g. Manhattan Plaza), and not long after the survey the Fund assumed leadership of the Rodney Kirk Center, which had been providing very limited on-site services to help senior residents of Manhattan Plaza. The Fund found resources to greatly expand the services offered at Manhattan Plaza by hiring an administrator, case managers, and a nurse.

The AI survey findings showed that the majority of arts professionals (68 percent) and 72 percent of non-arts professionals aged sixty-five-plus live alone. Furthermore, 66 percent of arts professionals and 52 percent of non-arts professionals have no living children. This may mean that this particular population will be more likely than those with spouses and/or children nearby to use the formal support system, and having access to assistance in navigating the health and social services systems, like that offered through the Rodney Kirk Center, will be invaluable to them.

Through the survey process, The Actors Fund also learned that efforts to make a community more aging-friendly go well beyond service provision. Like the example cited earlier, the many comments that survey respondents made about the neighborhoods' traffic problems raised the alarm about the safety of older adults who walk outside. The seniors not only felt unsafe but *were* in fact unsafe, as the pedestrian accidents in the neighborhood grew. The Actors Fund chief operating officer informed the local community board about the problem, and its transportation planning committee wrote to the New York City Department of Transportation asking it to act. As a result, crosswalk countdown timers were installed, a pedestrian refuge between bicycle and car lanes was created, and changes were made to traffic patterns to improve pedestrian safety.

The AdvantAge Initiative survey findings help organizations that are leading aging-friendly initiatives in their communities learn about older residents' experiences in the community and understand their points of view to inform planning. It is possible that older residents' priorities will not be in line with those of service providers or city agencies and may impact their work plans, but if creating an aging-friendly city or town is the goal, then getting input from seniors at the start of an aging-friendly community initiative makes it more likely that these end users will appreciate the outcomes of the initiative. Furthermore, the leaders of an aging-friendly initiative need to be ready to work with other sectors in their city or town (e.g., planning department, housing providers, transportation providers) that may not have been collaborators in the past, as illustrated in The Actors Fund and Pacific Northwest examples above. In fact, working with individuals from other community sectors should be the rule, because it takes a village to create an aging-friendly community.

Mia R. Oberlink is a senior research associate at the Center for Home Care Policy and Research (CHCPR) of the Visiting Nurse Service of New York (VNSNY). She manages the AdvantAge Initiative, a project that has collaborated with over sixty communities nationwide to measure their aging-friendliness and develop strategies to help older residents age in place. She was the director of the technical assistance office for the U.S. Administration on Community Living program, Community Innovations for Aging in Place (CIAIP). Before joining CHCPR, Ms. Oberlink spent thirteen years at the Department of Geriatrics and Adult Development at the Mount Sinai Medical Center and at the International Longevity Center, where she was director of communications.

Barbara S. Davis has been with The Actors Fund since 1984. As chief operating officer, she oversees the intersection of administration, finance, advancement, and programs including social services, health care, and workforce development for the Fund's three offices in New York, Chicago, and Los Angeles and at its supportive housing residences, as well as at the assisted living and skilled nursing home in New Jersey. Ms. Davis is co-chair of the Housing, Health and Human Services Committee for Manhattan Community Board 4 and is vice president of the Waldman Foundation. She has her BA in psychology from American University and a master's degree in social work from Columbia University.

References

AARP. 2014. *Livable Communities.* AARP. Accessed 15 January 2017. http://www.aarp.org/livable-communities.

Feldman, Penny, and Mia Oberlink. 2003. "Developing Community Indicators to Promote the Health and Well-Being of Older People." *Family & Community Health* 26: 268–74.

GIA. 2013. *Age-Friendly Communities: The Movement to Create Great Places to Grow Up and Grow Old in America.* Accessed 15 January 2017. www.giaging.org/documents/13042_GIA_AFC_primer.pdf.

Greenfield, Emily, Mia Oberlink, Andrew Scharlach, Margaret Neal, and Philip Stafford. 2015. "Age-Friendly Community Initiatives: Conceptual Issues and Key Questions." *Gerontologist* 55(2):191–98.

Hanson, David, and Charles Emlet. 2006. "Assessing a Community's Elder Friendliness." *Family & Community Health* 29(4): 266–78.

Lehning, Amanda, Andrew Scharlach, and Jennifer Price Wolf. 2012. "An Emerging Typology of Community Aging Initiatives. *Journal of Community Practice* 20: 293–316.

WHO (World Health Organization). 2007. *Global Age-Friendly Cities: A Guide.* Geneva: World Health Organization. Accessed 15 January 2017.http://www.who.int/ageing/publications/Global_age_friendly_cities_Guide_English.pdf.

PART III
Collaboration across Generations

THE AGE-FRIENDLY COMMUNITY MOVEMENT IS often criticized for its primary focus on old age alone, as if other age groups and populations were not subject to similar forces of exclusion from the mainstream. Some proponents have suggested that the effort can be defended with the argument that improvements for older populations will bring about residual improvements for others. For example, "no-step entrances" to housing and commercial spaces, it is typically argued, benefit everyone, not just elders. Of course, the same argument can be made for focusing purely on disability or purely on children, where interventions in the environment benefit other groups. Part III provides examples of efforts to fully resolve the debate and demonstrate how an intergenerational model of age-friendly community work can occur and may actually may be necessary for the movement to be successful.

We begin in chapter 7 with Corita Brown and Nancy Henkin's very comprehensive and persuasive argument that an all-ages approach to community change can perhaps be one of the most effective strategies for creating age-friendly communities. While the "good for elders, good for all" argument may have a grain of truth, it is not a sustainable strategy so much as a trickle-down theory of change. They suggest that a singular focus on older people represents a missed opportunity for the age-friendly movement to explicitly adopt an equity framework, enhance social capital, and build a broader, multigenerational base of support around shared issues such as safe streets, food access, transportation, and affordable, accessible housing.

While the global demographics of aging have been referenced in other chapters, Brown and Henkin also make a significant contribution in describing the impact on older people of the broader range of demographic changes occurring at the global level—migration of younger people, changing birth rates, and workforce changes bringing minorities into the system of care for older adults and others. Echoing Phillipson and Buffel, they demonstrate the limitations of constructing an understanding of old age through a simplistic, ready-made recitation of aging demographics.

This focus on changes across the life span and the development of a life-course perspective on age-friendly communities is an implicit critique of age segregation that might, ironically, reinforce aging stereotypes and conflict over limited resources that can be provided across the generations. Moreover, collective efficacy, as defined by Brown and Henkin, can promote more substantive and sustainable change, and the age-friendly movement misses the mark in not taking advantage of naturally occurring alliances that might be present in any community. They demonstrate the power of this approach in a major national Communities for All Ages project and describe ways in which "leadership for all ages" can play a critical role in the promotion of social, cultural, and economic change. Baggett's article provides a best-case example.

Emi Kiyota (chapter 8) extends this focus on inter- and multigenerational community development with a compelling example from post-tsunami Japan. An architect like Lennard, she demonstrates how participatory design involving the architect and the elders can result in a flourishing intergenerational environment that empowers elders while serving children. This approach to design is meant to counter the "hidden program" of care, safety, and security that typically informs the construction of environments for elders. She offers the concept of the Ibasho café as an alternative and provides a fascinating description of the development of one café in an area devastated by the Great East Japan Earthquake of 2011. Participation of elders in the project infused its development from beginning to end, ranging from purpose, to visioning, to governance, and even to the hiring of elder carpenters familiar with traditional Japanese building methods.

Arthur Namara and Kristin Bodiford (chapter 9) describe the inspiring work of young Ugandans who have collectively organized to address the significant daily needs of frail elders, in companionship with the elders themselves. Building collaborations across the generations resulted in joint economic development outcomes (with elders training youth in farming, crafts, and other areas) and improved health outcomes for elders (with youth identifying and responding to daily needs expressed by elders, needs as basic as the removal of tortuous pit latrines and the installation of toilets). As in the Japanese example, development work "exploits" the social, cultural, and human capital already in place as represented by young people and by elders—a timely, "asset-based" model in times of austerity.

7 COMMUNITIES FOR ALL AGES
Reinforcing and Reimagining the Social Compact

Corita Brown and Nancy Henkin

> *We are caught in an inescapable network of mutuality, tied in a single garment of destiny. Whatever affects one directly, affects all indirectly.*
> —Martin Luther King, Jr.

Introduction

The age-friendly movement has emerged as a powerful response to the rapidly growing aging population (Lui et al. 2009; Scharlach 2012; WHO 2007). Although the range of age-friendly community definitions reflects multiple approaches and methods (Lui et al. 2009), many models promote a vision that is inclusive of all ages and highlight the importance of strengthening the social compact. Consider these quotes:

> A Society for All Ages is multigenerational, [not] fragmented, with youths, adults, and older persons going their separate ways ... rather, it is age-inclusive, with different generations recognizing and acting upon their commonality of interest. (Kofi Annan, secretary-general of the United Nations, at ceremony launching International Year of Older Persons; Annan 1999)

> AARP's Livable Communities supports the efforts of neighborhoods, towns, cities and even states to become Great Places for ALL Ages. We believe that communities should provide safe, walkable streets, age friendly housing and transportation options, access to needed services, and opportunities for residents of all ages to participate in community life. (AARP, n.d.)

> Communities for a Lifetime are good places to grow up and grow old and offer physical, social and service features for residents of all ages and abilities. Through collaborative action and strategic planning, community leaders across sectors build places that support health and vitality for residents and the community as a whole" (Minnesota Board on Aging, Department of Human Services 2013)

The World Health Organization (2007: 6) and others further articulate this premise by defining aging as a lifelong process: "We are all aging at any moment in our life and we should all have the opportunity to do so in a healthy and active way. To safeguard the highest possible quality of life in older age, WHO endorses the approach of investing into factors which influence health throughout the lifecourse."

In practice, however, the age-friendly movement has focused primarily upon the needs and interests of older adults, their caregivers, and service providers (Lui et. al, 2009). The published research suggests that most *age-friendly* initiatives are not intentional about gathering data from all ages, including youth/education organizations and younger residents in planning efforts, or engaging multiple generations in joint advocacy and/or collective action to address shared concerns. For example, the WHO (2007) guide supports an age-friendly city for all ages and defines aging as a lifelong process, but it does not gather data from youth and families about what makes a city livable or about opportunities and barriers for engaging collaboratively with older adults and the aging network. Similarly, Emlet and Moceri (2012) facilitated a community forum to examine social relationships and social connectedness in elder-friendly communities. Their results highlight the importance of community-based intergenerational relationships, but they did not interview anyone under forty years of age.

What accounts for this discrepancy between vision and practice? One answer may lie in a common assumption of the age-friendly movement that *what is good for older adults is good for everyone* (Grantmakers in Aging, n.d.). In other words, if the age-friendly movement succeeds in making communities livable for older adults, those communities will then be livable for all generations. While there are many shared interests among different generations, recent studies in the United States and Europe indicate that young adults and older adults are demonstrating more polarized voting patterns and attitudes than they have since the 1970s (Taylor 2012; European Commission 2009). This emerging data suggest the need to critically examine what it will take to create age-friendly communities that are embraced and supported by all generations.

In this chapter we explore key trends, theories, and practices that underscore the importance of using an "all-ages" approach to meet the goals of age-friendly initiatives. We will examine (1) the shifting demographic landscape, particularly with regard to age, race, and ethnicity and the opportunities and challenges this presents for the age-friendly movement; (2) theoretical underpinnings of an all-ages approach; (3) the Communities for All Ages model as a case study; (4) benefits of using this lens to achieve age-friendly goals; and (5) concrete strategies for age-friendly communities to embed an all-ages approach.

The Demographic Imperative

Globally, the number of older persons is expected to more than doubled (from 841 million in 2013 to more than 2 billion in 2050), exceeding the number of children for the first time by 2047 (United Nations 2013). The older global population is growing faster in less-developed regions, where by 2050 nearly eight in ten of the world's older adults will live. Dependency ratios (working-age adults per older person in population), particularly in more developed countries, also continue to fall. This changing dependency ratio may impact, among other things, the service use and income supports for older adults relative to the taxes contributed by working-age residents. The shifting ratio will place greater responsibility on young people to support older adults than in any previous generation. Myers (2007, 2008) and others argue that building a sense of intergenerational interdependence and "rediscovering the intergenerational compact" are crucial as the older population grows.

In the United States, due to longer life expectancy and the aging of the population born during the post–World War II baby boom (between the years 1946 and 1964), the percentage of older adults within the total population is increasing at an unprecedented rate. In 1930, older adults (aged sixty-five and older) composed just 5 percent of the total population; by 2030, they are projected to compose over 20 percent (National Institute on Aging et al., n.d.). Rapid population aging is not the only trend altering the nation's demographics. Increasing racial/ethnic diversity, especially among children, is also dramatically increasing. Results from the 2010 census showed that racial and ethnic minorities have accounted for 91.7 percent of the nation's growth since 2000. The majority of the increase from 2000 to 2010 (56 percent) is among Latinos. Though "non-Hispanic whites" compose over 62 percent of the national population, they account for only 8.3 percent of its growth during this last decade. In 2011, U.S. census data marked a "tipping point" in which, for the first time since census data has been collected, whites accounted for less than half of the births (Tavernise 2011).

The intersection of the demographic shifts in age and race/ethnicity in the United States is marked by a growing gap between the median age differences among racial and ethnic groups. This emerging phenomenon has been characterized by demographers as a "racial generation gap" (Hochschild 2003). While today's population of adults over sixty-five is more diverse than any prior cohorts (Pew Research Center 2011), whites currently compose 80 percent of this population.[1] This percentage is attributed to both longer life expectancies among whites than other racial and/or ethnic groups, as well as racially restrictive immigration policies prior to 1965 that maintained a white majority of the total population (Chin 1996). In contrast, 47 percent of youth aged eighteen and under and over 50 percent of children aged five and under are African American, Latino, Asian American, and Native American (Heisler and Shrestha 2011). Thirty years ago, the difference in the percentage of African Americans, Asian Americans, and Latinos did not exceed 5 percentage points in any successive generations. In other words, people in their sixties had a similar racial/ethnic makeup as those in their forties and fifties, who in turn had a similar demographic to those in their twenties and thirties. This is no longer the case.

Demographic changes have the potential to create powerful connections and collaborations (Myers 2008). For example, the retirement years are increasingly viewed as a period of meaningful, productive activity versus one of disengagement (Chambré 1993; Moen 1996). Research suggests that the need to be *generative*—to ensure the continuity of one's own life span through investments in younger generations—is a powerful motivator for baby-boom-era older adults to give back to their communities (Taylor 2006; Freedman 1997). At the other end of the age spectrum are the millennials (those in their teens and twenties today), who have been characterized as unusually "confident, self-expressive, liberal, upbeat, receptive to new ideas and ways of living" (Taylor and Keeter 2010) and interested in opportunities to contribute to their communities. These generational trends suggest enormous potential for engaging people at different stages of life in mutually beneficial experiences that foster social connectedness and address critical societal needs.

It is unclear, however, what impact these demographic changes will have on public investments. Researchers and practitioners point to the potential for a national split over competing agendas between an older white electorate and a younger population that is increasingly Latino, Asian, and African American (Roberts 2007; Pastor and Carter 2012). Demographer William Frey notes, "This racial generation gap could create serious policy dilemmas if policymakers feel that they must choose between, say, higher budgets for health care for the elderly or higher budgets for schooling for youth. The gap could lead to severe social divisions" (in Hochschild 2003). Pastor and Carter (2012) warn that today's elders and decision makers do not see themselves "reflected in the faces of the next generation" and as such are investing less in education and community infrastructure for youth and families. Indeed, emerging state- and county-level data indicate that older white adults are less likely to support funding for public education when the children in the public schools are of a different race and ethnicity (Poterba 1998; Ladd and Murray 2001).

The potential for polarization across generational and racial/ethnic lines underscores the importance of reinforcing and reimagining the intergenerational social compact—the reciprocal ties that hold families, governance, and society together over time (Cornman and Kingson 1998). The social compact, based on Toqueville's ideal of a society that respects differences and honors the inherent worth of every citizen (Achenbaum1998), involves exchanges of resources and care across age groups and reflects a sense of mutual responsibility. Policies that support public education for all children and social security are at the core of the compact.

Policy makers and researchers have suggested that high poverty rates (particularly among children), growing stress on caregiving families, youth unemployment and job insecurity, violence, and growing social and economic disparities reflect a *fraying* of the social compact (Reich 1998). Over two decades ago, John Gardner (1990: 6) wrote that the "web of reciprocal dependencies that once existed has been destroyed" and called for "a renewed sense of community and a recognition of the interdependence across generations." In light of the major demographic changes we are experiencing today, how can the age-friendly movement contribute to strengthening generational obligations, promoting the common good, and building a civil and caring society for all?

Theoretical Frameworks

The all-ages lens proposed in this chapter draws upon several theoretical frameworks.

Life Span Theory and Life Course Perspective

Both the life span developmental theory and the life course perspective embrace a human development approach that views aging as a lifelong process. *Life span development* focuses primarily on individual life trajectories, suggesting that each major period has its own developmental challenges and offers opportunities for significant growth and change. It examines individual differences in physical, cognitive, personality, and social development and the interaction between heredity and environment (Feldman 2013). Accomplishing age-related developmental tasks and developing effective strategies for lifelong adaptation are key elements for achieving optimal health and well-being. This framework underscores the importance of understanding the needs and capacities of individuals as they move through the life cycle.

The *life course perspective* focuses on the intersection of individuals and social structures, particularly structures of inequality. Researchers conceptualize life course as a "sequence of age-linked transitions that are embedded in social institutions and history" (Bengtson, Elder, and Putney 2005) and suggest that "as we age, we are a product of our place in history, our place in the social structure, our agency, the decisions we make and the consequence of earlier decisions we made" (McPherson and Wister 2008).

From an *individual* lens, life course perspective focuses on the connection between early events and outcomes in later life. Rather than highlighting discrete stages, it focuses on an integrated continuum of exposures, experiences, and interactions and suggests that inequality among age peers increases as they move through the life course.

From an *institutional* perspective, the life course can be viewed as a "political and social construct that consists of explicitly defined age-graded stages that are reinforced in institutions like work and education" (Dannefer and Settersen 2010). This is exemplified by the traditional three boxes of life framework that presents youth as a time for education, middle age as a time for work and child rearing, and old age as a period for leisure. Researchers suggest that the crumbling of these life course patterns, particularly related to education, transitions to adulthood, and work/retirement, will require a deinstitutionalization of the life course, a movement away from restrictive social roles based on age, and the creation of more opportunities for people at all stages of life (Riley and Riley 1994).

From a *policy lens,* the life course framework highlights the challenges of growing inequities in communities. McDaniel and Bernard (2011) suggest that "life courses unfold in the context of disparities in resources with which individuals and families face shocks and make transitions" and that individual trajectories are built on past constraints and opportunities. This concept of cumulative advantage/disadvantage recognizes the adverse effects of childhood poverty as well as the impact of the social circumstances that individuals face as they move through the life course (McDaniel and Bernard 2011). For example, racial discrimination and lack of access to resources and opportunities have resulted in a myriad of health disparities such as limited life expectancies for men of color, two- to threefold disparities in birth weight and preterm birth between African American and white newborns (Braverman and Barclay 2009), and the fact that cancer mortality is highest among African American men (National Cancer Institute 2018). Research (Rumbaut and Komaie 2010) suggests that for millions of young adults who lack legal permanent residency, access to postsecondary education and prospects for social mobility are limited. Young children who are U.S. born but live with a noncitizen parent may also suffer long-term health consequences due to the fear and anxiety they experience, according to a recent Kaiser Foundation study (2017). It is likely that structural barriers to citizenship and anti-immigrant sentiments will continue to negatively impact many immigrants as they move through the life course. Social inequality impacts not only individual health and well-being, but also the transmission of disadvantage from generation to generation (Braverman and Barclay 2009).

Although critics have noted that the life course perspective focuses primarily on the importance of childhood investments, recognition that interventions are needed across the life cycle to buffer critical transitions is growing. McDaniel and Bernard (2011) stress that social policy should make more options available to more people over their lifetimes, enhancing capabilities of people at all stages and providing help when challenges occur (Hall and Lamont 2009). A report by the Maternal and Child Health Bureau (2010) of the U.S. Department of Health and Human Services also highlights the importance of reducing risk factors and increasing protective factors across the life span, not just in the early years.

The life course perspective is a valuable framework for planning, practice, and policy development. It provides a strong rationale for investing in human capital at all stages of life, moving toward an integration of services across the life course, and mobilizing generations to work together to address the root causes of inequities—all key tenets of an all-ages approach to community building.

Age Segregation

A common concern cited by researchers and practitioners within the age-friendly context has been to "change the culture of aging." Culture change in this context can be defined as "the transformation of individual and societal attitudes toward aging and elders, transformation of elders' attitudes toward themselves and their aging, changes in the attitudes and behavior of caregivers toward those for whom they care, and changes in governmental policy and regulation" (Fagan 2003). What will it take to change attitudes of the broader community toward aging and elders? The literature suggests that countering age segregation may be a useful strategy for these culture change efforts.

Age segregation is cited as both a cause and consequence of negative stereotypes and stigma attached to both old age and youth (Hagestad and Uhlenberg 2005; Vanderbeck 2007). In addition, social and spatial age segregation have been identified as a cause of increased loneliness and isolation for older people (Thang 2001) and decreased protective factors for youth (Engwicht 2005). Hagestad and Uhlenberg (2005) cite three main types of age segregation within community settings: institutional, spatial, and cultural. Institutional segregation describes the ways in which generations are separated through work, school, and religious environments, government funding streams, and research traditions. Spatial segregation refers to the lack of face-to face contact based on institutional segregation. Cultural segregation refers to differences in language, food, dress, and so on among different generations.

While physical proximity between generations may be important, commentators suggest that proximity alone is not sufficient to produce respect (Valentine 2008). Ageist attitudes are perpetuated, for example, by public images of aging as a period of decline and older people as dependent rather than capable (Robbins 2015.) Research indicates that age segregation reinforces these ageist attitudes by restricting opportunities for older and younger persons to form stable, interdependent, cross-age relationships that could counter stereotypes. The growing racial generation gap adds complexity to issues of age segregation and the forming of cross-generational networks. For example, Pain (2000) found that generational segregation has a distinct ethnic/racial dimension in neighborhoods in the United Kingdom experiencing rapid ethnic change. In this study, older (white) people's isolation and hesitancy to navigate public space independently are linked to fears of young people from immigrant groups in local areas. Given the complex demographic landscape, Valentine (2008) poses a fertile question to geographers, which could also be posed to the age-friendly movement: "What kind of work needs to be done—and in which kinds of spaces—to generate this [cross-racial/ cross-generational] interdependence?"

National research indicates that non-kin networks in the United States are currently highly age homogeneous (Vanderbeck 2007). These statistics, however, are not disaggregated by race and ethnicity. The literature suggests that levels of age segregation appear to differ somewhat within different racial and ethnic groups. For example, a study comparing social networks within specific racial and ethnic groups suggests that Asian American and Latino (native-born and immigrant) and African American cultural traditions may involve less generational segregation than is common in white communities (Kim and McKenry 1998). The age-friendly movement could benefit from further exploration of how non-kin intergenerational networks are formed within specific racial and ethnic groups and whether these networks impact perceptions and attitudes of aging and elders within those communities. Cultures with greater prevalence of age integration may provide valuable models for the age-friendly movement in supporting age-diverse non-kin networks.

Social Capital and Collective Efficacy

The age-friendly literature focuses on both the social environment and physical infrastructure as combined determinants of health and well-being at the community level. This is supported by the research evidence from environmental gerontology that indicates a link between the physical and social environment and the well-being of older adults (Buffel and Phillipson 2012) and neighborhood effects research that underscores the connection between the social and physical attributes of neighborhoods and quality of life for children and adolescents (Sampson, Morenoff, and Earls 1999).

Social capital has many competing definitions, but broadly speaking, it offers a useful theoretical construct to conceptualize the roles that social structures (personal and organizational networks) play in providing supports, information, and opportunities for individuals and within communities (Chaskin et. al 2006). It is important to note that though we will primarily examine the benefits of building social capital to support age-friendly communities, there has been research that indicates the potential for negative effects (Portes 2000; Jennings 2007). De Souza Briggs (2006) reminds us that "social capital is a *means*, that is, a resource that enables productive action, just as other forms of capital do, and not an end in itself." As such, the accruing of social capital through networks and civic associations has been leveraged both to improve neighborhood conditions and to support exclusionary processes such as racial segregation (Jennings 2007).

Social capital can focus on both the individual level and the community level. In the context of age-friendly communities, we focus at the community level and draw on the collective efficacy framework outlined by Sampson et. al (1999). The construct of social capital focuses on the social relationships themselves, while collective efficacy examines how those relationships are operationalized for the common good. Cagney and Wen (2008: 242) describe communities with high levels of collective efficacy as places where people "not only feel attached to their neighborhood and trust one another, but are willing to intervene on each other's behalf, even when they do not know one another." Social cohesion and social control are defined by Sampson et al. (2008) as the two key forms of social capital that impact the development of collective efficacy at the neighborhood level. Social cohesion is defined by levels of mutual trust and solidarity among community residents. Social control is defined as the extent to which the community is able to leverage social resources toward positive community outcomes, including a healthy environment.

The distinction between social cohesion and social control is an important one. A common criticism of intergenerational and cross-racial efforts is that they focus only on social cohesion, and less on the process of leveraging relationships to support collective action (Vanderbeck 2007; Valentine 2008). For example, Vanderbeck (2007: 213) critiques intergenerational practice for promoting "a relatively limited vision of what extra-familial intergenerational relationships are or can be, tending to emphasize relatively conventional and uncontroversial (and, one might also say, depoliticized) notions of intergenerational contact based on roles like honorary grandparenting, mentoring or serving as successful role models." The collective efficacy model provides an opportunity for the age-friendly movement. What will it require to build collective efficacy across a generational and/or a racial generational divide? How do we build a culture of interdependence and leverage our relationships to create neighborhoods and cities that are good for all generations? This exploration can provide a valuable contribution to the research on aging, intergenerational practice, social capital, racial equity, and politics of place.

From Theory to Practice

The life course, age integration, and collective efficacy theories can help inform the development of new strategies for community building and planning. The rapid demographic changes we are now experiencing provide an opportunity to break out of habitual patterns and identify new strategies for community building and planning. A number of organizations currently utilize age-integrated approaches and could serve as resources to the age-friendly movement. Some of these organizations explicitly address issues of racial/ethnic divides as well as generational differences, and others address these differences more implicitly. In the United States, one of the first organizations to address shared policy concerns across generations is Generations United (GU). Founded in 1986 by leaders of the National Council on Aging, Child Welfare League of America, Children's Defense Fund, and AARP, GU connects advocates for children and advocates for older adults to build a common agenda, forge new partnerships, and educate and empower leaders in the field. In the United Kingdom, the Beth Johnson Foundation established the Centre for Intergenerational Practice in 2001 to support the development of intergenerational practice throughout the UK and to promote an understanding of the potential of intergenerational practice to address social issues. A range of university centers and programs have been developed that support leadership and develop research on intergenerational practice and planning. In the United States, these include the Penn State Intergenerational Program, the Department of City and Regional Planning at Cornell University, and the Intergenerational Center at Temple University.

Building Communities for All Ages: A Case Study

Communities for All Ages (CFAA), developed by The Intergenerational Center at Temple University, was a national initiative that utilized an intergenerational and life course lens for community building. The CFAA model promotes a vision, a lens, and a framework for creating communities that are good for growing up and growing older. The vision imagines places that intentionally engage people of all ages in civic and community life and include quality supports and environmental design for all ages. The lens is a way of thinking that emphasizes values of interdependence, reciprocity, and collective responsibility. The framework is a way of acting, using collaborative intergenerational community change strategies to improve outcomes for all community residents, particularly vulnerable children, families, and elders. The Intergenerational Center conceptualized the Communities for All Ages framework in 2002 in response to the emergence of multiple age-segregated community building efforts in the United States. To operationalize the key elements of a "Society for All Ages" (Annan 1999) at the neighborhood/community level, literature related to age-friendly, child-friendly, and family-friendly community initiatives was reviewed, and focus groups with aging and youth practitioners were conducted. A set of common concerns across age groups emerged related to education/lifelong learning, health/social services, family support, public safety, and opportunities for civic engagement (Henkin et al. 2005).

Implementation

In 2003, the Intergenerational Center partnered with the Arizona Community Foundation to pilot Communities for All Ages in five communities. Based on promising early outcomes, the initiative was expanded in 2005 to four communities in Westchester, New York. In 2008, with a grant from the W. K. Kellogg Foundation, a request for proposals was nationally distributed to identify local foundations that would be interested in providing matching funds to support the development of CFAA sites in their communities. The local funders that were selected identified the neighborhoods or small towns in which they wanted to work. A total of twenty-three sites across the country participated in the CFAA National Network.

Rather than addressing a specific age group, the Communities for All Ages model intentionally brings together organizations representing diverse groups and residents of all ages (not just young and old) to engage in efforts that promote the common good across the life span. The twenty-three sites in the CFAA Network engaged in a three-step process of assessment, planning, and implementation, with local and national funding and technical assistance from the Intergenerational Center. During assessment, each local site developed a collaborative team including staff from organizations representing different constituencies (e.g., aging, education, family services, faith based, community development, neighborhood associations), policy makers, and residents of all ages. Using intergenerational assessment tools (e.g., focus group questions, surveys, asset mapping) developed by the Intergenerational Center and the Center for Assessment and Policy Development (CAPD), the teams collected data, identified major issues of concern to all generations, and developed community profiles that summarized their findings. Based on this profile and community feedback, each team identified an issue to use as their "doorway" into the community building process (e.g., improving health, increasing neighborhood safety, enhancing education and lifelong learning). All sites sought to increase trust and social connectedness across differences such as age, race, and/or ethnicity. The CFAA initiative chose to focus on race and ethnicity as well as age differences based on an understanding of race and age as intersecting categories that impact place-based inequalities. An assumption of CFAA is that to make a place good for all ages, we must address racial inequalities, and to advance racial equity, we must address generational differences.

Each team developed an action plan that utilized four key strategies:

1. Developing alliances across diverse organizations and systems
2. Engaging community residents of all ages in leadership roles
3. Creating places, practices, and policies that promote interaction across ages
4. Addressing critical issues (i.e., health, safety, and education/lifelong learning) from a life course perspective

Through the use of these strategies, opportunities to match complementary needs and skills emerged (i.e., older adults providing mentoring/tutoring to youth supports educational outcomes for kids and promotes healthy aging), and investment of all generations in community improvement efforts increased. Mobilizing different age groups to serve as resources for each other and their communities also helped counteract the negative effects of age segregation and build trust and connection across age, race, and other historical divides.

Evaluation

Communities for All Ages was designed to produce two types of outcomes: (1) improving residents' individual well-being in a particular issue area identified by local communities as important to multiple generations (e.g., health, safety); and (2) strengthening a community's capacity to apply cross-generational strategies to a range of community issues, making this approach "business as usual." A participatory cross-site evaluation conducted by the Center for Assessment and Policy Development (CAPD) documented the network's progress toward these outcomes and lessons learned that can strengthen community-building work in the future. Communities actively participated in defining their own outcomes and in gathering information to track their progress and document successes and challenges. The evaluators worked with the communities to create logic models and put in place a logic model reporting form to help communities provide evidence to track their implementation progress and report on agreed upon outcomes. The evaluators also conducted interviews and focus groups, and they collected survey data from aligned organizations in each community to better understand the extent to which individuals, the CFAA collaborations, and aligned organizations were embedding CFAA strategies into their own work, as additional indicators of key outcomes. Qualitative data were coded by two members of the evaluation team to develop inter-rater reliability.

Findings from these multiple sources were synthesized to describe progress of the initiative as a whole against the anticipated outcomes. Findings, stories, and lessons learned were documented in a final report (Henkin, Brown and Leiderman 2012). The participatory approach had both strengths and limitations. That the information was gathered from multiple sources added to its richness, though the fact that much of the information was qualitative and gathered by volunteers hindered comparability and completeness.

Findings

The cross-site evaluation documented some important benefits for older adults with regard to both types of outcomes. The following are a few examples of outcomes:

- Increased *community engagement* of older adults: In many sites, older adults volunteered as mentors and tutors, organizers and advocates, facilitators, master gardeners, and walking-group leaders. A range of individual benefits that research indicates contribute to healthy aging were reported by residents aged fifty-five and over, including decreased isolation and increased sense of purpose (Hinterlong and Williamson 2006).
- Increased *social capital* across generations: All twenty-three sites reported increased trust and interaction among different generations and other traditional divides such as race, ethnicity, and class. Through more inclusive practices such as team building and leadership development as well as intergenerational arts, oral histories, cross-age mentoring, intergenerational exercise, and community gar-

dening, likely and unlikely connections were formed. Participants from all of the sites shared stories of the ways in which older and younger people celebrate joys and help each other in times of deep loss or other major challenges. The skills and relationships that were built helped form a solid base of social capital between older adults and younger residents.
- Increased *involvement of the aging network* in community change efforts: In many communities, organizations within the aging network and older adult residents became engaged in community planning processes and collaborations from which they had previously been excluded. In every community, new partnerships were formed across organizations representing different age groups and sectors, and intergenerational strategies and approaches were infused into the policies and practices of many agencies and institutions. Shared community visions emerged across generations, additional resources were leveraged, and vital new multigenerational spaces (i.e., community centers, local parks, and shared sites) were created.
- Expanded *leadership and educational opportunities* for older adults: All twenty-three sites expanded opportunities for leadership and education among residents of different generations, including older adults. Organizations that provide support and leadership development to parents developed more inclusive practices that involved a broader range of caregivers, including grandparents raising grandchildren.

The following challenges to the implementation of CFAA were identified through the evaluation and technical assistance process:

1. *Policy.* Age-segregated funding streams and restrictions against interaction across ages on physical premises created significant barriers for several communities' attempts to develop multigenerational spaces and intergenerational activities.
2. *Finding common ground.* The drivers for change vary among different generations. Finding common ground across age, race, ethnicity, and class often required a complex mix of "caucusing," where people work with same-age peers, and collaborative approaches across group differences. Managing the "dance" of caucus and collaboration includes identifying outcomes for all generational cohorts and building a collective leadership approach in which generations organize and advocate on each other's behalf.
3. *Moving beyond programs.* It took months to years for organizational representatives and community leaders to digest the idea that CFAA emphasizes systemic change. It appears easier for many participants to think in terms of developing discrete programs.

4. *Logistics.* Negotiating the logistics involved in linking organizations and community residents from diverse networks often requires a significant investment of time, which can be a lot to ask of volunteers.

Discussion

Several key lessons learned from the initiative may add value to the age-friendly movement:

- *Multigenerational spaces hold great promise for building social capital and creating a tangible representation of a community that is livable and friendly for all ages.*
  The work that a community does to create or expand spaces serves as a microcosm of what a Community for All Ages is and what it takes to use an all-ages approach to community building. The space became a tangible result of the initiative—often before progress toward health, education, and lifelong learning, safety, or other issues were seen, and contributed to civic pride, a sense of history, and a sense of place.
- *Intergenerational community building is most successful when it engages individuals from ALL stages of life (not just young and old) and intentionally focuses on fostering meaningful relationships from the outset.*
  Intergenerational programs typically bring children and youth together with older adults in mutually beneficial experiences. The unique nurturing relationships that often develop when these "bookend" generations are connected are powerful and can contribute to both positive youth development and healthy aging (Taylor 2006; Schwartz and Simmons 2001). Increasing participation from these two groups, as well as other overlooked segments of the populations such as youth who have dropped out of school, kinship caregivers, and older immigrants and refugees, is critical. Moving beyond programs to create and sustain community change, however, also requires the involvement of residents of all ages and backgrounds. People trying to find employment, parents struggling to work and support multiple generations, and many others need to be at the table as well. The participation of residents of multiple age groups in collaboration with organizational representatives requires *intentionality and effort*. Investing time in team-building activities, designing meetings that take into account the needs and interests of different age groups, and offering intergenerational leadership training early in the process are all effective strategies. There are also a range of models for strengthening intergenerational collaboration; some groups developed same-age cohorts that they then integrated into an intergenerational group, while others began with a mixed-age group. No one approach fits all.

- *The intergenerational approach is particularly effective as an entry point to bridging historical divides (town/gown; race/ethnicity, class).*
  CFAA activities and supports contributed to new connections among people of different ages. This was anticipated, given the emphasis on intergenerational connection. One unexpected outcome, however, was that they also began opening some long-closed doors in the community, such as town/gown divides. For example, Mississippi Valley State University invested some of its resources into the local town of Itta Bena in new ways. The residents invited the university into the community for local events, and some residents who hadn't wanted to be on the campus before began taking advantage of the fitness center and other resources. This wasn't the first time that residents and the university had tried to bridge this gulf, but it is the first time that it appeared to be working. As in Itta Bena, many long-standing town/gown stressors exist in other neighborhoods where the CFAA initiative was building relationships between residents and university students, faculty, and administration, often for the first time. Stories emerged from many other communities that put in place history, art, craft, genealogy, or other strategies to engage people of all ages—most with a cross-race or cross-culture lens. These kinds of developments are likely not sufficient alone to bridge deep divisions across race/ethnicity, but it does appear that asking people to come together across ages seems to be a less threatening way to start the process.

Using an All-Ages Lens to Achieve Age-Friendly Goals

Benefits

The theoretical frameworks identified previously and the data gathered from the Communities for All Ages initiative suggest that using a more inclusive all-ages lens can increase community support, respect and inclusion, and civic/social participation—all key characteristics of age-friendly communities, as defined by the World Health Organization (WHO).

Community Support

Community building approaches that build upon the strengths of all generations, identify shared interests, and strive for positive outcomes across generational as well as racial/ethnic differences have the potential to build *public will* among different generations to invest in each other (Brown and Henkin 2014: Beth Johnson Foundation 2011). From a social capital and culture change perspective, forming strategic partnerships between aging-focused and youth-focused organizations and promoting the importance of reciprocity and interdependence can result in increased formal and informal support services for older adults and their families and help strengthen the social compact.

From an economic perspective, it is in the interest of older adults to support increased investment in children, especially the growing number of immigrant youth, upon whom many elders will depend in coming years. Younger generations will be the taxpayers and workers of the future in a society with a much greater percentage of older people relative to younger adults. Many of them will be working in jobs that provide care to the rapidly growing aging population. Failure to invest in the education and job training of youth and families will create broader challenges for cities and for older adults in particular. As such, the age-friendly movement will explicitly benefit from strategic partnerships with organizations that focus on supporting local and national investment in education, workforce development, and family support.

Respect and Inclusion
Research by Scharf et al (2002) on older adults living in low-income urban environments in the United Kingdom found that older people experienced a strong sense of exclusion from key organizations and institutions influencing the quality of life in their neighborhoods. These findings are echoed by Buffel and Phillipson (2012; chapter 1 in this volume), who assert that older adults are often the last to be involved in neighborhood planning processes. Similar arguments have been made about the exclusion of young people from community processes, particularly African American and Latino youth (Lewis and Burd-Sharps 2013). Data from the Communities for All Ages initiative suggests that an all-ages approach can increase inclusion of older adults and the aging network as well as disconnected children and youth in broader community development and planning efforts. All generations can benefit from more age-integrated social structures and reciprocal learning experiences. Research suggests that increased opportunities for ongoing, meaningful interaction across age, race, and ethnicity through purposeful, organized group activity (Amin and Parkinson 2002; Valentine 2008) can help foster empathy and dispel myths. When age-related biases are reduced, individuals of all ages have increased opportunities to reach their potential, contribute to society, and participate more fully in community life.

Civic/Social Participation
Intergenerational civic engagement has shown to produce benefits that are linked to healthy aging such as decreased isolation, increased social connectedness, and a greater sense of belonging (Hinterlong and Wil-

liamson 2006). It provides opportunities for older adults to fulfill their need to be generative and to engage in reciprocal interactions that build trust. Similarly, these experiences can contribute to a sense of social responsibility among young people and build important civic skills. Mobilizing multiple generations to support each other and collectively address community concerns can help build social capital, address historic community divisions, and foster understanding among diverse residents. Society benefits when young people learn the importance of giving to others and older adults have opportunities to pass on their wisdom to younger generations.

Strategies

Creating environments that are supportive, engaging, and equitable not only for older adults but for individuals throughout the life span will require a new set of place-based strategies.

Creating New Alliances

To date, the age-friendly movement has focused primarily on building partnerships between older residents/caregivers and organizations, businesses, and institutions that support older adults. Less emphasis has been placed on building strategic partnerships with organizations and initiatives that focus on younger generations, particularly those that engage low-income Latino, Asian American, and African American communities. This represents a missed opportunity for the age-friendly movement to explicitly adopt an equity framework, enhance social capital, and build a broader, multigenerational base of support around shared issues such as safe streets, food access, transportation, and affordable, accessible housing. Similarly, a scan of federally funded, place-based equity initiatives such as Promise Zones and Healthy Food Financing Initiative and national place-based equity initiatives such as Place Matters or Healthy Communities that typically focus on issues impacting low-income youth and families suggests a lack of involvement by the aging network and the older adults they serve. This dynamic may reinforce the polarizing notion that there is an older white electorate in competition with African American, Latino, and Asian American youth and families for scarce resources. Additionally, building strategic partnerships between aging and place-based initiatives that focus on racial equity and the social determinants of health can also serve to raise the visibility of the assets and challenges of elders of color, whose issues are not always front and center within both the aging network and the racial equity field.

Developing a More Inclusive Assessment and Planning Process

WHO ("age-friendly") and UNICEF ("child-friendly") have identified common issues such as walkability, affordable housing, accessible transportation, support services, and opportunities for social and civic engagement as critical to healthy development but have not yet worked collaboratively to address these concerns. In order to fully understand what constitutes a city that is friendly to people at different stages of the aging process and assess the opportunities and barriers to participation of older adults in the broader environment, it is critical to hear the voices of all residents, particularly immigrant youth and families, who compose a rapidly increasing percentage of the total population. Gathering data from multiple generations about what makes a city good for growing up and growing older will build a more robust understanding of aging as a lifelong process and identify shared concerns. It can also help elucidate how the growing racial generational divide may impact social participation, respect and social inclusion, civic participation, and community support of all generations.

The Department of City and Regional Planning at Cornell University (Warner, Homsy, and Greenhouse 2010: 51) contends that "as our population diversifies, meeting the needs of all residents regardless of age, ethnicity and income, requires new planning strategies." They outline a "planning across generations" strategy addressing shared concerns of younger and older generations and offer examples of intergenerational planning processes. Below is a description of the 2020 Community Plan on Aging in Charlottesville, Virginia:

> High school students were recruited as members of the planning committee. They acted as ambassadors to other young people through focus groups and student surveys. In the end, the high schoolers wrote a chapter of the plan titled "Strengthening Intergenerational Connections" with recommendations that included: recruiting students as healthcare workers encouraging alternative transportation options; promoting intergenerational volunteering to bring together older adults and youth in meaningful service; and educating youth on the need for lifelong financial planning. (Jefferson Area Board for Aging, n.d.)

Building the Capacity of Community Residents, Organizations, and City Planners

Civic engagement is a key principle in both age- and child-friendly community building efforts, though little effort has been made to date to build the capacity of youth and older adults to work as community leaders who bridge generational and other historical divides. As part of the Communities for All Ages initiative, a "Leadership for All Ages" curriculum was developed to build the capacity of multiple generations to serve as bridging leaders. The curriculum was piloted in eight communities. An evaluation of the curriculum indicated that nearly all respondents (aged fourteen to eighty) reported increased involvement in community events and efforts to develop solutions to community problems as well as stronger connections with people of different ages, races, and ethnicities as a result of the training. Residents in some communities advocated for policy changes that benefit all generations (Henkin et al. 2012).

In addition to building the community capacity of residents, it is also critical to build capacity in nonprofit organizations, public agencies, and institutions to address growing social and economic disparities (Porter 2014) and create community conditions in which all people can live healthy, productive lives across the life course. City planners and managers in particular are critical to building communities that support people across the life span.

These capacity-building efforts should enable city planners as well as other staff from nonprofits, public agencies, and institutions to leverage the talents and skills of multiple generations, facilitate cross-generational team building, and analyze the interconnectedness of issues and solutions across generations. Efforts are needed to understand the complementarities between the needs of children/youth and older adults and to recognize that economic development requires a balanced approach to the investment of resources. Developing enabling physical environments that promote healthy development for people at all ages and examining life span approaches to mobility, housing, and public spaces will be essential for years to come.

Using Intergenerational Strategies to Develop Physical and Social Environments That Support People across the Life Span

Service Integration

Issues like transportation, health, education, and affordable housing are important for both younger and older generations. Planning and health literature suggests that integrating services and facilities can effectively, and perhaps better, meet the needs of people across the life span and does not pit the old against the young (Warner et al. 2010; Maternal and Child Health Bureau 2010). According to the life course model, linking and/or integrating health services and systems across the life span can help maximize protective factors and minimize risks for multiple generations. Age-integrated services and systems also promote efficient use of resources and social connectedness through "economies of scope"—single solutions that address multiple challenges (Dressel and Henkin 2009). For example, the organizers of AARP in Richmond developed an intergenerational "walk to school" initiative promoting the idea of getting relatives over fifty to walk children to school. The initiative supported health outcomes for both generations, nurtured intergenerational social connections, and raised awareness for a successful campaign to repair sidewalks, crosswalks, and intersections near the schools and senior housing (Warner et al. 2010).

Shared Spaces

In Braithwaite's (2002) research on reducing stereotypes and prejudice against older adults, she notes that concerted efforts are necessary to create "spaces where young, middle aged and older people from all walks of life can get to know each other enough to build mutual respect, develop cooperative relationships, and re-ignite the norm of human heartedness" (Braithwaite 2002: 332). Examples of shared spaces include schools that function as centers for lifelong learning, school buses used during off hours as transportation for older adults, adult-child day care centers, conversion of senior or youth centers into all-ages community centers, and public parks that support healthy development for all ages.

Joint Advocacy

There are a range of examples of intergenerational advocacy and organizing at the local and national level. At the local level, the Chinatown Community Development Center in San Francisco has developed intergenerational collaborations on public policy advocacy campaigns affecting the individual and collective interests of youth, families, and older adults such as affordable housing, social security, and the Dream Act (Chin 2011). At the national level, the Caring Across Generations campaign provides a powerful example of innovative coalition building between older adults and younger immigrant families. Caring Across Generations is a grassroots movement designed to improve care for elders and people with disabilities in the United States and to improve conditions for the workers who provide that care, many of whom are immigrant women of multiple generations (Poo 2013).

Intergenerational Practice

Intergenerational practice has been defined as "[bringing] people together in purposeful, mutually beneficial activities which promote greater understanding and respect between generations and contributes to building more cohesive communities. Intergenerational practice is inclusive, building on the positive resources that the young and old have to offer each other and those around them" (Beth Johnson Foundation 2011). Examples from local initiatives include older adults tutoring and mentoring in schools and younger people supporting older adults' technology use and providing local transportation through car sharing. Communities in the United States and in Europe are implementing home-share programs where older adults provide free or low-cost housing to young adults at the university in exchange for basic home maintenance and socialization (Head and Symanowicz 1997). In some communities, older adults allow younger families to plant and steward food gardens on their property, and they share produce (Henkin et al. 2012).

Support to Families

Although families continue to serve as the primary source of support for their members, geographic mobility and financial stress have resulted in significant challenges. Whether supporting frail elders, grandchildren, young adults who have returned home, or family members of all ages with disabilities, many families struggle with the demands of caregiving. The range of family support issues suggests the value of a life course approach to caregiving.

The importance of developing new ways to support families is underscored by a growing trend toward multigenerational households. The growth of multigenerational households has increased substantially during the economic downturn. According to a report by Generations United (2011), there were 5 million households composed of multiple generations (4.8 percent of all households) in 2000. Between 2008 and 2010, this number grew significantly in the United States—from 6.2 million (5.3 percent of all households), to 7.1 million in 2010 (6.1 percent of all households). This growth can be attributed to a number of factors including (1) economic conditions, (2) an increasing number of grandparents assuming primary responsibility for their grandchildren, (3) young adults marrying later and living with parents longer, (4) immigration patterns that bring older family members to the United States to help care for children, and (5) health and disability issues that require additional caregivers (Generations United 2011). A substantially higher share of Latinos, African Americans, and Asian Americans live in multigenerational households, compared to whites (Generations United 2011). This reflects cultural traditions that stress the importance of generational obligations and a history of family members relying on each other in hard times.

While multigenerational households can provide significant advantages, they also can present challenges. For example, although multigenerational living has been shown to improve financial stability and/or make it possible for at least one member to enroll in job training or school, this arrangement can also contribute to increased stress. In many immigrant and refugee communities, where reciprocity and generational interdependence are at the core of family life, there appears to be a growing schism between grandparents and grandchildren due to language barriers, differing rates of acculturation, and conflicting demands on each generation (Yoshida, and Henkin 2012. Respite programs in which college students and/or older adults provide in-home support to caregiving families, targeted services to kinship families, mentoring programs that recruit older adults to support young parents and their children, and activities that strengthen intrafamilial bonds all are examples of ways that intergenerational interventions can build the capacity of families to care for their members.

Developing New Messages That Reflect Shared Values

How we talk about age-friendly communities matters. The words we choose shape our thinking toward conflict or toward solution. While there is value in unpacking the racial generation gap and potential for polarization, we also need new words and messages to reflect new possibilities and realities. How do we begin to create a new language that communicates an understanding and a vision of shared fate? Ongoing investigation is required to understand what messages resonate and motivate multiple generations. Broadly speaking, however, there are key values we believe can be highlighted in the framing of age-friendly communities:

- *Interdependence:* People feel a sense of shared responsibility for one another. The age-old social compact is strong as generations rely on each other for care, support, and nurturing. Elders are viewed as resources to families and communities. Young people feel valued as resources for elders and gain a sense of social efficacy.
- *Reciprocity:* People of all ages have opportunities to both give and receive support; to both teach and learn. Age groups rely on each other for support. Advocates for the young and the old are not pitted against each other for limited resources, but work together as allies toward the development of mutually beneficial policies and services.
- *Individual worth:* Each individual, regardless of age, race/ethnicity, gender, sexual orientation, or other variables, deserves respect and care, is entitled to equal access to the community's resources, and offers an ability to contribute to the community in some way.
- *Inclusion:* Policies and programs are designed for all members of the community, with the understanding that improvements to overall community quality of life will benefit community members across generational, racial, ethnic, and other differences.
- *Equity:* There is a commitment to analyzing the systemic factors that produce and maintain inequalities and taking deliberate steps toward ending racial and other disparities.
- *Social connectedness:* Social relationships build and deepen the social networks that provide support for all age groups.

Conclusion

This chapter focuses on ways to use an all-ages lens to enhance age-friendly initiatives and move toward a society for all ages. As the racial-generational gap grows and immigration trends continue to impact the distribution of resources and the nature of age relations, this approach can help strengthen the social compact and promote the concept of intergenerational solidarity—"an explicit vision that is built on an understanding of interdependence across the life course, the contributions of all ages, and a recognition of disparities and inequities that threaten the social compact" (European Foundation for the Improvement of Living and Working Conditions, 2012: 3).

Building on research, theories, and lessons learned from the national Communities for All Ages initiative, we have presented concrete strategies for supporting aging within a framework of reciprocity and identified how this broader lens can achieve some of the goals of the age-friendly movement. This approach is about more than services and programs; it is about culture change. A different view of aging as a lifelong process with flexible pathways, a sense of *collective* rather than *individual* responsibility for the health and well-being of individuals across the life course, and a willingness to work together for the common good are all needed to make this approach a reality. Moving forward will require breaking out of the silos in which we live and work and developing policies that balance the needs of all ages and invest in people at all stages of life. Only then can we build healthy, equitable communities that are good for growing up and growing older.

Corita Brown has over twenty years of experience in the nonprofit sector. She currently serves as the leadership and learning director for Encore. org's Generation to Generation Campaign. Prior to joining Encore.org, she worked as the national training director for the Intergenerational Center at Temple University. Dr. Brown has successfully built the capacity of diverse teams in the nonprofit, community development, and philanthropic realms to develop multigenerational leadership, build cross-sector collaborations, and design policies, practices, and programs to support intergenerational engagement. She holds a master's degree in organizational psychology and adult education from Teachers College, Columbia University, and a Ph.D. in urban studies from Temple University. She currently serves as a reviewer for the *International Journal of Intergenerational Relations.*

Nancy Henkin, founder and former executive director of the Intergenerational Center at Temple University, is currently a senior fellow at Generations United and a consultant to numerous agencies and foundations across the United States. For over 38 years, her work has focused on intergenerational community building and programming, intergenerational relationships in immigrant communities, and lifelong civic engagement. Dr. Henkin serves on the editorial board of the *International Journal on Intergenerational Relations* and the Mayor's Commission on Aging in Philadelphia. She is the recipient of numerous awards, including the Jack Ossofsky Award from the National Council on the Aging, the Maggie Kuhn Award from the Gray Panthers, and the Intergenerational Champion Award from Generations United. In 2006, she was elected into the Ashoka Fellowship, a global community of social entrepreneurs.

Note

1. Although the majority of older adults are white, since 1990, the number of foreign-born residents over sixty-five has grown from 2.7 million to 4.3 million and is expected to increase to 16 million by 2050 (Tan 2011). The Latino elderly population is projected to grow from 3 million in 2010 to 17.5 million in 2050, while the population of Asian elders will expand from 1 million to 7.5 million during the same period (Federal Interagency Forum on Aging, 2012).

References

AARP. n.d. *AARP Age-Friendly Communities Toolkit.* AARP. Accessed 5 May 2016. http://www.aarp.org/livable-communities/network-age-friendly-communities/.
Achenbaum, Andrew. 1998. "The Social Compact in American History." *Generations* 22(4): 15–18.
Amin, Ash, and Michael Parkinson. 2002. "Ethnicity and the Multicultural City: Living with Diversity." *Environment and Planning* 34(6): 959–80.
Annan, K. 1999. Opening Speech at UN International Conference on Ageing. Accessed 15 January 2016. http://undesadspd.org/Ageing/InternationalDayofOlderPersons/1998/SpeechdeliveredbySecretaryGeneralKofiAnnan.aspx.
Bengtson, V. L, G. H. Elder, and N. M. Putney. 2005. "The Life Course on Ageing: Linked Lives, Timing, and History." In *The Cambridge Handbook of Age and Ageing*, ed. M. L. Johnson, 443–501. New York: Cambridge University Press.
Beth Johnson Foundation. 2011. *A Guide to Intergenerational Practice.* http://www.centreforip.org.uk/res/documents/page/BJFGuidetoIPV2 percent20 percent2028 per cent20Mar percent202011.pdf.
Braithwaite, Valerie. 2002. "Reducing Ageism." In *Ageism: Stereotyping and Prejudice against Older Persons*, ed. Todd D. Nelson, 311–37, Cambridge, MA: MIT Press.
Braverman, Paula, and Colleen Barclay. 2009. "Health Disparities Beginning in Childhood: A Life Course Perspective." *Pediatrics* 124(3): 163–75.
Brown, Corita, and Nancy Henkin. 2014. "Building Communities for All Ages: Lessons Learned from an Intergenerational Community-Building Initiative." *Journal of Community and Applied Social Psychology* 24(1): 63–68.

Buffel, Tine, and Chris Phillipson. 2012. "Ageing in Urban Environments: Developing 'Age-Friendly' Cities." *Critical Social Policy* 32(4): 597–617.

Cagney, K. A., and M. Wen. 2008. "Social Capital and Aging-Related Outcomes." In *Social Capital and Health*, ed. I. Kawachi, S. Subramanian, and D. Kim, 239–58. New York: Springer.

Chambré, Susan M. 1993. "Volunteerism by Elders: Past Trends and Future Prospects." *Gerontologist* 33(2): 221–29.

Chaskin, Robert J., Robert M. Goerge, Ada Skyles, and Shannon Guiltinan. 2006. "Measuring Social Capital: An Exploration in Community–Research Partnership." *Journal of Community Psychology* 34(4): 489–514.

Chin, Gabriel J. 1996. "The Civil Rights Revolution Comes to Immigration Law: A New Look at the Immigration and Nationality Act of 1965." *North Carolina Law Review* 75: 273.

Chin, Gordon. 2011. *Intergenerational Leadership*. LISC Institute for Comprehensive Community Development. Accessed 19 January 2018. http://www.instituteccd.org/news/3260.

Cornman, John, and Eric Kingson. 1998. "What Is a Social Compact? How Would We Know One If We Saw It?" *Generations* 22(4): 10–14.

Dannefer, Dale, and Richard Settersen. 2010. "The Study of the Life Course: Implications for Social Gerontology." In *The Sage Handbook of Social Gerontology*, ed. Dale Dannefer and Chris Phillipson, 3–19. Los Angeles: Sage.

de Souza Briggs, X. 2006. "Social Capital and Segregation in the United States." In *Desegregating the City: Ghettos, Enclave, and Inequality*, ed. D. P. Varady, 79–107. Albany: State University of New York Press.

Dilworth-Anderson, Peggye. 2001. "Extended Kin Networks in Black Families." *In Families in Later Life: Connections and Transitions*, ed. Alexis Joan Walker, 104–6. Newbury Park, CA: Pine Forge Press.

Dressel, Paula, and Nancy Henkin. 2009. "The Viable Futures Toolkit: Promoting Sustainable Communities for All Ages." *Generations* 33(2): 85–86.

Engwicht, David. 2005. *Mental Speed Bumps: The Smarter Way to Tame Traffic*. Sydney, Australia: Envirobooks.

Emlet, Charles A., and Joane T. Moceri. 2012. "The Importance of Social Connectedness in Building Age-Friendly Communities." *Journal of Aging Research* 173224: 1–9.

European Commission. 2009. *Intergenerational Solidarity: Analytical Report*. Flash Eurobarometer 269. Accessed May 12 2015. http://ec.europa.eu/public_opinion/flash/fl_269_en.pdf.

European Foundation for the Improvement of Living and Working Conditions. 2012. "Intergenerational Solidarity." Accessed 2 September 2018. https://www.eurofound.europa.eu/publications/foundation-findings/2012/working-conditions-labour-market-social-policies/foundation-findings-intergenerational-solidarity.

Fagan, R. M. 2003. "Pioneer Network: Changing the Culture of Aging in America." *Journal of Social Work in Long-Term Care* 2(1–2): 125–40.

Feldman, Robert D. 2013. *Development across the Life Span*. 7th ed. Hoboken, NJ: Pearson.

Freedman, Marc. 1997. "Towards Civic Renewal: How Senior Citizens Could Save Civil Society." *Journal of Gerontological Social Work* 28(3): 243–63.

Frey, W. 2012. *America's Changing Demographic Landscape: New Projections from the Census Bureau*. Washington, DC: Brookings Institute. http://www.brookings.edu/research/expert-(qa/2012/12/13-frey-qa.

Ganz, M. 2009. *Reform Immigration for American Movement Building Training: Arizona Leadership; Workshop Guide*. Washington, DC: New Organizing Institute.
Gardner, John. 1990. "Building Community." *Social Contract* 1(1): 25–29.
Generations United. 2011. "Family Matters: Multigenerational Families in a Volatile Economy." http://www.gu.org/LinkClick.aspx?fileticket=L3k2KbjdsqY percent3d&tabid=157&mid=606.
Ghazaleh, Rana Abu, Esther Greenhouse, George Hormsey, and Mildred Warner. 2011. *Multigenerational Planning: Using Smart Growth and Universal Design to Meet the Needs of Children and the Ageing Population*. Chicago: American Planning Association.
Gonzales, R., and L. Chavez. 2012. "Awakening to a Nightmare." *Current Anthropology* 53(3): 255–68.
Grantmakers in Aging. n.d. "Age Friendly Communities." http://www.giaging.org/issues/community-development/.
Hagestad, Gunhild O., and Peter Uhlenberg. 2005. "The Social Separation of Old and Young: A Root of Ageism." *Journal of Social Issues* 61(2): 343–60.
Hall, P. A., and M. Lamont, eds. 2009. *Successful Societies: How Institutions and Culture Affect Health*. Cambridge: Cambridge University Press.
Hatton-Yeo, A., and J. Melville. 2013. "Intergenerational Shared Spaces." Stoke on Trent, UK: Centre for Intergenerational Practice. http://www.centreforip.org.uk/res/documents/publication/Shared percent20Site percent20final percent20English percent20version.pdf.
Head, Helen, and Stacey Z. Symanowicz. 1997. *A Vermonter's Guide to Homesharing*. South Burlington: Project Home.
Heisler, L. B., and L. B. Shrestha. 2011. "The Changing Demographic Profile of the United States." In *Congressional Research Service Report for Congress*. Accessed 19 January 2018. https://fas.org/sgp/crs/misc/RL32701.pdf.
Henkin, Nancy, Corita Brown, and Sally Leiderman. 2012. *Communities for All Ages Intergenerational Community Building: Lessons Learned*. Philadelphia: Intergenerational Center at Temple University. Accessed 10 November 2014 https://www.gu.org/app/uploads/2018/06/Intergenerational-Report-IntergenerationalCenter-Community-Building-Lessons-Learned.pdf.
Henkin, Nancy, Esther Holmes, Benjamin Walter, and Barbara Greenberg. 2005. *Communities for All Ages: Planning Across Generations*. Baltimore: Annie E. Casey Foundation. Accessed 6 December 2014. http://www.aecf.org/upload/PublicationFiles/CFAA.pdf.
Hinterlong, J., and A. Williamson. 2006. "The Effects of Civic Engagement of Current and Future Cohorts of Older Adults." *Generations* 30(4): 10–17.
Hochschild, J. L. 2003. "Rethinking Accountability Politics." In *No Child Left Behind? The Politics and Practice of School Accountability*, ed. Paul Peterson and Martin West, 107–25. Washington, DC: Brookings Institution Press.
Jefferson Area Board for Aging. n.d. "2020 Plan on Aging." Accessed 9 September 2014. http://www.jabacares.org/.
Jennings, J. 2007. "Social Capital, Race, and the Future of Inner-City Neighborhoods." In *Race, Neighborhoods, and the Misuse of Social Capital*, ed. J. Jennings, 87–108. New York: Palgrave Macmillan.
Kaiser Foundation. 2017. "Living in an Immigrant Family in America: How Fear and Toxic Stress are Affecting Daily Life, Well-Being and Health." Accessed 7 Feb-

ruary 2018. http://files.kff.org/attachment/Issue-Brief-Living-in-an-Immigrant-Family-in-America.

Kim, Hyoun K., and Patrick C. McKenry. 1998. "Social Networks and Support: A Comparison of African Americans, Asian Americans, Caucasians, and Hispanics." *Journal of Comparative Family Studies* 27(2): 313–34.

King, Martin Luther. 2000 (1964). *Why We Can't Wait*. New York: Penguin Random House.

Ladd, Helen F., and Sheila E. Murray. 2001. "Intergenerational Conflict Reconsidered: County Demographic Structure and the Demand for Public Education." *Economics of Education Review* 20(4): 343–57.

Lewis, Kristin, and Sarah Burd-Sharps. 2013. "Halve the Gap: Youth Disconnection in America's Cities." http://ssrc-static.s3.amazonaws.com/moa/MOA-Halve-the-Gap-ALL-10.25.13.pdf.

Lui, Chi-Wai, Jo-Anne Everingham, Jeni Warburton, Michael Cuthill, and Helen Bartlett. 2009. "What Makes a Community Age-Friendly: A Review of International Literature." *Australasian Journal on Ageing* 28(3): 116–21.

Maternal and Child Health Bureau. 2010. "Rethinking MCH: The Lifecourse Model as an Organizing Framework." U.S. Department of Health and Human Services, Health Resources and Services Administration. Accessed 14 October 2014. http://mchb.hrsa.gov/lifecourse/rethinkingmchlifecourse.pdf.

Matthews, Hugh. "Citizenship, Youth Councils and Young People's Participation." *Journal of Youth Studies* 4(3): 299–318.

McDaniel, Susan, and Paul Bernard. 2011. "Life Course as a Policy Lens: Challenges and Opportunities." *Canadian Public Policy* 37(Supplement): 132.

McPherson, B., and A. V. Wister. 2008. *Aging as a Social Process: Canadian Perspectives*. Oxford: Oxford University Press.

Minnesota Board on Aging, Department of Human Services. 2013. "Communities for a Lifetime" Accessed 13 March 2015. http://www.mnlifetimecommunities.org/en/About.aspx.

Moen, Phyllis. 1996. "A Life Course Perspective on Retirement, Gender, and Well-Being." *Journal of Occupational Health Psychology* 1(2): 131.

Myers, Dowell. 2007. *Immigrants and Boomers: Forging a New Social Contract for the Future of America*. New York: Russell Sage Foundation.

———. 2008. *Old Promises and New Blood: How Immigration Reform Can Help America Prosper in the Face of Baby Boomer Retirement*. Alexandria, VA: Reform Institute.

National Cancer Institute. 2018. "Cancer Statistics." Accessed 15 July 2018. https://www.cancer.gov/about-cancer/understanding/statistics.

National Institute on Aging, U.S. Department of Commerce, Economics and Statistics Administration, Bureau of the Census, n.d. "Aging in the United States: Past, Present and Future." Accessed 3 January 2018. https://www.census.gov/population/international/files/97agewc.pdf.

Pain, Rachel. 2000. "Gender, Race, Age and Fear in the City." *Urban Studies* 38(5–6), 899–913.

Pastor, Manuel, et al. 2010. *The COLOR of Change*. USC Center for Environmental and Regional Equity. Accessed 18 January 2018. https://dornsife.usc.edu/assets/sites/242/docs/color_of_change_web.pdf.

Pastor, Manuel, and Vanessa Carter. 2012. "Reshaping the Social Contract: Demographic Distance and Our Fiscal Future." *Poverty and Race* 21(1): 5–6.

Pew Research Center. 2011. "The Generation Gap and the 2012 Elections." http://www.people-press.org/2011/11/03/the-generation-gap-and-the-2012-election-3.

Phillipson, Chris. 2011. "Developing Age-Friendly Communities: New Approaches to Growing Old in Urban Environments." In *Handbook of Sociology of Aging*, ed. R. Settersten and J. L. Angel, 279–93. New York: Springer.

Poo, Ai-Jen. "The Caring Majority Building a Coalition around Domestic Workers' Rights." *Tikkun* 28(4): 36–39.

Porter, Eduardo. 2014. "A Relentless Widening of Disparity in Wealth." *New York Times*, 11 March.

Poterba, J. 1998. "Demographic Change, Intergenerational Linkages, and Public Education." *American Economic Review Papers and Proceedings* 88: 315–20.

Portes, Alejandro. 2000. "Social Capital: Its Origins and Applications in Modern Sociology." In *Knowledge and Social Capital*, ed. Eric Lesser, 43–67. Boston: Butterworth-Heinemann.

Putnam R. 2000. *Bowling Alone: The Collapse and Revival of American Community*. New York: Simon & Schuster.

Reich, Robert. 1998. "Why We Need to Renew the Social Compact." *Generations* 22(4): 19–24.

Riley, Matilda, and John Riley. 1994. "Age-Integration and the Lives of Older People." *Gerontologist* 34(1): 110–15.

Robbins, L. 2015. "Gauging Aging: How Does the American Public Truly Perceive Older Age—and Older People?" *Generations* 39(3): 17–21.

Roberts, S. 2007. "New Demographic Racial Gap Emerges." *New York Times*, May 17. Accessed 8 August 2014. http://www.nytimes.com/2007/05/17/us/17census.html.

Rumbaut, R., and G. Komaie. 2010. "Immigration and Adult Transitions." *Future of Children* 20(1): 43–66.

Sampson, Robert J. 2008. "Collective Efficacy Theory: Lessons Learned and Directions for Future Inquiry." In *Taking Stock: The Status of Criminological Theory*, ed M. Gottfredson and T. Hirschi, 149–67. New Brunswick: Transaction..

Sampson, Robert J., Jeffrey D. Morenoff, and Felton Earls. 1999. "Beyond Social Capital: Spatial Dynamics of Collective Efficacy for Children." *American Sociological Review* 64(5): 633–60.

Scharf, T., C. Phillipson, A. Smith, and P. Kingston. 2002. *Growing Older in Socially Deprived Areas: Social Exclusion in Later Life*. London: Help the Aged.

Scharlach, Andrew E. 2012. "Creating aging-friendly communities in the United States." *Aging International* 37(1): 25–38.

Schwartz, L. K., and J. P. Simmons. 2001. "Contact Quality and Attitudes toward the Elderly." *Educational Gerontology* 27: 127–37.

Simmons, Tavia, and Jane Lawler-Dye. 2003. *Grandparents Living with Grandchildren*. Accessed 9 September 2014. http://www.census.gov/prod/2003pubs/c2kbr-31.pdf.

Smith, Ben, Kwok Cho Tang, and Don Nutbeam. 2006. "WHO Health Promotion Glossary: New Terms." Accessed 19 April 2015. http://www.who.int/healthpromotion/about/HP percent20Glossay percent20in percent20HPI.pdf.

Tan, J. 2011. "Older Immigrants in the United States: The New Old Face of Immigration." *Bridgewater Review* 30(2): 28–30. http://vc.bridgew.edu/br_rev/vol30/iss2/10.

Tavernise, Sabrina. 2011. "Numbers of Children of Whites Falling Fast." *New York Times*, 6 April.
Taylor, A. S. 2006. "Generativity and Adult Development: Implications for Mobilizing Volunteers in Support of Youth." In *Mobilizing Adults for Positive Youth Development*, ed. E. Clary and J. Rhodes, 83–100. New York: Springer.
Taylor, P. 2012. *The Big Generation Gap at the Polls Is Echoed in Attitudes on Budget Tradeoffs*. Washington DC: Pew Research Center. Accessed 16 November 2014. http://www.pewsocialtrends.org/2012/12/20/the-big-generation-gap-at-the-polls-is-echoed-in-attitudes-on-budget-tradeoffs/.
Taylor, P., and S. Keeter. 2010. *Millennials: A Portrait of Generation Next: Confident. Connected. Open to Change.* Washington, DC: Pew Research Center. Accessed 18 January 2018. http://www.pewsocialtrends.org/files/2010/10/millennials-confi dent-connected-open-to-change.pdf.
Thang, Leng Leng. 2001. *Generations in Touch*. Ithaca, NY: Cornell University Press.
United Nations, Department of Economic and Social Affairs, Population Division. 2013. *World Population Ageing 2013*. ST/ESA/SER.A/348.
Valentine, Gill. 2008. "Living with Difference: Reflections on Geographies of Encounter." *Progress in Human Geography* 32(3): 323–37.
Vanderbeck, Robert M. 2007. "Intergenerational Geographies: Age Relations, Segregation and Re-engagements." *Geography Compass* 1(2): 200–21.
Warner, M., George Homsy, and Esther Greenhouse. 2010. "Multigenerational Community Planning: Linking the Needs of Children and Elders." Planning for Family Friendly Communities Briefing Paper. Ithaca NY: Cornell University. Accessed 18 January 2010. http://economicdevelopmentandchildcare.org/documents/techni cal_assistance/planning_family_friendly/issue_multigenerational. pdf.
Weiner, Audrey S., and Judah L. Ronch. 2003. *Culture Change in Long-Term Care*. London: Routledge.
WHO (World Health Organization). 2007. *Global Age-Friendly Cities: A Guide*. Geneva: World Health Organization. Accessed 18 February 2015. http://www.who.int/ageing/publications/Global_age_friendly_cities_Guide_English.pdf, 2013.
Yoshida, Hitomi, and Nancy Henkin. 2012. "Growing Older in a New Land: Understanding Healthy Aging and Intergenerational Relationships in Immigrant and Refugee Families." Accessed 7 March 2015. https://www.gu.org/app/uploads/2018/05/Intergenerational-Report-IntergenerationalCenter-GrowingOlderInANewLand.pdf.

8 IBASHO CAFÉ
Giving Elders a Role to Play in Making Communities More Resilient

Emi Kiyota

Introduction

IN MODERN SOCIETY, OLDER PEOPLE are generally thought of as a vulnerable group in need of care. Thus marginalized, elders lose opportunities to contribute to society, while younger people lose the benefit of their wisdom and talents. The Ibasho café concept was developed to challenge these perceptions and change the harmful outcomes they create.

The first Ibasho café was developed in a part of Japan that was affected by the Great East Japan Earthquake (GEJE) of 11 March 2011. With a magnitude of 9.0 off the Sanriku coast of northern Japan, the earthquake caused one of the most devastating tsunamis in recorded history. The developers of the Ibasho café recognized the power of their project to build the social capital and resilience needed in response to natural disasters like the tsunami by creating an informal gathering place that brings the community together. All generations connect in the space, with children coming to read books in the English library, older people teaching young people how to make traditional foods, younger people helping elders navigate computer software, and so on. In addition, elders are actively engaged in the operation of the café, giving them an important role to play and helping to change people's mind-sets about aging.

This case study discusses the philosophical principles of the Ibasho café and its application to a Japanese community that was affected by the GEJE.

Reintegrating Elders into Society

This Ibasho café concept empowers elders, transforming them from burdens to society who need care and resources from younger generations to contributing members of society with something to offer other members of their communities. We create socially, economically, and environmentally sustainable communities that value elders' knowledge and experience, redefine the concept of elder care, and challenge the restrictive social role of elders in both developed and developing parts of the world. The power of this approach allows something as familiar and seemingly simple as a café to become a practical policy response to several serious global challenges, including the rising life expectancy and decreasing birth rates that are creating increasing financial burdens on medical and social welfare systems, the forced irrelevance of older people, and the vulnerability of communities—particularly the elder members of those communities—during and after natural disasters.

Current elder care services not only cause dependency among elders, but also demand significant monetary resources. Through the Ibasho café, we aim to challenge the way we think and act toward aging and to redefine the concept of elder care as well as the social role of elders in society. We believe that key to the social change is to change our own mind-set, including that of elders, as infrastructure and services are further developed. The Ibasho café engages and includes community members and elders as active participants through the process of planning, designing, construction, managing, and operating the café. A community-driven and community-owned place like Ibasho café can help local residents to see and experience the importance of social connections to others in their neighborhoods. It also encourages them to develop an interdependent support system among community members of all ages by connecting them on a personal level, which strengthens community resiliency.

Building Resilience to Help Communities Survive Natural Disasters and Global Aging

The Ibasho café concept was developed as a practical response to two major policy challenges around the world: global aging and supporting populations vulnerable to disaster. Nearly two-thirds (62 percent) of the victims of the GEJE were over sixty years old, unable to evacuate quickly enough on their own or to access the support they needed (Ministry of Reconstruction 2014). That extra vulnerability persisted for elders during the post-disaster recovery phase. Research has documented the dangers of isolation and weakened social networks following disasters, especially among the elderly and infirm, who are most vulnerable to these hazards (Klinenberg 2002). Strong social networks decrease the likelihood that affected neighborhoods will be deserted, help survivors overcome collective problems, and provide mutual aid and informal insurance (Aldrich 2012).

Yet despite the fact that deeper reservoirs of trust and social connections make communities more resilient following a disaster (Aldrich 2012), many disaster responses undermine these critical resources. After the 1995 Kobe earthquake, for example, more than 250 seniors died "lonely deaths" due to their isolation and separation from friends and family (Gakuta 2013). In their rush to move these individuals away from their damaged homes and apartments, disaster managers cut off their ties to the familiar, placing them alone in high-rise apartments. Similarly, many of the elderly survivors of the GEJE may reside for several years in the temporary housing where they were placed just after the tsunami, far from their social networks (Sasa, Tanaka, and Doi 2012).

A related problem for Japan, Germany, and other industrialized societies is the challenge of "global aging," in which rising life expectancy and decreasing birth rates drive the median age higher. More than one-fifth of Japan's population is over the age of sixty-five, and its population has been shrinking since 2010. Elders are projected to be more than 35 percent of the population by 2050, due to the nation's low birth rate and long life expectancy (Ministry of Health, Labor, and Social Welfare Japan 2014). Aging populations create financial burdens for younger generations, who must pay into medical and social welfare benefit systems. The elderly consume the largest proportion of medical benefits of any age group. They also require additional publicly funded services such as home care, adult day care, nursing homes, and palliative care.

More than 180 million older people are currently living in poverty worldwide (UNFPA 2012). This creates more challenges involving income security and affordable housing for elders, particularly in low-income countries. Global aging is also causing a boom in the number of elders with Alzheimer's and other forms of dementia, making the problem of finding appropriate support for such people that much more urgent. This global age wave is usually presented as a threat or a challenge, but it has positive aspects as well. Today's elders are generally healthier than people over sixty-five once were, and they can and want to continue to contribute to society. Moreover, having more elders than children provides ample opportunities for children to obtain help and attention from elders.

A central tenet of the Ibasho philosophy is that elders can and should play a vital social role in our communities. Their wisdom and experience are valuable assets—especially when standard systems do not function adequately to meet people's needs, as is often the case during unprecedented demographic changes or natural disasters.

The Ibasho Café Approach and Framework

Ibasho cafés create a place where elders contribute to their communities. We engage elders as change agents to explore new ways of providing both informal and formal support to community members of all ages. We use this approach to challenge the widespread perception of elders as passive, often burdensome recipients of care and to alleviate the problems this perception causes for elders, which include social isolation, a loss of dignity and respect, and a lack of positive roles to play in society.

An Ibasho café is an informal gathering place that brings the community together. Elders take a leadership role, sharing their knowledge and experience with younger people while serving snacks and tea to visitors. We believe that sharing elders' life experiences and wisdom not only benefits younger generations, but also makes communities more resilient by creating and strengthening social ties and passing on vital knowledge from one generation to the next. Our objective is not to operate a profitable café, but to connect the other members of the community with their elders and to foster collaboration and a strong sense of attachment, ownership, and leadership among those elders.

Ibasho cafés achieve these objectives through three main elements: the physical environment, the social environment, and the Ibasho mission.

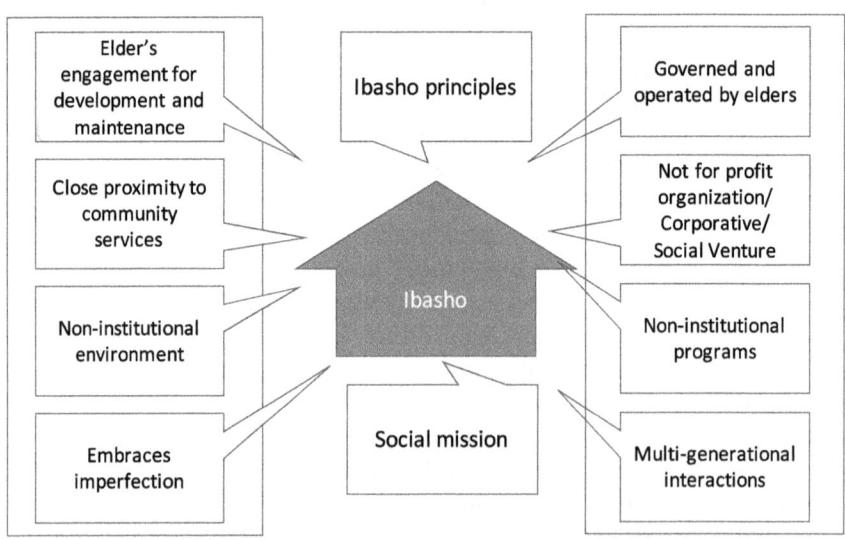

FIGURE 8.1. Ibasho café framework (chart by author)

Ibasho Mission and Philosophy

An Ibasho café is a place where elders go not to passively receive services, but to actively transfer their knowledge and experiences to younger generations. Each café is unique, since each reflects its local culture, but they all share the same mission and principles.

Ibasho's mission consists of three factors:

1. Embrace the Ibasho principles (see below)
2. Create a place in the community where elders are valued as a community resource
3. Collaboratively determine a unique social mission that contributes beyond the community

Ibasho recognizes that place plays an important role in how we view our elders in our society. For example, elder care facilities give us the image of dependency and age segregation, while the naturally occurring retirement community (NORC) and Village to Village models emerging in the United States allow elders to receive the services they need while remaining independent in their own homes. However, even these new models often foster isolation, since they do not offer opportunities for elders to develop meaningful relationships with other members of community.

Ibasho creates a place where people can meet each other. We believe that frequent encounters among community members at an Ibasho café help them form new relationships. Having a place to go also makes it easier for elders to find roles and make concrete contributions. Most importantly, a café allows people to experience the everyday world of a place where Ibasho principles are embraced.

An Ibasho café empowers elders to support others beyond their own community as well, tapping into the strong sense of social purpose that is common among elders and sending a positive message about their contributions to society at large. As a social mission of the Ibasho café in Japan, elders are setting aside some profit and collecting donations for a disaster relief fund to help elders who will be affected by future natural disasters.

Ibasho's Eight Principles

Ibasho's eight principles are as follows:

1. *Older people are a valuable asset to the community:* Ibasho believes in a society where the elderly can contribute with confidence and their wisdom and knowledge are valued.

2. *Community members must create informal gathering places:* Living in institutions with strict rules and schedules is confining and limiting. Ibasho creates places of normalcy where elders can stop by at their leisure to do what they want.
3. *Community members must drive development and implementation:* Each Ibasho place, whether a café or elder care facility, is created not *for* elders but *with* them. Other members of the community must also be involved in the development and operation of the new place, so all can share a sense of ownership and pride.
4. *All generations must be involved in the community:* Connecting within one's own generation is easy and comfortable, but stopping there cuts you off from other perspectives and sources of knowledge, not to mention other individual relationships. Ibasho creates places where the young learn from the elderly and the elderly learn from the young.
5. *Local culture and traditions must be respected:* Each community has its own history and culture, even if it is not something one can easily identify. Ibasho creates places where people can discover and reflect on the treasures of their communities.
6. *All residents must participate in normal community life:* An Ibasho, like a community, succeeds only when it is a welcoming home for everyone, regardless of age or ability, gender, ethnicity, stage of life (e.g., raising a family; caring for aging parents), or any of the other traits that differentiate us. Even the socially disconnected should be able to find a place there. Ibasho is a place not to worry about what one *cannot* do, but rather to enjoy what one *can* do.
7. *Communities must be environmentally, economically, and socially sustainable:* An Ibasho protects the nature that brings bounty to life, is economically self-sufficient, and cherishes and nurtures the connections among individuals.
8. *The community must grow organically and embrace imperfection gracefully:* Ibasho does not strive for perfection. It is adaptive and flexible, as life is forever changing. Each community has its own path to balance, believes in the possibility of change, and gently embraces imperfection.

Physical Attributes

Because Ibasho involves creating an actual place to nurture community, the physical environment is an important factor in a project's success. Specifically, we have found that three key factors must be present:

1. *Elders must be engaged in the development process:* While most environments for elders are designed and programmed by professional

third-party organizations, Ibasho uses the design, development, and construction phases of a project as a vehicle for community development, including elders and community members. When designing a café, we emphasize "users as experts," rather than asking outside experts to drive the design process with the idea of "what is good for them." This helps ensure that the project meets the elders' needs and fosters a sense of ownership, which helps make the café sustainable once the building is complete.

2. *The environment must be noninstitutional:* Our environments have a strong impact on our behavior. Traditionally, services and programs for elders are provided in institutional environments that create hierarchical relationships between caregivers and care receivers. This fosters a sense of dependency among elders, defining them as people to be taken care of rather than people with something to contribute. As Silverstein and Jacobson (1978) pointed out in explaining the concept of a "hidden program," these buildings are derived from our notion that good care consists of "protecting elders in a secured place," and their design then reinforces that idea. We strongly believe that this cycle must be broken, both by changing social perceptions and by educating architects and designers about what constitutes anIbasho—a place where one can feel truly at home, being oneself. Institutional environments are designed to maximize efficiency, hygiene, convenience, and safety, but these are the attributes of a health-care facility, not a home or community. To remove the stigma of living in or visiting such places, Ibasho creates environments that are as noninstitutional and normal as possible.

3. *The place must be close to the people it serves:* Ibasho's goal is to naturally connect community members of all ages, since we believe in the importance of unplanned and unprogrammed encounters. Traditional elder care services are often located outside of town or in a designated social service area, so only people of the same age group used the space. To integrate people of all ages, an Ibasho café is designed to be a community social hub, close to many everyday activities. It should be visible from a main source of pedestrian traffic, so people can discover it and stop in easily.

Social Attributes

Ibasho Is Formally Owned by the Community Elders

Ibasho café is a community-driven project that is owned and operated as a community initiative, rather than policy-driven initiative. Community-driven projects can often face the challenge of long-term sustainability due to limited external grants or lack of personnel resources. Therefore, it is key to establish a formal organization governed by elders in the community. To ensure long-term sustainability, the Ibasho café should be structured as a self-sustaining not-for-profit organization or a cooperative. It should be owned and operated by a group of elder community members.

Ibasho Offers Noninstitutional Services

The social service programs provided by professional staff in places such as adult day centers, senior centers, and long-term care facilities serve a purpose, but they do not make many allowances for spontaneous, informal interactions or activities, and regimented schedules dictate what happens when. Ibasho aims to provide noninstitutional services in a normal place where people can simply stop by when they are in the mood.

The essence of noninstitutional services is captured by the reactions of elders at Japan's Ibasho café when the city asked the Ibasho café to offer a "dementia café" program once a week. The elders declined to accommodate the request, saying they felt that type of program should be coordinated in elder care organizations, not in the Ibasho café. As one elder said, "Who would like to go to the program called dementia café, if you or your family has dementia? Ibasho café wants to be a place where people would like to stop by at anytime. We do not have to provide a service that local elder care facilities can do. People with dementia can always come to Ibasho café, when they want to."

Ibasho Is Governed by Elders

Community elders take the lead in operating Ibasho cafés, collectively deciding on the governance process. Board meetings are held regularly to decide the overall direction of the café, approve financial reports, and decide other important issues such as what research to accommodate, when and who to hire, and whether to apply for grants. The core operation team, which is in charge of day-to-day operations, meets every month to discuss operational matters. They also plan and organize events that are suitable with Ibasho principles. Both the board and the core operation group consist of local elders.

Case Study: Ibasho Café Japan as a Post-Disaster Reconstruction Project

The GEJE was significant not only because of the large magnitude of the damage, but because the disaster occurred in regions that were already facing the rapid growth of elders and shrinking number of young people. Some communities had even struggled to remain viable, due to the combination of a high proportion of elders, frequent migration of young people, and a low fertility rate.

The Ibasho team visited the affected area, conducting interviews with elderly survivors still living in temporary housing communities eleven months after the disaster. Both elderly residents and the younger generation spoke of elders who saved younger people's lives by guiding them to higher ground and teaching them how to survive with extremely limited resources. Older people also expressed a great deal of gratitude for all the aid they received and wanted to give back. Many said that they want to be useful to others but did not know how.

These conversations made it clear that elders' wisdom and experience became valuable resources when the standard system was interrupted. We felt strongly that elders who were in the affected area should be given ways to actively participate in the recovery of the community, rather than being treated as liabilities that need to be protected and cared for.

Gathering Support and Developing the Core Team

This project was initiated eleven months after the GEJE with the support of Honeywell Hometown Solutions, Operation USA. One week after the GEJE, Ibasho organized a presentation regarding the disaster relief idea in Washington, DC. The donors heard about the idea from one of the participants at the event and contacted Ibasho, asking if the donation would be used to develop a place to help elderly victims. Ibasho proposed to create a project that empowers elders to develop their community support system in the process of recovery, rather than creating another place where they would be served.

After three months of discussion between Ibasho and funders about the direction and objective of this project, Ibasho contacted several nursing home operators in Japan and asked if they would be interested in developing the Ibasho café with us. We explained to them that this is a drastically different approach to care for elders.

One of those groups we contacted, a social welfare organization called Tenjinkai, agreed to help with outreach to elders in the communities where they served. With local support from Tenjinkai, Ibasho visited four communities in Ofunato and conducted informal interviews with elders who lived in temporary housing communities. We also met with local leaders and city officials to understand the needs of community members.

We decided to work with the community of Massaki in Ofunato city because of the strong commitment we got from leaders in this community.

After identifying the community, we visited the mayor of Ofunato and explained our objective, giving a brief overview of the process involved in creating and operating the project. The mayor agreed to provide his support, which was very important to us, since we were expecting to encounter various regulatory issues during the development phase.

Next, we communicated with city workers and design professionals, explaining our vision of the project and asking for their cooperation. Many city workers and architects volunteered to work with us and the community elders.

After assembling that core team, we explained the project to elders and other local stakeholders, who volunteered to be catalysts for the project, connecting us to people in the community, because they knew so many of them. The elders and community members we talked to agreed that elders' knowledge and experience are valuable to improve the community's ability to survive and recover during and after a natural disaster, when standard systems and institutions do not function properly.

Physical Attributes: Because This Building Is Old, It Is Beautiful

Community members supported the idea of the Ibasho café. The project inspired many to recover their sense of community, which had been damaged by the tsunami. To support the project, a local family donated their old farmhouse to add a symbolic meaning. We all felt that it was important to build a culturally significant, permanent structure in the area damaged by the tsunami, since so many temporary structures were erected after the disaster. We saw such a unique beauty in the building because it was old. This old structure quietly projects the people's life and history of this community. There was something special about this old structure that newly constructed buildings would not be able to achieve. Moreover, the design of the building made it possible for elder carpenters to play an important role during the reconstruction process, as it was built with a traditional Japanese architectural technique that did not use nails.

The Ibasho team then searched for a location, along with local leaders, supporting organizations, and the city of Ofunato. We needed a large enough property close to services on high ground, so a large-scale tsunami will not reach it. This was challenging because properties on high ground were in high demand from people who lost their houses. Local leaders and elders played an important role, using their networks of friends, colleagues, and family members to identify the property and negotiate to secure it. In the end, they found an excellent location, close to temporary housing communities and a middle school, where many community members pass by every day.

The farmhouse was disassembled, moved, and reconstructed as an Ibasho café in the Massaki area. A local construction company rehabilitated the old farmhouse, with the agreement that it would hire elder carpenters for the project. This gave elder carpenters opportunities to transfer their knowledge and skills to younger generations.

The landowner has agreed to ten years of free rent. This arrangement could not have happened if we had not worked closely with local elders and the city of Ofunato.

Social Environmental Attributes: Writing the Scenario, and Then Building the Stage

While planning the infrastructure, we organized community workshops to learn what community members would like to create through this project. We employed the concept of "place making," using the design process as a vehicle to educate people about the Ibasho concept and strengthen the capacity of the community support system. We held ten workshops over eighteen months with community members of all ages, including sessions on vision, participatory design, and operation, empowering elders to help design, construct, and operate this Ibasho project.

When designing a place, we advocate a process we call "writing the scenario first, then building the stage." The main actors and actresses in this process are the community members. Our development team is the support staff, and the stage is designed to fit the story that community members create.

The development team's role is to challenge preconceived ideas regarding a "proper" place for elders and engage elders to collectively create a scenario that reverses the current social perception of the role of elders from being cared for to caring for and contributing to the community. As they developed the scenario, elders developed a shared vision that informs how the building should be designed.

It was challenging for elders and community members to envision what they wanted to create but easy to talk about what they did not want to create. To help them visualize the life of Ibasho café, we have asked elders to describe the differences between an Ibasho café and an adult day center. This question seemed to help them think outside the box and start sharing their vision of a new and better way. Here are some of their comments:

> In adult day center, we are treated as a group of old people who need to follow the schedule while the young caregivers tell us what to do. But in Ibasho café, we envision for us to do what we want to when we want to. We do not have to go there when we don't feel like it.

> A lot of old people go to adult day center because there is nothing else to do. I would like to see Ibasho café being a place where I can find something useful to do with my friends.

Community members collectively came up with the idea of creating a café space where community members can gather in an informal manner. They also discussed how to create programs and a space to welcome young people, so they would like to come too. They decided they would create a space where babies can safely play with elders when mothers are taking a short break. They also wanted to prepare traditional local meals and drinks for visitors, which brought up a regulatory challenge: If we registered this place as a café, community members could not cook there without following strict rules, and they could not bring meals from their homes to share with others. Moreover, the capacity of the kitchen and water tank would have to follow commercial regulations, which would exceed our budget and strip away some of the cozy feel we wanted to create.

To reconcile this issue without compromising the elders' vision, we consulted the city and decided to register as community center, not a café. Because it is registered as a community center, elders cannot charge for foods and drinks. Instead, community members came up with the idea that we ask visitors to support the Ibasho café operation by making donations for the drink and foods. Elders are only allowed to warm up meals on-site, but they prepare light meals together and also bring foods they cook at home. This is one example of our need to find creative solutions to fit within the regulatory environment, because the place we were creating was unlike anything the city had seen before.

To ensure the long-term sustainability of the Ibasho café as a community initiative, the Ibasho Sozo Project, a not-for-profit organization, was formed by a group of local elders. At the initial development stage of the project, elders were unenthusiastic about starting up a formal organization due to their age. Their reaction made our Ibasho project team realize that how deeply social perceptions of what older people should and should not do was embedded in our thinking—and not just among younger people. Elders are often very careful when they sign up for anything new, we learned, because they are afraid of being embarrassed if others would not accept their commitment, in addition to other concerns such as the level of commitment for their time and financial liabilities. As a 74-year-old retired school principal said, "Aren't we too old to start the new organization?"

Once they were encouraged to apply for nonprofit status with the support of local leaders, however, they were determined to make the project succeed.

Learning to Operate in Accordance with Ibasho Principles

During the first year after its June 2014 opening, the project grew as a truly community-owned initiative. The local elders made efforts to integrate individuals of all ages, including children and people with dementia, both as a part of operations and as customers. They established strong governing and operational teams, which organize a monthly operational meeting with nine elected board members from the community. They also organized more than fifty events with the purpose of transferring their knowledge to younger generations, in addition to serving more than five thousand people. The donations they are given for those drinks and snacks, as well as the grants applied for by the Ibasho Sozo Project, cover the cost of operating and maintaining the cafe.

The Ibasho café has become a place where locals meet. Elders living alone come for some conversation, children come to read books and play, students come to study, mothers bring their children, and community members of all ages come to learn local traditions from the elders.

However, the transition was not always smooth.

Beginning Phase

The first four or five months of operation were an adjustment phase for us all. The community members had to decide many details, such as how to communicate with each other about the operation, who would be in charge of day-to-day operational decisions, who should manage the keys, and what the hours of operation should be. The Ibasho development team, which consisted of external professionals, supporting organizations, and community leaders, talked to community elders about what kind of support we could provide without interfering with their process of making it a truly community-owned operation. We were all collectively trying to figure out what it meant to operate the Ibasho café as a community initiative that benefited people of all ages.

There were many occasions of misunderstanding or mistrust during this initial period, between the community leaders and the external experts and professionals but also among members of the community. Examples included how this place should be used, who should be involved in the operation, the role of volunteers, and how external experts would assist the operation. This unfamiliar place and the new roles it created were causing confusion and forcing community members, including elders, to discuss things that made them uncomfortable, rather than pretending as if those issues did not exist. This kind of conflict does not commonly occur in traditional elder care settings because the elders are not involved in finding solutions to their problems. But conflict, we realized, is a part of life and not necessarily something that should be avoided, especially when the need to work out their differences motivated people to find better solutions to their problems. Through this process the depth of the community tie became stronger and even helped to form new friendships among the elders.

Through the numerous discussions among community members and external support organizations, a core Ibasho café operation group was naturally formed. We also learned that even an informal gathering place needs more structure than could be provided by the small group of volunteers we had initially envisioned managing the place. The elders still hope to operate the place on a volunteer basis in the near future, but first they must invest considerable time in reaching out to community members to help them understand the meaning of this place and motivate them to participate. As one core operation member put it, "We want to operate this place as a completely volunteer effort among the community members; however, it takes time to establish the system. Until then, we need to hire someone who can be here."

When the Ibasho Sozo Project was formed, it was awarded a small grant from the city. The board members approved use of the fund to hire a part-time staff member. That new position caused confusion at first, because the roles of paid staff and volunteer members were not defined clearly. The operation group developed a clear hiring process and defined the paid staff responsibilities.

Transition Phase: Five to Six Months after the Opening

Once the basic operational structure was established, other concerns emerged as we learned how challenging it could be to create a "normal" environment. That fear elders often have of being embarrassed by failing at something they were asked to do arose again as the core operation group felt the pressure of determining the financial status and direction of the café for the long term. Elders shared their fear of not being able to maintain the philosophy of the Ibasho café when new members joined the current operation team. They also felt that the board members involvement was not helpful, because the future direction of the Ibasho café had not been clearly communicated to them.

We organized meetings between the board members and the core operation group to air those concerns, and the responsibilities of each group were clarified. During these discussions, we shared my concerns about the danger of making this place too rigid and structured, creating an institutional operation that would lose the informality and sense of normalcy needed to allow people to come and go as they wish. At the same time, we were made aware of community politics and human dynamics in which outsiders cannot intervene. It may take more time and effort, but engaging community members in operational discussions is critical, so we can communicate our vision and they can come up with solutions that fit their community. Cleaving to the eight principles of Ibasho was helpful in explaining the fundamental purpose of the project to community members.

Settling In: One Year after the Opening

In July 2014, the community celebrated the first anniversary of the Ibasho café. Elders organized the event and welcomed more than three hundred visitors. Looking at the report and images from the elders, I found that they have embraced Ibasho principles in their own ways. Collaborating with local members as well as volunteers, the Ibasho core operation group arranged for traditional foods prepared by elders with ingredients from local elderly farmers, a concert by a local musician, and many activities for children, to appeal to people of all ages.

One year after the opening, the elders feel the operation has become stable. They are ready to take the Ibasho café to the next level. In the second year, they want to teach local traditions and disaster survival skills to more children. They want to encourage more participation by young people, people in temporary housing, and elders with dementia and their families. They would also like to create more opportunities for elders to learn from young people.

To achieve those goals, they intend to organize events with local groups and schools. They have asked more local elders to serve as board members, to strengthen the long-term operation. With the community's help, the core group hopes to slowly move to an all-volunteer operation.

Conclusion

This case study discussed the philosophical principles of the Ibasho café and its application to the post-disaster recovery project in Japan. The first Ibasho café ever created, this project has had a positive impact on the lives of elders and other community members, but it also created many challenges for them. Some of those challenges involved regulations, but most stemmed from communications issues and other human dynamics among the individuals involved in the project.

This project challenged our accustomed way of caring for elders. Developing and operating a new kind of place forced us to go beyond our comfort levels, thinking and acting in new ways, which led to feelings of uncertainty and frustration. While this process was challenging, I found it beneficial for the elders and other community members. Thinking about their roles in the community made many elders realize that a gap existed between the types of places and services they would like to have and what was available as they aged. Many mentioned that Ibasho café created a place for them to go and do something meaningful for their community members. Some also said they formed new friendships by being involved in the Ibasho café. Perhaps most importantly, they learned that community is something that they have to negotiate and create with others, not something that they can passively receive. After a year of the Ibasho café operation, one community member told us, "I was so frustrated in the beginning because you were asking us so many questions that we normally don't think about. I did not understand why you were asking what we wanted and how I could be helpful. I thought we could figure out when the building is completed. Now, it makes sense."

Looking back at the evolution of this new place, I was reminded that we were working with elders, not children. They not only have long life experience and skills, but also relationships with many community members. The Ibasho café could not have happened without the external individuals and organizations that provided support during the development phase, but we had to learn to trust community members when it came to managing this community-driven project. A comment from a core operation group captures the essence of this important issue: "Please fully trust us to operate this place, if you would like us [elders] to be in charge. We will not do this if you organize half of the work for us to complete the rest."

The physical environment of the Ibasho café changed as elders used the space to fit with their needs. When I walk into the Ibasho café now, I have a sense of "their place." There are many handcrafts decorating the space, the furniture arrangement was changed, and assistive devices such as grab bars were installed to welcome visitors safely and comfortably. I feel that the Ibasho café is no longer a building that we developed, but a place that belongs to the elder members of the community.

Lessons Learned

The lessons learned as we develop Ibasho sites will enable us to develop theoretical and practical knowledge about how to create and manage an effective Ibasho café. These lessons will also inform us about effective ways to develop community-driven initiatives, making possible a new way of providing services for elders in their communities. We have learned many lessons from this experience, but four are particularly important.

The most important of all is that we should not hand over the whole operation to local elders without providing initial financial and personnel support for the operation. Community-owned projects need time to learn and grow before members of the community have enough skills and knowledge to take care of day-to-day administration and plan for the future. It is critical to have a coordinator who helps elders make a smooth transition in the early stage of the operation. At the Ibasho café in Japan, the coordinator role was filled by a full-time researcher who understood the concept of the Ibasho café and was able to help elders with administration matters, computers, outreach, and communications.

The second lesson is that we should not impose the funders' timeline on the community. Funders would normally like to see a project completed in a short period of time, but community members may not feel the same sense of urgency or have enough time to invest in the project to complete it quickly. Accommodating that kind of organic growth rate may mean that the duration of the initial grants or decisions about how the funds are utilized may need to be adjusted.

The third lesson is that the role of outside experts must be carefully managed in a community-owned project. One of the experts involved in the development of the Ibasho café said, "We are tested how much we as experts can trust community members and their inputs when we facilitate a community-driven project. It is difficult to balance how much we allow the community's input into our design and creating a successful project." After one year of Ibasho operation, I realized that this comment was not only disrespectful but also wrong. When working with any community, but particularly one that experienced such a traumatic event, the experts should realize the key to a successful project is how much community members can trust experts, not the other way around. Experts and professionals should act as facilitators, working to empower elders to create the community they want and to help them become fully integrated as active participants.

The fourth lesson is the importance of exploring ways of collaborating with local government. To achieve stable operation of the Ibasho café or other community-owned projects, it is critical to explore how to involve local government without compromising the initiative's community-driven nature.

Final Thoughts

I have often encountered discussions regarding the importance of investing in social development, not just physical infrastructure, when creating services for elders or providing disaster relief. When I do, I always wonder why we treat these two important issues as separate matters. Why not use the development of any new infrastructure as an opportunity to enhance the social development of the community?

Community development can be challenging because an enhanced sense of community is hard to measure and varies for different individuals. Including infrastructure development as a part of community development gives participants and other members of the community a tangible way to measure their progress and see the results of the work they have invested. A physical infrastructure also makes it easier for community members to develop a sense of ownership in a project and to invest the effort needed to ensure long-term sustainability.

Of course, our grassroots approach will not solve all the issues around global aging or the vulnerability of elders during and after natural disasters. However, we need community-driven projects as well as government-driven ones to bring about needed social changes. Engaging elders in the planning, design, and implementation of solutions to these problems makes the effort more effective and efficient by tailoring it to local needs and creating greater buy-in. I am not suggesting that current elder care services are ineffective, but I am advocating for more options and for more ways of allowing elders with something to contribute to their communities to be useful to others. No one wants to be a burden, regardless of age.

Emi Kiyota is an environmental gerontologist, educator, and organizational culture change expert, focusing on initiatives to improve the quality of the built environment for health-care settings and long-term care services for elders. She has been a consultant to numerous age-friendly design projects for senior housing, hospitals, and clinical care centers in the United States, Europe, Asia, and Africa. She is a founder of the not-for-profit, international organization entitled Ibasho, embodying the Japanese concept of "a place where one feels at home being oneself." Ibasho aims to create a socially, economically, and environmentally sustainable communities that value their elders. She has been involved in the development of housing and services for elders in Bhutan, Sri Lanka, and Ivory Coast. She also facilitated the building of the first innovative "Ibasho café" in a disaster area after the Great East Japan Earthquake and tsunami and is implementing this initiative in Philippines. She was awarded a Bellagio Fellowship for a one-month residency on an "Innovative Response to Global Aging" from the Rockefeller Foundation. In 2016–17, Dr. Kiyota was a Loeb Fellow at the Harvard Graduate School of Design.

References

Aldrich, Daniel P. 2012. *Building Resilience: Social Capital in Post-Disaster Recovery.* Chicago: University of Chicago Press.

Gakuta, I. 2013. *Kodokushi: Hisaichide Kangaeru Ningen no Fukko.* Tokyo: Iwanami Gendai Press.
Klinenberg, Eric. 2002. *Heat Wave.* Chicago, IL: University of Chicago Press.
Ministry of Health, Labor, and Social Welfare Japan. 2013. *Annual Vital Statistics Report.* Accessed 1 June 2018. http://www.mhlw.go.jp/english/database/db-hw/lifetb13/index.html.
Ministry of Reconstruction Japan. 2014. *Higashi Nihon Dai Shinsai niokeru Shinsai Kanrensi.* Annual report. Accessed 1 June 2018. http://www.reconstruction.go.jp/topics/main-cat2/sub-cat2-1/20140527_kanrenshi.pdf.
Sasa, Y., N. Tanaka, and M. Doi. 2012. "Koureishamuke Jutaku Kyojusha no Gaishutsu ni Kansuru Kenkyu." *Nihon Kenchiku Gakkai* 52: 165–68.
Silverstein, Murray, and Max Jacobson. 1978. *Restructuring the Hidden Program: Toward an Architecture of Social Change.* In *Facility Programming,* ed. Wolfgang F. E. Preiser, 11–51. Stroudsburg, PA: Dowden, Hutchinson and Ross.
UNDESA. 2012. *World Population Prospects.* Accessed 1 June 2018. http://esa.un.org/wpp/Documentation/publications.htm.
UNFPA. 2013. *The State of World Population 2012 – By Choice, Not By Chance: Family Planning, Human Rights and Development.* New York: United Nations. Accessed 1 June 2018. https://www.unfpa.org/publications/state-world-population-2012.
Wilhelmi, Olga V., and Mary H. Hayden. 2010. "Connecting People and Place: A New Framework for Reducing Urban Vulnerability to Extreme Heat." *Environmental Research Letters* 5(1): 014021.

9 YOUTH AND OLDER PERSONS AS AGENTS FOR CHANGE
Creating an Inclusive and Age-Friendly Society for All

Arthur Namara and Kristin Bodiford

THE UNITED NATIONS DEFINES A society for all ages as one that "enables the generations to invest in one another and share in the fruits of that investment, guided by the twin principles of reciprocity and equity" (UN, n.d). In this chapter, we will provide a perspective of inclusive and age-friendly communities in an African context, with a specific example of intergenerational community development in Uganda. We will explore an inclusive and age-friendly community as one where youth and older persons are equally engaged in co-creating and optimizing opportunities for health, participation, and security in order to enhance quality of life for all ages. Both age groups have special gifts to contribute to this. Thinking of inclusive and age-friendly communities as places that promote the well-being for all persons opens possibilities for how we might all work together to develop community approaches that support people across the life span. The Madrid International Plan of Action on Ageing developed at the United Nations Second World Assembly on Ageing in 2002 asserts that solidarity between generations, where younger and older persons are able to address the issues in their lives and communities, is fundamental to build a vision for and work toward a society that is inclusive of all ages. Embracing the theme of the Twenty-Fourth Anniversary of the UN International Day of Older Persons and the focus of the post-2015 development framework, "Leave No One Behind: Promoting a Society for All," reinforces the importance of improving the lives of people of all ages and supports an intergenerational approach where multiple generations are seen as core assets to post-2015 development goals. "When we encourage generations to come together, our mutual understanding is enhanced; our capacity to care for each other, expanded; and our shared effort of addressing community issues, empowered" (Bodiford 2013: 126).

In this chapter, we will lay a foundation of demographic changes and issues related to older persons and youth in Africa, review principles of family-centered and intergenerational community building, explore what counts as evidence and "what works," and share the work of Health Nest Uganda related to intergenerational community building. The stories in this chapter illustrate how people of all ages can work together to create inclusive and age-friendly communities.

Demographics Changes and Related Issues and Opportunities in Africa

It is important to state several assumptions before proceeding. First, for the purposes of this chapter, we will reflect the designations from the United Nations of "more developed" and "less developed or developing" countries and reinforce that by using this language we are not implying a judgment about the stage reached by a particular country in the development process. Much of the statistics we will be using are from sub-Saharan Africa.

Secondly, although we will be representing demographics and issues related to countries and people in Africa, we recognize that Africa is not homogeneous and has regional and country variations and historical, political, socioeconomic, religious, and cultural diversity.

Lastly, for purposes of demographic comparison, when we speak of youth, we are referring to ages fifteen to thirty, unless otherwise indicated. When we speak of older persons, we are referring to ages sixty and above. We will first begin exploring the demographic changes and related issues and opportunities related to older persons and youth in Africa.

Older Persons in Africa

Madrid International Plan of Action on Ageing (UN 2002) recognizes that while most of the concern around population aging has been a focal point for more developed countries, there is growing momentum in developing countries as well. It is projected that over 60 percent of the world population aged sixty and older lives in developing countries and is expected to increase to over 70 percent by 2030 and 80 percent by 2050 (UN 2015: 9; Velkoff and Kowal 2006). In Africa, the older population is projected to grow from 64 million in 2015 to 220 million by 2050 (UN 2015: 10). Between 2015 and 2050 the number of older persons in sub-Saharan Africa is projected to more than triple, with a growth rate for the 2040s that is projected to be faster than any other region since 1950 (UN 2016).

The population in Africa is growing older because of increasingly healthy lifestyles and improving health conditions. This is especially relevant in Africa because of the vital role that elders play in society, including the care they provide for children orphaned by HIV/AIDS. Adults with HIV/AIDS are often cared for by their parents, and a large majority of the over 50 million children in Africa who have been orphaned are cared for by their grandparents (UNICEF 2017; WHO, n.d.). Between one-fifth and one-third of women aged sixty years or over are living in skipped generation households, composed solely of grandparents and grandchildren (UN 2011: 8).

Chronic health conditions including depression, hypertension, and poor vision are common among many older persons (Scholten et al. 2011). One of the challenges in addressing these issues is the limited research, awareness, and knowledge in Africa of the issues older persons face. Primary care facilities remain the main source of health care; however, the major focus of these health-care centers is on infectious illnesses, by people with little knowledge of geriatric care. Older persons are also challenged in their attempts to access care at primary care facilities due to lack of transportation and cost of health care.

Older persons in sub-Saharan Africa often face additional challenges including elder abuse, financial insecurity, poverty, and social exclusion. The United Nations sixty-sixth session General Assembly Follow-Up to the Second World Assembly on Ageing (UN 2012) acknowledges that fundamental to aging with dignity is the ability to age with "good health, economic security, adequate housing, an enabling environment, and access to land or other productive resources." UN Secretary-General Ban Ki-Moon reinforces the importance of looking at human rights mechanisms to address the specific circumstances of older men and women (NGO Committee on Ageing, n.d.). Rights of older women are particularly important because of the inequalities and limited access to resources and opportunities they face. The UN sixty-sixth General Assembly report recognizes the impact of gender inequalities that become more pronounced in older age, where older women are more likely than older men to be poor. At the same time, older women often take on greater responsibilities for family care, with little social and economic support, leaving them and those for whom they care extremely vulnerable (UN 2011: 4).

The United Nations Sustainable Development Goals have shifted the global goals that used to include specific targets for children and youth, with older persons largely left out, to including people across all ages. The most pressing challenge to the welfare of older persons is poverty (UN 2011: 5). In 2016, it was estimated that only 10 percent of older persons in Africa receive any form of pension support, and over 70 percent remain highly vulnerable to falling into extreme poverty (UN 2017; UN 2011: 26). Older populations in many developing countries like Uganda have little real social protection (such as social assistance or cash transfers) from the state. Older persons in Africa easily find themselves in a community plagued with social exclusion, including age discrimination, inability to access work in the formal sector, and limited access to financial services (HelpAge International 2008; UN 2011). In response, countries are evaluating social protection initiatives. For example, the Ugandan Ministry of Gender, Labour and Social Development is implementing the social protection program called Expanding Social Protection with Senior Citizens Grants. It began with a pilot in fifteen districts in 2010 and expanded to forty districts in 2016. Through this program, persons sixty-five years and above and families with low labor capacity and high dependency will receive UGX 25,000 (approximately $8.00 U.S.) monthly. The purpose of this program is to provide social protection and reduce poverty for older persons and families, support people to contribute to society, and provide income security for people as they age (Ministry of Gender, Labour and Development, n.d.).

The increase of the older population in Africa and the rising cost of caring for them have also significantly limited the social safety net that has been in existence. In Uganda, institutionalized care does not exist for the older population. It is commonly thought that older persons will be supported by their family and the communities in which they live. Caring for older persons in these societies has long been considered a family responsibility and finds its roots within cultural traditions. It was typical to see large families, and as such the responsibility of shared care for parents was divided between siblings, to minimize cost. When older persons faced times of crisis or illness, they generally had families as sources of support.

> In sub-Saharan Africa, older people have traditionally been viewed in a positive light, as repositories of information and wisdom. And while African families are generally still intact, development and modernization are closely connected with social and economic changes that can weaken traditional social values and networks that provide care and support in later life. (National Research Council 2006)

Nayiga Zaam, director of Elders' Concern Uganda (ECU), shares her concern for how a current cultural shift impacts older persons' ability to live and age with respect and dignity:

> Way back in Uganda's past, older persons were traditionally cared for by relatives, friends, and the kind donations of neighbors. The times have changed, though, and these people can no longer support the elderly owing to increasing caretaker poverty. This is leaving older persons more vulnerable and causing them to lose hope in life. Older persons seem to have been abandoned

despite the challenges they face, including stress, poor health, loss of income and poor nutrition. (Health Nest Uganda 2013)

While many African countries work to bridge policy and practice, older persons often occupy a vulnerable position in society as they go through aging transitions, deal with health challenges, and rely on family or community support. In Uganda, there is a focus on developing effective policy organized around the decentralized provision of family and community-based responses. The Uganda Report on the Implementation of the Madrid International Plan of Action on Ageing (Baryayebwa 2010) focuses on areas such as economic empowerment of older persons and strengthening formal and informal community supports in efforts to support quality of life and well-being of older persons. Uganda has put in place a National Council for Older Persons as established by the National Council of Older Persons Act 2013. The National Council is a body mandated to guide, coordinate, monitor, and advise all stakeholders on quality service delivery to older persons as provided for in the National Policy on Older Persons and the Constitution of the Republic of Uganda (2009).

While it is important to recognize the issues that older people face, it is also critical to engage and support the strengths of older people. Emi Kiyota (chapter 8 in this volume) reminds us that when we view older persons primarily in terms of their vulnerabilities, we miss out on the tremendous contributions that older people are making and can make in society. They play a critical role in advocating for policies and being an active partner in developing community-based responses to address not only their health and well-being, but also the health and well-being of their families and communities. As countries like Uganda are experiencing an almost doubling of the population over the age of sixty, a shift in thinking about older people as vulnerable to a recognition of the strengths and resources that older people contribute to society is an economic and social imperative.

Youth in Africa

As Africa's older population continues to grow, it also remains the world's youngest continent, bringing both challenges and opportunities to Africa's development. The United Nations (UN 2013b) reported that 60 percent of Africa's population is made up of people twenty-four years and younger; half of these (or 217 million) are youth between the ages of fifteen and twenty-four. By 2050, nine in ten youth will live in developing countries (Population Reference Bureau 2009). The "youth bulge" occurring in Africa is in part due to the successful efforts of reducing infant mortality rates, while the fertility rates remain unchanged (Lin 2012).

According to Ministry of Gender, Labour and Social Development, 78 percent of Uganda's population is under the age of thirty (International Youth Foundation 2011). This calls for a coherent youth development action plan to turn the "youth bulge" to "youth gain." Although the government of Uganda has made investing in young people one of its fundamental social obligations, Uganda's fast-growing population is of concern because it is not matched with the country's ability to create jobs. Youth unemployment is a significant issue throughout Africa. Almost 40 percent of Africa's workforce is youth. Only 113,000 of the more than 400,000 young Ugandans who enter the labor market each year are absorbed in formal employment, leaving the rest to find jobs in the informal sector (Ssenkabirwa 2012). Due to high unemployment levels, youth may engage in unproductive or risky activities, which in the end may expose them to infections like HIV/AIDS and further contribute to intergenerational cycles of poverty.

Instead, what if the strengths of youth were engaged in community development work? The African Union (2010) reinforces the importance of mobilizing and equipping youth to help drive Africa's integration, peace and development agenda. The African Union Youth Volunteer Corps supports youth empowerment and effective participation of young people as the architecture of human capacity development across Africa.

Currently, Africa is experiencing a strong wave of youth activism. Youth activism generally refers to the actions that youth take to address a variety of social, economic, and political issues impacting society. Youth activism is a conscious and collective effort that youth employ to work for equity and social justice in their communities. Youth activism includes young people taking direct action through forms of protests or initiatives to better themselves or the society in which they live. While youth activism might be viewed as a social destabilizing force, it can also be seen as an opportunity for youth to address issues that affect the lives of older persons in their communities—making youth a powerful agent of change to create more inclusive and age-friendly communities. Youth can be society movers through participating in meaningful dialogue, being involved in decision-making, and contributing to positive change.

At the same time, the African Position on Youth Development (African Union 2010) recognized the "limited opportunities to civic participation, governance, and education that engenders human rights around issues of equity, equality, and the relevance of social inclusion." Youth are often not considered as participants in African state policies, with few real conversations with leaders that could lead to concrete policy changes. African youth have the potential to be global catalysts of change for their communities and countries when they are part of the political process. While there is a growing commitment to support youth empowerment, youth continue to face challenges to their participation in decision-making processes. The *African Youth Report* by the United Nations Economic Commission for Africa (UN 2009) recommends that African governments work to create opportunities for youth to participate in political affairs through youth quotas in parliament, memberships in village councils, and efforts to increase their knowledge of national policies through participation and training.

Often, even as youth move from rural communities, the connection and bond to their community remain. Their actions to support older persons in their communities can be seen as a form of activism born from a connection to their community. In an attempt to understand the role youth activism can play in building inclusive and age-friendly communities, we might pose a question, "What are motivating factors of youth activism and engagement in Uganda?" Eunice Musubika, a Health Nest Uganda youth volunteer, shares how through a strengths-based approach, youth discover their strengths and discuss together and identify projects they would like to start in partnership with older persons:

> Young people know and understand the challenges in the communities they have grown up in and are in the best position to overcome them when youth can agree to make a difference in their communities. Youth can do something to change their current situations by taking the lead and by including peers and elders to solve challenges through co-creation. All of us are uniquely talented and if we put our talents together we can make a difference through our collective creativity. (Personal communication 2014)

Youth activism and engagement can be seen as multistoried and complex, as acts of volunteerism, as a culture of collective community responsibility—and as a holistic approach of addressing societal challenges.

Family Strengthening and Intergenerational Solidarity

Because of the centrality and role of families in African countries, a movement to create more inclusive and age-friendly communities would focus on strengthening families and supporting what families need at all ages. While there has been significant progress of global development goals, with the extreme poverty rate halved globally, many families are living in extreme poverty, with almost half of the people in sub-Saharan Africa needing to feed, clothe, heal, educate, and build for the future on less than the equivalent amount of $1.90 a day (UN 2017). Productive and decent employment is rare, accompanied by high rates of hunger (ibid.). As a result, family dynamics continue to shift from the effects of industrialization, globalization, urbanization, migration, and smaller families and challenge the long-standing cultural practice of family support. With this change in extended family systems, youth and older persons often experience less support than they used to have.

The African Union Plan of Action on the Family (African Union 2004) underscores the importance of supporting families with policies, programs, and community development efforts. The UN report in preparation for the twentieth anniversary of the International Year of the Family (UN 2014a) recognizes that policies that strengthen families as building blocks of society support social development and urges member states to "promote and implement family-friendly policies aimed at providing sustainable, affordable and quality living conditions for families and to empower families and recognize their role in social cohesion and economic development." The fifty-second session of the Commission for Social Development, United Nations Economic and Social Council (UN 2014b) encourages member states to strengthen efforts to develop policies that address family poverty, social exclusion, work-family balance, and intergenerational solidarity.

The following is a definition of *intergenerational solidarity* in the *Report of the Secretary General: Intergenerational Solidarity and the Needs of Future Generations* (UN 2013a: 3):

> Intergenerational solidarity is widely understood as social cohesion between generations. Most frequently, however, it refers to relations between the younger and older generations of those living, including child-parent relationships, social participation of elderly people and children in communities, affordability of pensions, and care of the elderly. Increasingly, the scope of family policies related to intergenerational solidarity has been gradually expanding, from a focus on families with young children to the inclusion of all generations, an expansion warranted by rapidly ageing societies where family-oriented policies need to take into account the changing roles and demands of all generations.

A focus on intergenerational relationships recognizes the interdependence of generations to support healthy families and societies where people are able to make contributions across the life course (Butts, Thang, and Yeo 2012). The African Union (2012: 5) recognizes that a focus on intergenerational solidarity, "reflected by the provision of reciprocal care, support and exchange of material and non-material resources between younger and older family members, will help re-strengthen what has been a key function of families in Africa."

The participation of youth and older persons in informing and shaping public policy is central to a human rights perspective and helps address social exclusion and isolation (UN 2011: 18).

Promotion and protection of all human rights and fundamental freedoms is important in order to achieve a society for all ages. In this, the reciprocal relationship between and among generations must be nurtured, emphasized and encouraged through a comprehensive and effective dialogue. (UN 2002)

In the face of the challenges and opportunities families, youth, and older persons experience, there is a unique potential to bring together multiple voices into dialogue to create communities that are inclusive and age-friendly. Through meaningful dialogue, multiple generations can expand knowledge, develop strategies, improve practice, and influence policy. Stimulating and strengthening intergenerational cooperation help people develop a sense of responsibility for each other and promote intergenerational relationships where youth appreciate older persons and older persons appreciate youth, each supporting each other and helping each other.

Evidence of Impact

Before we begin to explore intergenerational responses in Uganda, let's first consider the call for evidence and guidance for what "works" to better inform our efforts. The Madrid International Plan of Action on Ageing (UN 2002) encourages the international community to promote and support research, training, and capacity building. The Strategic Framework and Plan for Research in Sub-Saharan Africa (Oxford Institute on Ageing 2005) calls for enhanced research on aging in Africa to act as a catalyst for promoting and informing development policy responses to aging and to gain an understanding of how the roles and links of generations within society are changing and shaping development processes. Strengthening the capacity for developing and implementing evaluation practices and sharing knowledge in a community of practice would help to further understand how to develop more inclusive and age-friendly communities.

In the international development field, learning from experience helps efforts to be more effective and accountable and to manage limited resources well. With the limited resources that global south countries often face, the challenge remains how to use resources wisely to grow locally developed strategies and at the same time evaluate impact.

If we think of research as a relationally engaged activity (McNamee and Hosking 2012), meanings and actions are a by-product of coordination and human action, not objective, neutral, or empirical truths (Gergen 2009). This opens the possibility for engaging more forms of social processes for knowledge production and co-creating new possibilities. Action research is a resource that supports participation from community members to collectively design solutions to complex issues and supports community ownership. Youth and older persons can become co-researchers to generate solutions and new knowledge. This participatory and often emancipatory approach to research shifts the power of evaluating community change to those most impacted by the issues they face in their lives, grounded in lived experience and developed in partnership (Bradbury and Reason 2003). It defines people not as passive recipients but as active agents of change and owners of the discourses that affect them. This move also supports an ongoing action learning cycle from the very beginning where the community defines the problems and develops local solutions that make sense to them. In this case, outside "researchers" are also committed engaged co-participants and co-learners in the process. Another approach to action research shifts the focus from problems to strengths. Appreciative Inquiry is an example in which stories of success and positive change are identified, illuminated, and grown. This approach to evaluation and research engages multiple stakeholders, including those voices most often left out, as resources for learning and generating new knowledge.

The UN Programme on Ageing (Sidorenko 2006) reinforces the importance of a participatory "bottom-up" approach to research that enriches policy making with qualitative information and establishes priorities for policies and programs that reflect people's interests. It provides an opportunity for people to voice their needs and aspirations. The World Health Organization age-friendly cities and communities guide (WHO 2007: 7) also encourages a bottom-up participatory approach that involves and empowers older persons to contribute to society and participate in decision-making processes. Communities can engage youth and older persons in dialogue to learn from them as experts in their own lives:

1. What are the features of an inclusive and age-friendly community?
2. What challenges do people encounter in their lives? How do they address these challenges? What strengths do they draw upon?
3. What is missing that would enhance people's health, participation, and security?
4. What strengths can communities draw upon to address these possibilities?

All ages have skills to contribute to research efforts. Youth and older people are valuable assets who can be trained as researchers in participatory methods. Youth Participatory Action Research (YPAR) increases youth involvement in social movements and brings energy and enthusiasm for social change. In the process of developing their capacity as co-researchers, they are also building their leadership within their communities (Powers and Allaman 2012). In addition, when youth participate in inquiry with older persons, relationships are transformed. As youth listen to older persons, they also begin asking what they can do to help. Through this intergenerational process, generations are supported to come together, increase their understanding of each other, and begin to work together in new ways to address issues in their communities. In dialogue, the generations are able to both listen to the best of what has been and spark their imaginations for what could be—what is possible. Intergenerational cooperation also enables wisdom, culture, and values to be shared and passed on through the process of research (Bodiford 2013).

Supporting and empowering people to participate in the research process may lead to more just and locally relevant evidence-based models of community development. The question then moves from "What is the 'evidence' for this form of community development?" to "What new ideas, knowledge, possibilities, and understandings are emerging? What are we creating together?" (Bodiford and Camargo-Borges 2014).

Narrative inquiry is another resource for research that lifts up positive aspects of community development efforts, including community members' values, hopes, and dreams. By sharing stories between generations, communities become more richly storied or narratively resourced, providing alternative options for meaning making and social action (Bodiford 2013). Marshall Ganz (Moyers 2013), a veteran activist and organizer, reminds us of the importance of narratives for social movements: "Movements have narratives. They tell stories. They are not just about rearranging economics and politics, they also rearrange meaning. And they're not just about redistributing the goods, they are about figuring out what is good."

The following illustration in Uganda will help us learn from intergenerational efforts to create more inclusive and age-friendly communities. Youth and older persons from Uganda can be our guides, sharing narratives and what they are learning as they work to support their lives and their communities. In these communities, what both ages say they need is the opportunity and power to influence their communities using local solutions with a blend of the ages working together to bring out the potentials of each age group. Narratives of these change makers provide illustrations of the strengths that each generation can bring to create more inclusive and age-friendly communities.

Intergenerational Community Development in Uganda

Relational practice, as introduced in the chapter by Marian Barnes, underpins intergenerational community development with a recognition of our interdependence and the importance of collaborative efforts to improve people's lives in our communities. There are many intergenerational efforts worldwide that recognize the importance of bringing generations together as resources for each other and for communities. For example, Marta Benavides with the Alliance for Sustainability for Sustainable Peace and Cesar Cartagena with the Association on Neuva Vida Pro-Ninez y Juventud in El Salvador have partnered for an intergenerational and intercultural alliance with a bottom-up participatory process. Their approach works to end exclusion and invisibility and helps to build an effective civil society in which all people are included in the Sustainable Development Agenda. Pfizer and HelpAge USA have partnered to explore how intergenerational interventions can support healthy aging through the life course in rural Tanzania. In their background paper, *Policies and Programmes Supporting Intergenerational Relations*, Butts, Thang, and Hatton Yeo (2013) illustrate throughout North America, Europe, Asia, Africa, Latin America, and the Caribbean the importance of developing intergenerational cohesion and share examples of how through intergenerational solidarity we are stronger together.

At the same time, approaches in Uganda to support older persons often do not account for what youth, older persons, and their communities can do for each other. To address this gap, there are organizations such as HelpAge and Health Nest Uganda that are doing important work to develop intergenerational approaches to address the needs of older persons. However, program and geographical coverage remains low, with almost a complete dependence on external funding and support. These organizations play mainly a supportive role as they work to develop sustainable and scalable approaches that increase awareness and knowledge about issues that affect older persons. The approaches involve the families and communities of older persons in identifying their own strengths and coming up with innovations to support older persons. In these efforts, youth can play, and in fact are playing, an important role in advancing support and social justice with and for older persons, in particular more vulnerable older persons, in their communities.

As Corita Brown and Nancy Henkin state (chapter 7 in this volume), "The reciprocal ties that hold families, governance, and society together over time" build a sense of interdependence and mutual responsibility to care for each other across the generations. The example from Uganda illustrates Brown and Henkin's proposal that social cohesion and intergenerational relationships are important resources for collective action and demonstrate that youth and older persons together can raise awareness, advocate for issues people face, and develop programs and responses to create more inclusive and age-friendly communities.

Health Nest Uganda (HENU)

In Uganda, there are a high number of young people living with older persons either as the carers of the older persons or as orphans under their care. During Health Nest Uganda (HENU) home visits to assess health and well-being needs of older persons, volunteers observed that whenever they were in a discussion with older persons, younger family members tended to sit aside, listening but without contributing to the discussion. HENU decided to bring them on board through intergenerational activities. For example, HENU offered an essay competition in schools, where they asked the young people to write about topical issues in regard to the well-being of older persons within their communities. This activity created awareness and raised a sense of responsibility among the youth to contribute to solutions addressing the challenges older persons face in their daily lives. It also created inspiration among the youth. Now youth are active advocates for older persons' issues.

Youth with HENU share that when they work with older persons, they are becoming better at helping both their peers and older persons to become active agents of change by realizing their own and their community's strengths as a resource to address issues and concerns. As youth work to support older persons in their communities, they are also learning important skills, knowledge, values, and histories both from the work they are engaging in and from their elders. There is value in the passing of knowledge from one generation to another that strengthens solidarity through equity and reciprocity (Kelly, n.d.). This builds community resilience with "deeper reservoirs of trust and social connections" (Kelly, n.d.: 2) and a strengthening of social networks to address issues communities face.

In order to support older persons to be heard, HENU volunteers invite leaders to listen to the concerns of older persons in community meetings during the International Day for Older Persons celebrations. Youth also advocate for older persons as they engage local leaders in the villages to join them during home visits to learn more about the issues that older persons are facing and how older persons work to strengthen family unity and their communities. These home visits serve to increase awareness and encourage local action. For example, on one home visit, a local religious leader learned about an older person who was living in unsafe housing. The church has now constructed her a house with the help of the chairperson of the area.

During HENU home visits to listen and learn from older persons' lives, volunteers also encourage young people to work together with their grandparents to fight poverty. HENU then links and facilitates income-generating training activities in areas such as candle and soap making, mushroom growing, keeping poultry and pigs, environmentally friendly briquette making, and tailoring. These activities promote a partnership between older persons and the youth as they work as a team to fight poverty. With support, youth and older persons can be seen as job creators rather than job seekers and produce and market quality products nationally and internationally. Together older persons and youth share information, collaborate, support, and build up one another. This approach also supports young people to develop their skills, create their future, and contribute to their families and communities. Revolving fund income-generating projects present opportunities for youth and older persons to discuss and plan together on how they can liberate themselves from poverty sustainably. Revolving savings funds offer a tool to spread risk among members "drawing upon sub-Saharan African traditions of shared support and kinship networks" (National Research Council 2006).

At the age of seventy-five, Agnes Mbalire began the Bakadde Bakannya group in the Kabable/Kitubulu villages. *Bakadde Bakannya* means "Older Persons Living in Harmony." Agnes was encouraged to start this group after attending a Health Day organized by Health Nest Uganda in 2013 where older persons' psychosocial and medical concerns were addressed. The Bakadde Bakannya group helps its members in managing loneliness by coming together to share, learn, and laugh together. They also make mats, cakes, and beads and practice market gardening. The youth help them to market their products. Agnes observed the role of the youth in helping older persons attend this day and the importance of peer support among older persons themselves:

> You have to be careful with the way that you handle young people because they are not our peer group, our group is not like their group. You have to be considerate, the way they see things may not be the ways we see things. You have to understand the young people, that is the first step. If you do not understand them, you will drift apart and will not be able to make compromise. You have to work with them, because sometimes you need them. For example, they understand technology. We need each other. (Personal communication 2014)

Magala Simon Peter, a 25-year-old counselor in Entebbe, agrees that cross-generational collaboration can be achieved and is a good tool in creating harmony between the youth and older persons to put to proper use the strengths of the two generations, where youth have the energy and will and older persons have the knowledge and experience. He acknowledges, however, that low self-esteem can get in the way of the ability of youth to contribute:

> Many youth do not think they have any talent or the ability to do something meaningful. Confidence and esteem are very low and thus the youth take no

effort to use or discover their talents. I believe we should bring up our children in such a way that they feel they can be the next president instead of degrading their abilities. (Personal communication 2014)

Dr. Ndora Katuramu is involved with the older persons project in Kitubulu in which neighbors of all ages originally from Sudan, Kenya, and Uganda have come together to develop income-generating projects, including mat and basket weaving and farming. The group also has a saving scheme where members borrow small capital to start these income-generating activities. Dr. Katuramu reinforces the importance of supporting mothers and grandmothers in community projects because of their role of supporting the whole family and in particular orphans—for example, paying school fees for children.

Retired bishop Samuel Balagadde Ssekkadde is a member of the Health Nest Uganda board and advises and guides the organization on issues regarding older persons. Bishop Ssekkadde shares that "what brings hope to older persons is love." When volunteers visit with older persons, they hug, sit with them, cry with them, and bring therapeutic support. They begin to see people coming out of depression and frustration. Many of the older persons whom volunteers visit have experienced a loss of friendship and family and feel a sense of abandonment. The UN report on the status of older persons (2011: 6) notes that while many older persons who are living alone are in good health and are active, studies show that "older persons living alone are more likely than those living with a partner or in a multigenerational household to be lonely and depressed, to have small social network, and to have infrequent contact with children." The bishop's wife, Ellen Ssekkadde, points to the importance of bringing fellowship to dispel depression and loneliness. When groups of older persons organize to come together and address the issues in their community they bring support, laughter, and friendship:

> In spite of anything, despite poverty, despite hardship, you can still smile. People keep on smiling. Even if you have never met, it will feel like you have been with the person for a long time. So, it creates laughter and peace of mind. Peace and hope. It is a Godly peace where there is God and everything is possible. (Personal communication 2014)

In addition, Bishop Ssekkadde shares how stereotypes and fixed assumptions that the generations might hold about each other begin to dissolve with relationships and participation. Once people are in an ongoing relationship, they begin asking, "What can we do?" When youth volunteers visit older persons, they begin to help them with things that are challenging, like fetching water from wells and nursing the frail.

Using the EASY Care Tool, Health Nest Uganda volunteers discovered that squatting during and getting up after using a pit latrine is an infernal torture for many older persons, whose bones, joints, and muscles are no longer able to respond the way they used to. The Uganda National Policy for Older Persons (Republic of Uganda 2009) acknowledges "pit latrines are not user-friendly as older persons usually have squatting problems." Although the National Plan of Action for Older Persons (Republic of Uganda 2012) envisages "a society where older persons are living in a secure and a dignified environment that fulfills their needs and aspirations," older persons' comfort and convenience when using pit latrines have been conspicuously ignored. Squatting, even briefly, is a painful ordeal that tends to discourage and/or delay older persons from going to the pit latrine when the urge arises, consequently leading to digestive and other health complications. In addition, older persons report eating only one meal a day to minimize using the pit latrine. Older persons themselves, together with their household members, have identified the need for user-friendly toilets. Health Nest Uganda volunteers are actively working to install one hundred user-friendly pit latrines for older persons.

In 2017, Health Nest Uganda partnered with HelpAge USA to pilot an approach called Collaborating for Health, in which older people lead an effort to promote healthy and active lifestyles for themselves, their families, and their communities. These efforts focused on the growing issue of noncommunicable diseases in developing countries, as highlighted in Philip B. Stafford's introduction to this volume. This initiative works to promote healthy aging through a life course approach and employs a data-informed approach that supports people's health and well-being into older age. The process empowers individuals, families, and communities to engage in greater levels of health-seeking behavior, manage health conditions, and advocate for policies that increase access to improved health services. Collaborating for Health designs and implements health solutions *with* older people rather than for them (Access Accelerated 2018).

Older people in this project report that they feel happy they can share their experience and wisdom with younger people and lay a hand and give support. In an intergenerational community, everyone is together, the older people and the younger people. These examples of collective action address the contexts, resources, and social relations that Marian Barnes describes as being critical to support well-being as a generative concept, in which people are recognized as experts in their own lives and can work together toward common goals (see chapter 12). In addition, it recognizes the importance of sustainability, as Alan DeLaTorre presents (see chapter 4), in which development efforts to meet the needs of present generations also support the well-being and ability of future generations to meet their needs as well. As older persons work with youth in partnership, they are contributing to the development of another generation, and at the same time they are supported in the role that many older persons have of raising their grandchildren. This blurring of the generational lines leads to a sense of collective responsibility for each other, for communities, and for future generations.

Closing Reflections

The UN Principles for Older Persons (UN 1991) reinforces the importance of active participation of older persons in society and their communities:

1. Older persons should remain integrated in society, participate actively in the formulation and implementation of policies that directly affect their well-being, and share their knowledge and skills with younger generations.
2. Older persons should be able to seek and develop opportunities for service to the community and to serve as volunteers in positions appropriate to their interests and capabilities.
3. Older persons should be able to form movements or associations of older persons.

These principles support not only the participation of older persons but also their role in actively informing and implementing policies that impact their lives. This represents an important move from participation of marginalized groups of people to influence and involvement in decision-making. Older persons in Uganda want people to hear: "We exist. We matter. We want to contribute."

Youth also desire an ability to be seen as active and legitimate agents of change in their communities. The Global Partnership for Youth consulted with seventy-seven thousand youth in Africa in the Voice of Africa's Future campaign (Onyango 2014) to create the following vision for the Post-2015 Sustainable Development Agenda:

> Our vision for Africa is a self-reliant and independent Africa that prioritizes taking care of its people. An economically diverse Africa, whose economy creates equal access and equal opportunity for all. We dream of an Africa whose people are educated and are able to maximize their potential through innovation and enterprise. We envision an Africa that lives in peace and harmony—a politically stable Africa with democracy being the foundation for governance.

Without active participation and influence in all levels of the decision-making process, youth and older persons will remain at the periphery. Both generations are advocating to be heard, to be supported, and to participate in the development of their country. Engaging and mobilizing the strengths of youth and older persons is an inclusive process that works to create a society for all ages. The work of Health Nest Uganda demonstrates the important role of civil service and advocacy organizations in supporting the participation and action of youth and older persons in development and in co-creating ways to address the issues they face in their lives and communities.

Arthur Namara (Namara Arthur Araali) is a gerontologist and director of Health Nest Uganda, which works for and with older persons in Uganda. He is a member of the National Council for Older Persons, where he chairs the Research and Documentation Committee, which is responsible for documenting issues affecting older persons and to advise stakeholders. His research interests include assessment of the health system in Uganda to manage dementia, healthy aging, intergenerational linkages, and strengthening community care systems. He obtained his master's degree in gerontology from Southampton University in the United Kingdom and his bachelor of arts degree in community-based development from Nkumba University in Uganda.

Kristin Bodiford has long been involved in age-friendly and intergenerational community building and focuses on strengthening relational resources for social innovation. She is an adjunct faculty member at Dominican University School of Social Work, with an interest in research, policy, and practice related to community development and public health, intergenerational community building, trauma healing and restorative practices, and age-friendly communities. She is also a health advisor for HelpAge USA and a representative for Generations United to the NGO Committee of the United Nations Economic and Social Council (ECOSOC), focusing on family and intergenerational policy.

References

Access Accelerated. 2018. "Improving Healthy Aging through a Life Course Approach." Access Accelerated. Accessed 7 January 2018. https://accessaccelerated.org/initiative/collaborating-health-improving-healthy-aging-life-course-approach/.
African Union. 2004. *Plan of Action on the Family in Africa*. Addis Ababa: African Union.

———. 2010. *African Position on Youth Development.* Accessed 26 July 2018. http://www.un.org/en/africa/osaa/pdf/au/cap_youthdev_2010.pdf.

———. 2012. *African Common Position on the Family for the International Year of the Family.* Accessed 27 July 2018. http://www.un.org/esa/socdev/family/docs/egm12/AUCOMMONPOSITIOFAMILY.pdf.

Baryayebwa, Herbert. 2010. *Uganda Report on the Review and Appraisal of the Implementation of the Madrid International Plan of Action on Ageing.*

Bodiford, Kristin. 2013. "Intergenerational Community Building." In *Aging in Community*, ed. J. M. Blanchard and B. Anthony. Chapel Hill, NC: Second Journey.

Bodiford, Kristin, and Celiane Camargo-Borges. 2014. "Bridging Research and Practice." *Appreciative Inquiry Practitioner*, August 2014. Accessed 27 July 2018. https://aipractitioner.com/product/appreciative-inquiry-practitioner-august-2014/.

Bradbury, Hilary, and Peter Reason. 2003. "Action Research: An Opportunity for Revitalizing Research Purpose and Practices." *Qualitative Social Work* 2(2): 155–75.

Butts, Donna, Leng Leng Thang, and Alan Hatton Yeo. 2013. *Policies and Programmes Supporting Intergenerational Relations.* Accessed 27 July 2018. http://www.un.org/esa/socdev/family/docs/BP_INTERGENERATIONALSOLIDARITY.pdf.

———. 2012. "Policies and Programmes Supporting Intergenerational Relations in Family-Oriented Policies for Poverty Reduction, Work-Family Balance and Intergenerational Solidarity." In *Family-Oriented Policies for Poverty Reduction, Work-Family Balance, and Intergenerational Solidarity.* Accessed 27 July 2018. https://www.un.org/development/desa/family/2012/09/01/family-oriented-policies-for-poverty-reduction-work-family-balance-and-intergenerational-solidarity/.

Gergen, Kenneth. J. 2009. *An Invitation to Social Construction.* Los Angeles: Sage.

Health Nest Uganda, 2013. *Towards Caring Communities: Strengthening the Participation of Older Persons in Local Community Responses in Uganda.*

HelpAge International. 2008. *Older People in Africa: A Forgotten Generation.* Accessed 26 July 2018. http://www.helpage.org/download/4c48ac8a30145.

International Youth Foundation. 2011. *Navigating Challenges. Charting Hope: A Cross-Sector Situational Analysis on Youth in Uganda.* Accessed 27 July 2018. http://www.youthpolicy.org/national/Uganda_2011_Youth_Mapping_Summary.pdf.

Kelly, Peggy. n.d. *Integration and Participation of Older Persons in Development.* Accessed 27 July 2018. http://www.un.org/esa/socdev/documents/ageing/Integration_participation.pdf.

McNamee, Sheila, and Dian Marie Hosking. 2012. *Research and Social Change: A Relational Constructionist Approach.* New York: Routledge.

Ministry of Gender, Labour and Social Development, Expanding Social Protection Programme. n.d. Website. Accessed 26 July 2018. http://www.socialprotection.go.ug.

Moyers, Bill. 2013. "Marshall Ganz on Making Social Movements Matter." BillMoyers.com, 10 May 2013. Accessed 27 July 2018. http://billmoyers.com/segment/marshall-ganz-on-making-social-movements-matter.

National Research Council (U.S.) Committee on Population. 2006. *Aging in Sub-Saharan Africa: Recommendation for Furthering Research.* Edited by B. Cohen and J. Menken. Washington, DC: National Academies Press. Accessed 27 July 2018. http://www.ncbi.nlm.nih.gov/books/NBK20293/?report=classic.

NGO Committee on Ageing. n.d, *Protecting the Rights of Older People: 10 Reasons Why We Need to Act.* Accessed 27 July 2018. http://www.ngocoa-ny.org/protecting-the-rights-of/.

Onyango, Willice Okoth. 2014. High-Level Event on the "The Contributions of Women, the Young and Civil Society to the post-2015 Development Agenda." Accessed 27 July 2018. http://www.un.org/en/ga/president/68/pdf/letters/2262014TD_Women_the_Young_and_Civil_Society-26_February_2014.pdf.
Oxford Institute on Ageing. 2005. *Understanding and Responding to Ageing, Health, Poverty and Social Change in Sub-Saharan Africa: A Strategic Framework and Plan for Research.* Accessed 27 July 2018. https://www.ageing.ox.ac.uk/files/afran_oxford_conf_research_ageing_africa_final_report.pdf.
Population Reference Bureau. 2009. *2009 World Population Data Sheet.* Washington, DC: Population Reference Bureau. Accessed 27 July 2018. https://assets.prb.org/pdf09/09wpds_eng.pdf.
Powers, Cara Berg, and Erin Allaman. 2012. "How Participatory Action Research Can Promote Social Change and Help Youth Development." Accessed 27 July 2018. https://cyber.harvard.edu/sites/cyber.law.harvard.edu/files/KBWParticipatoryActionResearch2012.pdf.
Republic of Uganda. 2009. National Policy for Older Persons: Ageing with Security and Dignity. Accessed 27 July 2018. http://www.mglsd.go.ug/policies/National%20Policy%20for%20Older%20Persons.pdf.
———. 2012. The National Plan of Action for Older Persons 2012/13–2016/17. Accessed 27 July 2018. http://www.mglsd.go.ug/Plans/NATIONAL%20PLAN%20OF%20ACTION%20FOR%20OLDER%20PERSONS.pdf.
Scholten, Francien, et al. 2011. "Direct and Indirect Effects of HIV/AIDS and Anti-retroviral Treatment on the Health and Well-Being of Older People." In *Well-Being of Older People Study: A Study on Global AGEing and Adult Health (SAGE) Sub-study.* Accessed 26 July 2018. http://opa.psc.isr.umich.edu/pubs/abs/1362/.
Sidorenko, Alex. 2006. "Research Benefits for the Ageing Population Dissemination Conference for European Research Results." In *Follow-Up of the Madrid International Plan of Action on Ageing.* UN Programme on Ageing.
Ssenkabirwa, Al-Mahdi. 2012. "Rising Youth Unemployment in Uganda, a Ticking Time Bomb." *Daily Monitor,* 7 April. Accessed 27 July 2018. http://www.monitor.co.ug/SpecialReports/688342-1381200-ara4ho/index.html.
UN (United Nations). 1991. A/RES/46/91 Implementation of the International Plan of Action on Ageing and Related Activities. *UN News Center.* Accessed 27 July 2018. http://www.un.org/documents/ga/res/46/a46r091.htm.
———. 2002. *Madrid International Plan of Action on Ageing.* Department of Economic and Social Affairs (DESA)—Economic and Social Council (ECOSOC). http://www.un.org/esa/socdev/documents/ageing/MIPAA/political-declaration-en.pdf.
———. 2009. *African Youth Report 2009.* Economic Commission for Africa. Accessed 26 July 2018. https://www.uneca.org/publications/african-youth-report-2009.
———. 2011. *Current Status of the Social Situation, Well-Being, Participation in Development and Rights of Older Persons Worldwide.* Accessed 27 July 2018. http://www.un.org/esa/socdev/ageing/documents/publications/current-status-older-persons.pdf.
———. 2012. Sixty-Sixth Session: Resolution Adopted by the General Assembly on 19 December 2011 on the Report of the Third Committee Follow-up to the Second World Assembly on Ageing. Accessed 27 July 2018. http://www.un.org/en/ga/search/view_doc.asp?symbol=%20A/RES/66/127.
———. 2013a. *Intergenerational Solidarity and the Needs of Future Generations.* Re-

port of the Secretary-General. Accessed 27 July 2018. http://sustainabledevelopment.un.org/content/documents/2006future.pdf.

———. 2013b. *World Population Prospects: The 2012 Revision, Highlights and Advance Tables.* Department of Economic and Social Affairs, Population Division. Working paper no. ESA/P/WP228. Accessed 27 July 2018. https://esa.un.org/unpd/wpp/publications/Files/WPP2012_HIGHLIGHTS.pdf .

———. 2014a. 20th Anniversary of the International Year of the Family—Declaration of the Civil Society. Accessed 27 July 2018. https://www.un.org/development/desa/family/international-day-of-families/2014-3.html.

———. 2014b. Report on the fifty-second session. Accessed 26 July 2018. Commission on Social Development. https://www.un.org/development/desa/dspd/united-nations-commission-for-social-development-csocd-social-policy-and-development-division/52nd-session-of-the-commission-for-social-development.html.

———. 2015. *World Population Ageing.* Accessed 26 July 2018. http://www.un.org/en/development/desa/population/publications/pdf/ageing/WPA2015_Report.pdf.

———. 2016. *Population Facts: Sub-Saharan Africa's Growing Population of Older People.* Department of Economic and Social Affairs. Population Division. Accessed 26 July 2018. http://www.un.org/en/development/desa/population/publications/pdf/popfacts/PopFacts_2016-1.pdf.

———. 2017. 28 July 2016–27 July 2017 Agenda items 5, 6 and 18 (a) High-level political forum on sustainable development. *Progress towards the Sustainable Development Goals Report of the Secretary-General.* Department of Economic and Social Affairs. Accessed 26 July 2018. https://unstats.un.org/sdgs/files/report/2017/secretary-general-sdg-report-2017--EN.pdf.

———. n.d. "Raising Awareness: The Society for All Ages." Department of Economic and Social Affairs (DESA)—Division for Inclusive Social Development Ageing. Accessed 25 July 2018. https://www.un.org/development/desa/ageing/resources/international-year-of-older-persons-1999/operational-framework/raising-awareness-the-society-for-all-ages.html.

UNICEF, 2017. *Orphans.* Accessed 27 July 2018. https://www.unicef.org/media/media_45279.html.

Velkoff, Victoria A., and Paul R. Kowal. 2006. "Aging in Sub-Saharan Africa: The Changing Demography of the Region." In *Aging in Sub-Saharan Africa: Recommendation for Furthering Research,* ed. B. Cohen and J. A. Menken. Washington, DC: National Academies Press.

WHO (World Health Organization), 2007. *Global Age-Friendly Cities: A Guide.* Geneva: World Health Organization.

———. n.d. "Life Expectancy." WHO Global Health Observatory Data. Accessed 27 July 2018. http://www.who.int/gho/mortality_burden_disease/life_tables/situation_trends_text/en/.

Yifu Lin, J. 2012. "Youth Bulge: A Demographic Dividend or a Demographic Bomb in Developing Countries?" *Let's Talk Development,* World Bank, 5 January 2012. Accessed 27 July 2018. http://blogs.worldbank.org/developmenttalk/youth-bulge-a-demographic-dividend-or-a-demographic-bomb-in-developing-countries.

PART IV
Rural Aging

PART IV IS BASED ON the observation that the age-friendly movement need not be entirely urban in character, as is often the case. Indeed, rural areas and small towns may be the most challenging places to improve, given the problems of resources and out-migration of youth.

Zachary Benedict (chapter 10) offers an exciting model for revitalizing midwestern U.S. small towns through elder-centric design. While the "good for elders" model has some limitations, as described in chapter 7, Benedict bases his work on the insight that a major driver of community change in small cities (and elsewhere) is economic development, something that draws the attention of groups in power, perhaps more than anything else. Hence, he exhaustively describes the economic asset represented by an older population (whether wealthy or not) and explains how that asset can be transformed into economic development. His work is an explicit call for the revitalization of small-town America through the tapping of the assets of our older population. He provides multiple suggestions for changes in infrastructure, housing, education, work, and even zoning practices relating to age that can provide a cascading economic benefit to small towns and cities in the United States.

Nanami Suzuki (chapter 11) provides an international example in which economic development was also the driving force for creating an age-friendly community. She describes a wonderfully moving and inspiring revitalization of a small Japanese mountain town through the employment of native knowledge and skills. As the only "super-NORC" case study in the volume—a naturally occurring retirement community in which over 50 percent of the population is aged sixty-five-plus—the study is an important one for the age-friendly movement. Far from originating within the World Health Organization age-friendly blueprint, this community change effort was initiated through the dedication and insights of an agricultural agent sent to help the community revive native industry. He recognized that elder members of the community possessed knowledge and skills that could be invaluable, while building the appropriate kinds of supports that would actually put elders in a position to contribute. The result of the multiyear project was a remarkable, pervasive change in the quality of life for elders and all ages and the creation of Japan's first zero-net energy community as well as an elevation of status of elder adults, who gain "face." The message to age-friendly community advocates is to avoid unreflective reliance on "models" and search for whatever points of entry make sense in the local context.

10 RETROFITTING SMALL TOWNS
How Aging in Place Could Transform Rural America

Zachary Benedict

Introduction

THE LAWS AND REGULATIONS THAT define economic development within cities have had a direct impact on public health for centuries. In fact, conventional zoning policies are a direct outgrowth of a cholera outbreak London experienced during the 1850s. Prior to this, land use patterns were determined primarily by the private sector, but when a contaminated water pump began to spread the disease across the city, a local physician named John Snow published a zoning map of the outbreak. These simple diagrams highlighted the impact rapid industrialization was having on our communities.

As cities across the world dealt with the growing frequency of health epidemics (e.g., cholera, typhoid, typhus), strategic zoning requirements were developed to protect citizens' health. This was the beginning of land use zoning. In the early twentieth century, this trend inspired movements like Fredrick Law Olmsted's "City Beautiful" and Ebenezer Howard's "Garden City." These were new models for city planning that dedicated themselves to improving the quality of life for the masses. Today, a new challenge faces many cities—a challenge that again will force communities to refine development regulation to safeguard community health and well-being.

The growth of older adult populations across the world is well-known. In the United States, the number of individuals aged sixty-five and older are expected to double between 2010 and 2030 (Administration on Aging 2003). However, what many communities are less sensitive to, especially in smaller cities and towns, is how ill-equipped they are to support an aging population.

What is clear is that existing senior living environments will not be able to meet the growing needs of these populations. Currently less than 5 percent of age-qualified households reside in intentional senior care communities (e.g., continuing care retirement communities, nursing homes, assisted living apartments), leaving the balance to age in place in America's cities and towns (Schafer 1999). This is especially relevant considering that over 74 percent of households aged fifty and older currently reside in nonurban areas (AARP/Roper 2005: 50–51)—individuals living primarily in rural communities and small towns. The projected growth of these populations will force small towns to develop strategies that can incentivize the development of age-friendly communities.

These strategies begin, as Jeb Brugmann (2009: 202–3) emphasizes in his book *Welcome to the Urban Revolution: How Cities Are Changing the World*, "with the belief that progressive transformation in our cities is possible. We often perceive cities to be tethered to their problematic legacies and fixed development patterns. We tend to define them by their entrenched politics, social divisions, sunk capital investments, and gridlock. But cities are engines of self-transformation, more powerful than any established development pattern." It's a discussion that will require effective local leadership and rely heavily on a redefined approach to place making—one that again marries economic growth with community health.

The Power of Place

The impact suburban sprawl has had on community health is well-documented, producing living conditions that fall disproportionately hard on the elderly. The creation of segregated land use policies spawned development patterns that have affected multiple indicators of well-being ranging from loneliness to obesity. Yet, only recently have many *economic development* professionals fully acknowledged a correlation between the built environment and public health. It's a realization that has prioritized the social determinants of health as a meaningful metric for economic growth.

In 2008, the Knight Foundation and Gallup teamed up to launch the Soul of the Community project, which examined citizen attachment in twenty-six communities across the country by interviewing over forty-three thousand people. They sought to tease out factors that explain why certain communities have residents who are enthusiastic about where they live and have a deep sense of pride, while others are indifferent. Their research indicated that successful cities consistently prioritize communal attachment through three qualities: (1) *social offerings* (opportunities for social interaction and citizen caring); (2) *openness* (how welcoming a place is); and (3) *aesthetics* (its physical beauty and green spaces) (Knight Foundation 2008).

While traditional variables such as jobs, economics, and safety are also analyzed, the above three factors appear to routinely have more impact on one's attachment to place and community. The research indicated that the communities with the highest levels of attachment had the highest rates of gross domestic product (GDP) growth. Additionally, citizens who are engaged and give something back to their communities (be it time, money, or goodwill) have higher rates of personal well-being (Gallup 2011).

Improving place attachment not only positively enhances economic growth, it directly impacts public health. However, the perception of these qualities varies across the life span. As the measurement of social offerings, openness, and aesthetics can be made, there must be specific consideration given to understanding these elements through the lens of populations such as older adults. As our understanding of the value of engaging and age-friendly neighborhoods increases, so does the market's appreciation for their functionality (Cortright 2009).

In defining the current state of American well-being, Gallup-Healthways publishes annual *Community Well-Being Rankings* (Gallup-Healthways 2016). In it, they measure communities on five indicators:

- *Purpose:* Liking what you do each day and being motivated to achieve your goals.
- *Social:* Having supportive relationships and love in your life.
- *Financial:* Managing your economic life to reduce stress and increase security.
- *Community:* Liking where you live, feeling safe, and having pride in your community.
- *Physical:* Having good health and enough energy to get things done daily.

This analysis highlights one glaring observation—the U.S. Midwest is growing increasingly unwell. For example, in the most recent rankings of states' Well-Being Index Score, the tristate area of Ohio, Indiana, and Kentucky placed 45th, 47th, and 49th, respectively. In 2016, Fort Wayne, Indiana, placed 166th out of the 190 communities evaluated. While the city placed 58th in the "financial" rankings, it placed last (190th) within the "social" category. The well-being of even smaller midwestern cities relative to these indicators is much lower.

This capacity to foster "supportive relationships" and cultivate social well-being is a direct outcome of the methods in which these communities have been developed over time. As Joseph Coughlin, director and founder of MIT AgeLab said, "People in the United States are now living longer than prior generations, a trend that stands to continue. As a nation, we must improve upon advances in well-being, while developing new strategies to help Americans age well and thrive in later life" (Gallup-Healthways 2015).

The midwestern United States is uniquely positioned to benefit both socially and economically from the reengagement of these marginalized populations. This will require cities to reevaluate the ability of the public realm to, as Jane Jacobs stated, foster camaraderie through "a feeling for the public identity of people, a web of public respect and trust, and a resource in time of personal or neighborhood need" (Jacobs 1993: 73).

Where neighborhoods prioritize a sense of place through their ability to maximize informal contact among neighborhoods, the streets are safer, citizens are healthier, and people are happier with their surroundings (Putnam 2000). However, to develop such neighborhoods, rural communities will be forced to understand how their growing older adult population can not only be engaged in a more meaningful way, but consider it as a key resource in their continued pursuit to attract and retain intergenerational talent. It's an inconvenient truth with, as yet, no convenient solution.

The Current State of Small Towns

The well-being of midwestern towns isn't the only thing that makes these communities unique. America is home to approximately twenty-seven thousand small towns and villages, communities that support over thirty million people. These places of fewer than twenty-five thousand residents make up most of the country's "urbanized areas." While they may be remote and small, they rival highly urban areas in density. If roughly 80 percent of the population is urban, roughly 80 percent of urban areas are small towns (Daigle 2013); however, their demographics vary greatly from their metropolitan counterparts.

This becomes increasingly clear when one looks at a state like Indiana. If basic data is compiled for every city and town within the state that has a population between ten thousand and twenty-five thousand people, referred to here as "target cities,"[1] a series of notable trends emerge. Each community offers unique characteristics seldom found in other communities. Most of the cities (twenty-five out of thirty-one) are county seats, offering a centralized courthouse square surrounded by mixed-use development. All enjoy a single school district, eliminating the potential gentrification that competing districts often promote. All provide a substantially lower cost of living than the state or national averages. And, more subjectively, each community provides a unique and authentic history (e.g., Wabash Indiana, a city of ten thousand people, became the first electrically lighted city in the world on 31 March 1880), stories that can be helpful in increasing place attachment. However, there is another side to these cities.

When these communities are compared to state and national averages across basic economic indicators, it becomes clearer what challenges currently exist (see figure 10.1). They are already disproportionately old. Their levels of educational attainment are excessively low. And local jobs pay wages far less than those elsewhere. Add to this the limited access to everyday goods and services (most commonly provided through a single big-box retail chain) and the massive reduction in available health-care providers and it's easy to imagine the quality of life that awaits many older adults.

While this current condition is alarming, prevalent out-migration and diminishing municipal resources will cause these problems to only worsen if these communities do not systematically address the issues associated with their rapidly aging populations.

Between 2005 and 2040, Indiana's overall population is projected to increase by 15 percent. During that same time, the state's sixty-five and older population will grow by 90 percent, a statistic that varies according to communities' respective size. Larger metropolitan areas within the state will see a higher overall growth projection than the state, while, conversely, the growth of older adult populations in rural communities will be much larger.

To outline the immediate impact these shifting demographics will impose on small towns, special attention should be given to the current activity patterns of seniors. In a survey of Indiana residents aged sixty or older, participants indicated that they were highly engaged in social and civic activity, with over 88 percent claiming to have attended a least one social, religious, or cultural activity in the last week (Center for Home Care Policy and Research 2008). These seniors are key participants in the local econ-

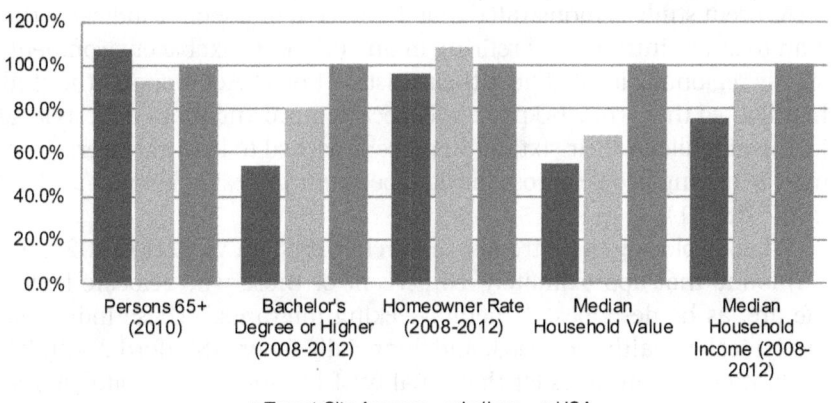

FIGURE 10.1. Indiana small-town summary (source: U.S. Census)

omy, the voter pool, and the regional transfer of wealth, providing a critical value many communities simply cannot afford to lose.

Existing as one of the few growing resources for many of these communities, this aging population could be leveraged as an invaluable resource for the future economic development of rural America. If policy and planning efforts can prioritize the needs and desires of this demographic, communities may be able to implement meaningful strategies that could not only retain an aging citizenry, but also attract migrating baby boomers searching for the ability to age in place.

If these elderly populations can be engaged in ways that fill immediate economic gaps for struggling small towns, "the result will be a windfall in American civic life" in the Midwest for years to come (Freedman 1999: 19–26).

The Changing Landscape

Baby boomers are projected to make over two hundred million residential moves between 2010 and 2020. With their preference for non-metro areas, rural and small-town population segments of persons fifty-five to seventy-five years old are projected to grow from 8.6 million to 14.2 million (Cromartie 2009). While retirement-related migration may begin long before retirement (e.g., empty nesters downsizing their homes), the tendency of this cohort is to relocate near town centers offering lower costs of living, walkability, and reduced crime (Brown and Glasgow 2010: 176–96). This preference outlines a market demand for an experience that small towns are uniquely positioned to provide.

A recent study demonstrated that 32 percent of boomers indicated they plan to or are intrigued by retiring in an "urban, walkable environment," ideally regionally located near their existing home. Additionally, the study highlighted that while 60 percent expect to move and make a lifestyle adjustment while in their sixties, 86 percent wished to live in a diverse community among people across the age spectrum (Ault, Engblom, and Fisher 2007: 48–51).

When exploring these trends, researcher William Walters (2002: 243–76) found that approximately 46 percent of those who relocate later in life are, as he describes, "amenity-seeking migrants." These individuals are typically healthy, married, and financially secure (Stafford 2009: 21), evaluating communities for their quality of life and social capital, a trend that places the concept of "senior migration" at the forefront of economic development concerns for small towns. To attract these migrants, however, communities will need to provide supportive living environments and effective marketing campaigns aimed at promoting a quality of life that can engage an active older adult audience seeking vibrant, intergenerational lifestyles.

Research has indicated a direct correlation between civic engagement and successful aging. A senior's ability to stay involved within their community shapes their perception of successful aging. As illustrated by a recent AARP survey (AARP/Roper 2005: 44), a community's ability to offer an engaged existence for seniors directly relates to their perceived quality of life. When respondents were asked to respond to macro-level questions regarding their quality of life (e.g., "I am satisfied with my life the majority of the time"), those who strongly agreed were those who claimed to have a high level of community engagement. Those who admitted to a lower level of engagement tended to be less satisfied. (see figure 10.2) This relationship will be an emerging metric in attracting and retaining active older adults.

One of the greatest hurdles preventing the elderly from "ushering in a renaissance of civic life in America," as Christopher Johnson (2003) advocates, "is that the articulation of a new vision for later life, at least at the national level, is outpacing the construction of programs and institutions needed to realize the vision." While it is critical that the built environment accommodate these populations, evolving development policies will need to prioritize the civic engagement of people of all ages and abilities if a sustainable solution to this problem is to be found.

In his book *Livable Communities for Aging Populations: Urban Design for Longevity,* Scott Ball (2012: 4) notes, "The gift of longevity very well may be the catalyst that returns America to an appreciation of the urbanism we once had and can have again. We grow more reliant on close proximities in both physical and social relationships as we advance in age." This notion of

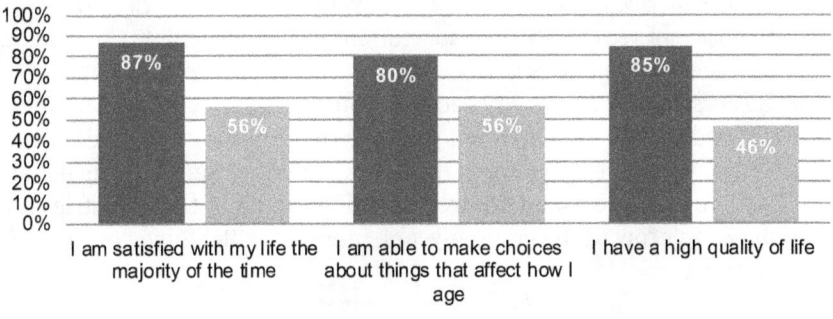

FIGURE 10.2. Correlation between successful aging and community engagement (source: AARP/Roper Public Affairs & Media Group of NOP World, *Beyond 50.05 Survey* [2004], 44)

proximity is the basic equation for effective urbanism, allowing a sense of community to exist at a smaller, more intimate scale—a scale that small-town America has perfected over the last two hundred years.

Various trends in urban planning have begun to reconsider the need and value of denser, more livable development models. From transit-oriented development (TOD) to form-based codes, urban planning policy has evolved its approach to "livability"—none perhaps more than the recent concept of "lean urbanism." Managed by the Center for Applied Transect Studies and funded by the John S. and James L. Knight Foundation, the Project for Lean Urbanism is focused on devising "tools so that community-building takes less time, reduces the resources required for compliance, and frustrates fewer well-intentioned entrepreneurs, by providing ways to work around onerous financial, bureaucratic, and regulatory processes." In a publication entitled *Lean Opportunity Resides in Small Towns* (Daigle 2013), the author outlines key elements that make small towns ripe for these new urban models. These components include the following:

- *Governance:* Small towns often offer simple and straightforward governance models. With an efficient collection of individuals responsible for regulatory issues changes can be implemented quickly.
- *Geography and physical form:* The dense street grid of many small towns provides a walkable and accessible public realm. Town centers provide a clear hierarchy of infrastructure and offer various building types for mixed-use development.
- *Building and development:* The classic Main Street mercantile buildings common in small- and medium-sized cities represent the second largest quantity of commercial building stock in the United States.
- *Economics and resources:* The cost of living and doing business in small-town America is usually much less expensive than in cities, including the price of real estate, transportation, insurance, child care, general services, and business needs.
- *Business:* Small towns embrace new businesses. Government employees and elected officials often promote their openness toward new investments and engage them on a personal level. Small towns usually have unmet needs and are well-suited for many of the industries predicted to grow in the coming years, many of which have low barriers to entry.

As small towns begin to more effectively embrace their ability to offer an inclusive neighborhood model, their ability to address these growing challenges will improve. However, in most cases, the current tools and resources are insufficient to support this needed transition. This has resulted in a growing grassroots interest in exploring innovative policies that can promote age-friendly development.

Incentivizing Age-Friendly Development Patterns

Individual definitions of what constitutes a "livable" or "lifetime" community vary. AARP/Roper (2005: 16) defines it as "one that has affordable and appropriate housing, supportive community features and services, and adequate mobility options, which together facilitate personal independence and the engagement of residents in civic and social life."

In 2007 the World Health Organization (WHO) published *Global Age-Friendly Cities: A Guide* to provide cities with tangible information to aid them in becoming "more age-friendly so as to tap the potential that older people represent for humanity." The guide provides eight categories that define a comprehensive picture of a city's age-friendliness, as illustrated in the introduction. These topics include housing, social participation, respect and social inclusion, civic participation and employment, communication and information, community support and health services, outdoor spaces and buildings, and transportation (WHO 2007).

While projects such as the Atlanta Regional Commission's Lifelong Communities initiative has introduced a broader appreciation for how larger metropolitan cities can address aging in place (Berger and Lawler 2009), more service-related strategies have also had success through programs such as naturally occurring retirement communities (NORCs) and "Village" models that focus on building active support networks for older adults (Baldwin and Willet 2014). While these tactics begin to address the underlying problem, their fundamental structure does not comprehensively address rural communities' urgent need to leverage the growing numbers of seniors to create an age-friendly economic development model. Inversely, the rural communities that fail to acknowledge this trend will continually suffer from a stagnated economic climate and disengaged citizenry, especially when coupled with the persistent growth of brain drain (Carr and Kefalas 2009: 4).

In response to this phenomenon, a new planning concept has been recently explored in Indiana to specifically incentivize development that promotes physical, social, mental, and economic well-being for persons of all abilities, across the entire life span. Coined as a "Lifetime Community District" (LCD), this planning typology is considering how existing rural downtowns can be transformed into intergenerational neighborhoods that understand and systematically prioritize all facets of wellness, utilizing these elements not as health-care strategies, but as planning principles.

Existing as a basic overlay zoning district, this LCD concept can be adopted by any local land-use regulating authority to allow certain types of development to occur within a defined geographic area. Overlay zoning may generally stipulate conditions under which specific functions or uses may be developed by right without further conditions, or they may be "plan contingent"—requiring review and approval of the specific plan and adherence to such requirements once entitlements are provided. The zoning can be enacted in an area before a specific project is identified and can be an enormous asset in attracting the targeted and specific kinds of projects desired by the community. Pattern books and other means of stipulating specific uses or building forms are encouraged to help proactively recruit the kinds of functions that would be most beneficial to the district (Ball 2012: 114–15).

The impetus for this strategy focused on exploring how requirements such as those outlined in the WHO *Global Age-Friendly Cities* guide could be used as planning principles—defining a framework that could potentially determine how local governments would incentivize private development within small towns. Under this premise, key concerns commonly found in smaller markets that make aging in place problematic were addressed by specialized recommendations and requirements. The theory is that, through this overlay zoning district, local governments could advance the practice of public/private partnerships by funneling municipal investment (e.g., tax abatements, tax increment funding) into focused development efforts that improve the community's ability to provide age-friendly neighborhoods (see table 10.1 for an example of LCD recommendations).

Within these districts, specific attention should be given to the accessibility of the defined area. Beyond the basic sensitivity to requirements outlined by the Americans with Disabilities Act (ADA), issues of proximity and way-finding must also be taken into account not merely through a disability lens, but also through an age-friendly lens. For example, conventional urban planning defines "walkable" environments by calculating a ten-minute walk shed at one-half mile (or 2,640 feet). This is unrealistic when considering the physical ability of older adults. Research supports that individuals sixty-five and older with an average life expectancy would average approximately one-third mile (or 1,574 feet) in that same ten minutes (Andrews, Bohannon, and Thomas 1996). Therefore, when an effort is made to provide urban conditions that can provide everyday goods and services (e.g., milk, produce, post office) within walking distance, the LCD would consider not only the walkability of an able-bodied teenager, but the physical limitations of older adults.

While many organizations and services are provided within existing communities to assist people of all ages and abilities, an LCD could allow

TABLE 10.1. LCD District Components and Considerations (in relation to the "age-friendly city topic areas" defined by the World Health Organization's *Global Age-Friendly Cities: A Guide*)

Age-Friendly Component	Common Issues in Rural Small Towns	Potential District Considerations
Housing	A lack of diverse housing options isolates many residents from commercial and recreational areas, while markets fail to provide affordable and accessible units for all incomes and abilities.	• Prioritize diversifying housing stock through new living models (e.g., multi-family, co-housing, accessory dwelling units, supportive housing) with access to commerce and community amenities. • Incentivize rehabilitation of owner-occupied homes to improve accessibility (e.g., universal design). • Consider visitability policy for new housing. • Ensure district provides affordable service and/or volunteer corps to assist in home maintenance.
Social Participation	Sprawling development patterns have made the occurrence of regularly scheduled events and activities difficult, resulting in a lack of regularly scheduled events and activities.	• Provide centralized civic spaces designed to host regularly scheduled events. • Support the development and management of quality "third places" within walking distance to all residents.
Respect and Social Inclusion	Existing support services for marginalized populations often segregate their consumers.	• Social services within the district agree to market themselves as inclusive municipal offering (e.g., senior center vs. Mather's Café model). • Ensure civic space provides an experience that is inclusive to district residents with physical or cognitive disabilities (e.g., signage, paving patterns).
Civic Participation and Employment	Growing isolation of older adults makes it difficult for communities to understand or access elderly talent and volunteer activity.	• Provide a virtual network that connects volunteers with people in need. • Develop co-working suites that incentivize intergenerational relationships by subsidizing older adult membership. • Encourage partnerships between senior housing providers and early childhood development (e.g., day care).

(continued)

TABLE 10.1. *continued*

Age-Friendly Component	Common Issues in Rural Small Towns	Potential District Considerations
Communication and Information	Disengagement and limited virtual capabilities make it difficult for older adults and pre-driving teens to remain engaged in the community.	• Create supportive living networks to allow local agencies and institutions to collaborate and define synergies that can be communicated to district residents. • Provide wi-fi internet access to all residents and throughout all public areas.
Community Support and Health Services	Local health-care providers are being acquired or shrinking, reducing the access to health-care services within the community.	• Provide localized health-care services within the district that can be reached by various means of transportation. • Provide a full spectrum of residential care facilities (e.g., assisted living, nursing homes) within the neighborhood. • Support home care services within the district that include health services, personal care, and housekeeping.
Outdoor Spaces and Buildings	Suburban development is favored over urban redevelopment, promoting growth that is often scattered and isolated.	• Adopt a form-based code and/or a pattern book for the district to define development patterns that encourage independence and accessibility for all ages. • Require age-friendly pavements and seating/rest areas within walkable zones. • Prioritize pedestrian access to public green spaces for all residents. • Provide adequate public toilets (especially near walkways and bicycle paths). • Provide quality public parks within a 10-minute walk of all district residents. • Provide access to fresh produce and healthy food choices within 10-minute walk of all district residents.
Transportation	The automobile is the main, and often, exclusive mode for transportation (while other transportation options, such as public transit, are limited or nonexistent).	• Develop local partnerships to provide a multimodal network and/or complete streets initiative with access to daily goods and services (e.g., sidewalks, trails, transit). • Prioritize availability of daily goods and services within 10-minute walking distance (1/3 mile) from homes and/or transit stop.

communities to consider rethinking how the successes of these programs are collectively measured. If the goal of each of these services is to empower residents to be more active members of their surrounding community (e.g., shopping, working, volunteering), these aging populations can serve as a catalyst for local economic growth. As this relationship expands, it increases the ability of these neighborhoods to attract portions of other market segments searching for the same product (Florida 2004: 232).

For the first time in modern America, the consumer behaviors of multiple generations are aligning. Baby boomers, Gen Xers, and millennials are buying the same music, watching the same movies, and migrating to the same neighborhoods. They are also prioritizing communities in very similar ways (APA 2014), and no other region is better suited to capitalize on this growing demand for an authentic urban village experience than the small towns scattered throughout the Midwest.

While the provision of supportive care and wellness-based services are paramount, the structure of LCDs are designed to be measured by their ability to impact four key indicators, all of which qualify the level of engagement of older adults:

1. *Housing:* Various innovative senior and intergenerational housing models have been realized in the last several years, creating diverse housing options within existing communities. These developments are especially successful when positioned adjacent to cultural amenities and complete streets. The locations for such housing can create mixed-income neighborhoods ripe with pedestrian activity.
2. *Commerce:* At its most basic level, an LCD's ability to attract seniors introduces an increased tax base and elevated purchase power in small towns. In doing so, intergenerational relationships can be built through mechanisms such as voucher programs to encourage seniors to support locally owned businesses (e.g., movies, pharmacy, coffee shops). Business models like Mather Lifeway's *More Than a Café* have understood the power of this relationship by disguising senior centers as trendy bistros (Rosenbaum, Sweeney, and Windhorts 2009).
3. *Workforce:* With 93 percent of U.S. labor force growth between 2009 and 2016 being produced by those age fifty-five and older (Pew Research Center 2009), it is crucial that seniors remain vital members of the local workforce. With a growing number of retired knowledge workers, programs such a co-working initiatives can be created to incentivize intergenerational relationships between an elderly workforce and emerging professionals.

4. *Volunteerism:* Increased senior populations bring a proportionately larger volunteer base. Research has indicated that seniors' willingness to donate their time and treasure is directly related to their level of attachment to the local community. Seniors that define themselves as "very attached" to their community are twice as likely to volunteer time and donate funds to local organizations than those classifying themselves as "not very attached" (AARP/Roper 2005: 35–38).

The focus of many investment subsidies is already moving toward prioritizing age-friendly development. In 2013, the Indiana Housing and Community Development Authority (IHCDA) refocused the criteria for awarding housing tax credits and has since identified housing-vulnerable populations as a primary goal in their Qualified Allocation Plan (QAP). This has forced developers pursing these credits to provide housing that supports aging in place to receive the competitive financing. With luck, this trend will grow into other development incentives at both the state and federal level.

The true intent of the LCD model is found in its goal to elevate the well-being of people of all ages and abilities. To do so, the district provides an engaging and dynamic environment that is (a) sensitive and accommodating to the needs and limitations of an increasingly frailer audience

FIGURE 10.3. Lifetime Community District concept plan, Bloomington, Indiana (source: MKM architecture + design)

while (b) providing a product that is desirable for multiple demographics (e.g., children, teenagers, empty nesters, retirees).

The goal of the district is intended not to determine a prescriptive aesthetic but to provide a framework in which various styles and development types can occur. Its focus is on the relationship between the built environment and the civic realm (see figure 10.3). By providing a built environment designed to instinctively support the engagement of older adults, the LCD structure improves the quality of life for people of all ages and abilities.

As small towns explore how these synergies can be leveraged, there should be an understanding that real progress will only come when planners, political leaders, and the general public realize that the resiliency of small towns rests in their ability to encourage generations to work together (Ghazaleh, Greenhouse, Homsy, and Warner 2011).

Conclusion

The way in which our cities and towns have regulated economic development has grown out of a desire to safeguard communities against emerging health concerns. As the understanding of health and well-being changes, so should the ability to develop new planning typologies that can nimbly react to the urgent issues surrounding a rapidly aging population.

While more research is needed in this area, further advancements in concepts such as "Lifetime Community Districts" could formalize well-being indicators as an effective ordering system for traditional neighborhood redevelopment. The goal with these efforts is grounded in the acceptance of older adults as a potential catalyst for urban renewal, viewing this demographic as a key instrument in creating and sustaining intergenerational communities within declining small towns across rural America.

As the agrarian poet Wendell Berry said, "The community—in the fullest sense: a place and all its creatures—is the smallest unit of health and that to speak of the health of an isolated individual is a contradiction in terms." The health and well-being of small towns is a collective effort, one that is reliant on context and connectivity. The resiliency of these communities in the years to come will rest on their ability to provide engaging places for people of all ages and abilities.

Zachary Benedict is a principal at MKM architecture + design (www.MKMdesign.com), focusing his career on the connection between people and places. With a background in urban sociology and neighborhood revitalization, he has lectured nationally on the benefits of inclusive social networks and quality civic spaces. In recognition of his work, the American

Institute of Architects (AIA) recognized him with the Young Architect Award. Additionally, Ball State University's College of Architecture and Planning Alumni Society recently recognized him with the Alumni Award of Outstanding Achievement. He is the youngest individual to ever receive this award. As a leading figure in the "Lifetime Community" movement, Zach publishes and speaks internationally on the importance of livable neighborhoods and inclusive design.

Note

1. The thirty-one cities explored within this research identified as "target cities" within the state of Indiana, were as follows (from largest to smallest): Crown Point, Franklin, La Porte, Logansport, Seymour, New Castle, Vincennes, Shelbyville, Huntington, Greenfield, Frankfort, Crawfordsville, Lebanon, Connersville, Beech Grove, Jasper, New Haven, Lake Station, Bedford, Warsaw, Peru, Auburn, Madison, Martinsville, Washington, Wabash, Plymouth, Greensburg, Princeton, Greencastle, and Kendallville.

References

AARP/Roper Public Affairs & Media Group of NOP World. 2005. *Beyond 50.05 Survey*. Accessed 2 September 2018. https://assets.aarp.org/rgcenter/il/beyond_50_05_survey.pdf.

Administration on Aging, U.S. Department of Health and Human Services. 2003. *A Profile of Older Americans: 2003*. Accessed 2 September 2018. https://assets.aarp.org/rgcenter/general/profile_2003.pdf.

Andrews, A. Williams, Richard W. Bohannon, and Michael Thomas. 1996. "Walking Speed: Reference Values and Correlates for Older Adults." *Journal of Orthopaedic & Sports Physical Therapy* 24(2): 86–90.

APA (American Planning Association). 2014. "Investing in Place: Two Generations' View on the Future of Communities." https://planning-org-uploaded-media.s3.amazonaws.com/legacy_resources/policy/polls/investing/pdf/pollinvestingreport.pdf.

Ault, Greg, Stephen Engblom, and Lisa Fisher. 2007. "The Urban Boom(ers)." *Multifamily Trends*, May/June.

Baldwin, Candice, and Judy Willett. 2014. "With a Little Help from Our Friends: Community-Building through Villages." *Generations—Journal of the American Society on Ageing* 37(4): 40–42.

Ball, Scott. 2012. *Livable Communities for Ageing Populations: Urban Design for Longevity*. Hoboken, NJ: Wiley.

Berger, Cathie, and Kathryn Lawler. 2009. "Lifelong Communities: Re-imagining the Atlanta Region from the Ground Up." *Generations: Journal of the American Society on Ageing* 2: 76–78.

Brown, David L., and Nina Glasgow. 2010. *Rural Retirement Migration*. Ithaca: Springer.
Brugmann, Jeb. 2009. *Welcome to the Urban Revolution: How Cities Are Changing the World*. New York: Bloomsbury.
Carr, Patrick, and Maria Kefalas. 2009. *Hollowing Out the Middle: The Rural Brain Drain and What It Means for America*. Boston: Beacon Press.
Cortright, Joe. 2009. "Walking the Walk: How Walkability Raises Home Values in U.S. Cities." *CEO for Cities*. Accessed 2 September 2018. https://nacto.org/references.cortright-joe/.
Cromartie, John. 2009. *Baby Boom Migration and Its Impact on Rural America*. United Stated Department of Agriculture. USDA: ERS Economic Research Report No. 79.
Daigle, Ann. 2013. "Lean Opportunities Resides in Small Towns." The Project for Lean Urbanism. Accessed 2 September 2018. http://leanurbanism.org/publications/lean-opportunity-resides-in-small-towns.
English, Cynthia, and Julie Ray. 2011. *Worldwide, Personal Well-Being Related to Civic Engagement*. Gallup. Accessed 2 September 2018. https://wellbeingindex.sharecare.com/wp-content/uploads/2018/02/Gallup-Sharecare-State-of-American-Well-Being_2017-State-Rankings_FINAL.pdf?t=1518473023878.
Florida, Richard. 2004. *The Rise of the Creative Class: And How It's Transforming Work, Leisure, Community, and Everyday Life*. New York: Basic Books.
Freedman, Marc. 1999. *Prime Time: How Baby Boomers Will Revolutionize Retirement and Transform America*. New York: Public Affairs.
Gallup-Healthways. 2015. *State Well-Being Rankings for Older Adults*. https://wellbeingindex.sharecare.com/wp-content/uploads/2017/12/State-Well-Being-Rankings-for-Older-Americans-2016.pdf.
———. 2016. *Community Well-Being Rankings*. Accessed 2 September 2018. https://wellbeingindex.sharecare.com/wp-content/uploads/2017/12/2016-Community-Well-Being-Rankings-2017.pdf.
Ghazaleh, Rana Abu, Esther Greenhouse, George Homsy, and Mildred Warner. 2011. "Multigenerational Planning: Using Smart Growth and Universal Design to Link the Needs of Children and the Ageing Population." American Planning Association. Accessed 2 September 2018. https://www.planning.org/publications/document/9148235/
Jacobs, Jane. 1993. *The Death and Life of Great American Cities*. New York: Random House.
Johnson, Christopher, Miriam Parcel, Mei Cobb, and David Uy. 2003. "Infrastructure of Volunteer Agencies: Capacity to Absorb Boomer Volunteers." In *Reinventing Ageing: Baby Boomers and Civic Engagement*, 91–125. Cambridge, MA: Harvard School of Public Health–MetLife Foundation Initiative on Retirement and Civic Engagement. Accessed 2 September 2018. https://assets.aarp.org/rgcenter/general/boomers_engagement.pdf
Knight Foundation. 2008. *Soul of the Community Fort Wayne, Indiana*. Accessed 2 September 2018. ttps://www.cityoffortwayne.org/knight-gallup-study.html
Oberlink, Mia. 2008. "Opportunities for Creating Livable Communities." AARP Public Policy Institute. Accessed 2 September 2018. https://www.aarp.org/home-garden/housing/info-04-2008/2008_02_communities.html.
Pew Research Center. 2009. *Recession Turns a Graying Office Grayer*. Pew Research Center, Social & Demographic Trends. Accessed 2 September 2018. http://www.pewresearch.org/2009/09/03/recession-turns-a-graying-office-grayer/

Putnam, Robert. 2000. *Bowling Alone: The Collapse and Revival of American Community.* New York: Simon and Schuster.
———. 2003. "Generations and Life Cycles in Civic Engagement and Social Capital." Harvard School of Public Health–MetLife Foundation Conference on Baby Boomers and Retirement: Impact on Civic Engagement, 8 October 2003, Cambridge, MA.
Rosenbaum, Mark S., Jillian Sweeney, and Carla Windhorts. 2009. "The Restorative Qualities of an Activity-Based, Third Place Cafe for Senior: Restoration, Social Support, and Place Attachment at Mather's More Than a Cafe." *Senior Housing & Care Journal* 17: 39–54.
Schafer, Robert. 1999. "Determinant of the Living Arrangements of the Elderly." Joint Center for Housing Studies, Harvard University, Cambridge, MA.
Stafford, Philip. 2009. *Elderburbia: Ageing with A Sense of Place in America.* Santa Barbara: ABC-CLIO, LLC.
Walters, William. 2002. "Place Characteristics and Later-Life Migration." *Research on Ageing* 24: 243–76.
WHO (World Health Organization). 2007. *Global Age-Friendly Cities: A Guide.* Geneva: World Health Organization.

11 CREATING AN AGE-FRIENDLY COMMUNITY IN A DEPOPULATED TOWN IN JAPAN
A Search for Resilient Ways to Cherish New Commons as Local Cultural Resources

Nanami Suzuki

Introduction

THIS CHAPTER[1] REFLECTS UPON THE process by which the act of care that is conscious of older adults' well-being carried out in a progressively graying depopulated town has led to the creation of living places for people from diverse cultural backgrounds and multiple generations. The setting of those activities is Kamikatsu-cho (Kamikatsu Town), nestled in the mountains of eastern Shikoku some forty kilometers southwest of the city of Tokushima.

The research on age-friendly communities, as can be seen in projects of the World Health Organization, spread from "the age-friendly cities movement," has been of particular interest from the perspective of environmental equality for every older adult (Stafford 2009a; Phillipson 2011; Scharlach and Lehning 2016; Caro and Fitzgerald 2016). In Japan, promoting research on the practice of creating age-friendly communities related to relatively small provincial towns is an urgent issue, considering the importance of the aging in place of older adults, the living in place of the younger generation, environmental protection, and preservation of the local culture.[2]

Japan has become well-known for its rapidly progressing aging and the often paired phenomenon of depopulation. Since 1994, it has witnessed the emergence of the so-called aged society, with 14–21 percent of the population aged sixty-five or older, and became classified as a "super-aged society" (21.5 percent) after the population estimation conducted in 2007. The rate of population aging was 25.1 percent and total fertility rate (the number of children that one woman gives birth to in her life) was 1.42 in 2016. Although the total fertility rate recovered to 1.4 units in 2012 in the sixteen years since 1996, declining population continues.[3]

There are frequent reports of depopulated towns or villages falling into a critical situation, with the local community, public service, and social infrastructure no longer functioning and the natural environment being destroyed. Since the beginning of 1990s, this situation has been such a concern that areas with more than 50 percent of the population aged sixty-five or older have been called *Genkai Shuraku* (region in limit situation) (Ono 2005), expressing worries especially for isolated older adults. These days, graying and aging in "new towns" developed on a wide scale after the 1960s are also a concern, as they are in the United States (Stafford 2009b).

In an effort to halt depopulation and isolation of older adults, researchers of economics and demography have insisted on the importance of promoting primary industries in regions experiencing depopulation (Matsutani and Fujimasa 2002: 94–99, 161–166). This is because in Japan the ability to continue work and other roles is a significant factor contributing to the well-being of the older adult. According to one international comparative study on the traits of those aged sixty and older in five countries including Germany, Korea, Thailand, and the United States, older adults in Japan have a greater tendency to attach importance to having a paid job and to getting along well with their neighbors (Maeda 2006; Yuzawa 2003: 176). In the history of Japan, older adults have had important roles working in the community, such as tending pineland as commons that protect people from strong winds and give people fuel, and caring for and educating children (Miyata et al. 2000: 22–23; Miyamoto 1984: 33–43). Aging and depopulation may deprive both older adult and younger generations of the opportunity of cultivating intergenerational relations (Thang 2001; Matsumoto 2011) and going through life as a whole.

Kamikatsu-cho, located on the island of Shikoku, is an example of an area that has suffered from progressive aging and depopulation. Several prior studies reported the reconstruction of regions as carried out by both local governments and a semipublic joint venture (defined as a category of the third sector in Japan). Honma (2007) and Oe (2008) referred to Kamikatsu in their comparative studies on successful cases in promoting primary industries in various depopulated municipalities, focusing on the government's designation of special districts in structural reform. These reforms were an attempt to avoid restrictions in certain fields and to stimulate the administration of local districts. Oe has termed these attempts as "welfare promoted by industry" (Honma 2007: 70–71; Oe 2008: 69; Suzuki 2009: 6–8). One of the leaders of the semipublic joint venture of Kamikatsu has reported on his efforts toward cultivating new products as an agricultural instructor and on the importance of having jobs for the well-being of older adults (Yokoishi 2007, 2009). The former mayor of Kamikatsu has also reported on a recycling system developed in the town (Kasamatsu and Sato 2008).

This chapter, based on ethnographic fieldwork and interviews I conducted starting in 2005, literature reviews, and exchange of letters, examines how a depopulated town can be revived by promoting a new business through indigenous products[4] and how the venture has escalated not only to promote well-being for older adults, but also allowing for more new ideas to surface by younger people. I shed light on how technologies and the ways of supporting the older adult's activities have affected the lifestyle of the younger generation and the town itself by examining the process of developing technologies and working out plans toward the creation of new events and activities. I also explore how older adults in particular came to expand their system of mutual aid with the cooperation of people outside of their town, sharing leisure time in addition to work by creating various new commons in town that are different from common land called *Iriaichi* that only qualified personnel can use.[5] Finally, I will discuss the challenges of townspeople's sharing values in cultural resources (cultural capital) in the days of changing lifestyle in town from the viewpoint of sustainable development of the town.

Development of a New Industry

Crises and Changes of Kamikatsu Town

Kamikatsu is situated upstream of the Katsuragawa River in the central region of Tokushima Prefecture of eastern Shikoku. The town is dominated by a range of mountains higher than 1,000 meters above sea level. Low-lying lands under 200 meters compose only 4 percent (4.2 square kilometers), and lands 200–500 meters are 28 percent; thus two-thirds of the town is nestled in the upland region. Some fifty-five settlements are scattered in the mountain slopes of the *V*-shaped valley, around 100–700 meters. Forest area reaches 86.1 percent of the town. Sixty-eight percent (73.96 square kilometers) of agricultural land is located over 500 meters and can be seen up to 600 meters (Kamikatsu-cho 1979: 3–8).

In 2014, the population of the town was 1,823, the number of households was 854, and the percentage of the town's population aged sixty-five or older was 50.3 percent, according to the national census. In the years between 1915 and the World War II, the number of households increased, but the overall population decreased. The population peaked at 6,356 in 1950, when returned servicemen and dislocated workers came back to the town. After 1955, the population began to decrease, and after 1960, it fell fast due to drastic out-migration to the three major metropolitan areas as well as to such cities in Tokushima prefecture as Tokushima, Komatsushima, Anan, and Katsuura (Kamikatsu-cho 1979: 23–26, 1216). Kamikatsu thus has been regarded as a *Genkai Shuraku* in critical condition.

After Japan's period of rapid economic growth, in the 1970s and 1980s, the sales of the main products of the town—timber and tangerines—were on the decrease, with an increase in imported products and products from other parts of Japan. Even worse, in February 1981, the tangerine orchards were completely destroyed by a cold wave (Suzuki 2009: 4). Trees of the special indigenous varieties of aromatic, sour citrus fruits—such as *yuko* and *sudachi*—were also on the verge of dying. An agricultural instructor, Mr. Yokoishi, was transferred from Tokushima to help develop new crops suitable to the chill of high ground. Various other crops such as scallion, nozawana and shiitake mushroom, were planted experimentally, but people's livelihoods barely improved (Yokoishi 2007: 36–43). Having lost hope, many of the local residents became depressed or even turned to alcohol. Deprived of the opportunity to cooperate in farming and seasonal festivals they were happy with in the past, people lapsed into saying nasty things about others at *Idobata Kaigi* (gossip meetings).[6] It thus became an urgent task to revitalize not only the town's economy, but its spirit as well.

Discoveries of the Resources of a Town: The Potential of Older Adults and Decorative Leaf Production

The town's residents tried to create a new industry suitable to the town. Mr. Yokoishi, the agricultural instructor brought to Kamikatsu, got the idea of picking seasonal leaves of various colors and shapes and providing them to Japanese restaurants and stores preparing fancy lunch boxes. Once, when he had supper alone at a Japanese restaurant after finishing his work in Osaka, he saw three women enjoying dishes garnished with seasonal leaves. At that moment, he realized that people highly regarded food served in a way that was pleasant to the eye (Yokoishi 2007: 51; Suzuki 2009: 4). Indeed, leaves are often placed upon *kaiseki* and other types of Japanese cuisine as a garnish, with the cooks normally obtaining the leaves themselves in the vicinity. The work of picking the mountain leaves was perfect for the older adult of Kamikatsu, who were quite familiar with local vegetation. Moreover, the work did not require much physical energy.

The next step was to find actors fit for this enterprise. Older men, who were mostly farmers and retirees from the local forestry and mandarin orange industries, were generally not interested, as they didn't consider going to the mountainside and gathering boxes of leaves as being "real work." However, older women, who were mostly housewives and had more free time as their children had left home, were more enthusiastic about the scheme, and so Yokoishi was able to convince several women from farming households to participate.

After launching the enterprise properly, the town entered into a semi-public joint venture with an agricultural cooperative association and began to tackle this industry on a full scale. Indigenous leaves and branches of plants growing in the village, including the leaves of persimmon and maple trees, nandina, giant elephant ear (a kind of taro), camellia plants, and bamboo grass, along with azalea flowers and the flowers of plum, cherry, and peach trees, became commercial products as food decorations.

The industry was successful beyond everyone's expectations. By 2005, nineteen years after the beginning of the venture, around three hundred kinds of leaves were being shipped from Kamikatsu, representing more than 80 percent of the sales of such products at the Osaka Central Wholesale Market. Annual revenue from sales was exceeding 250 million yen (around 2.45 million USD). City-dwelling customers now enjoy dishes decorated with beautiful leaves and willingly pay for them as well. More than 150 households (around 20 percent of all households) in the town were participating in the production of the leaves in 2005, with the average age of those engaged in the collecting, washing, and packing the leaves being at around sixty-eight. The average monthly wage of the workers was 200,000 to 300,000 yen (around 1,960–2,950 USD). Some of the elderly, especially women, got jobs and started to pay tax. The industry created in Kamikatsu demonstrates how older adults can be utilized to successfully produce a top-selling product.

Exploitation of Technologies to Increase Accessibility

While the work of the older adult may seem outwardly simple, it is in fact hardly simple at all. It is not enough for them just to pick some leaves here and there—the harvest must be planned and designed in a way that meets market needs, with the leaves being sent to the market at an appropriate time. In order that the older adults, particularly older women, who are collecting the product are able to adequately supply the product to the agricultural cooperatives that transport the leaves to the wholesale market in Osaka, various forms of support have been developed by younger employees, mainly working in the third sector that has been created in the town. The special efforts made to bring out the older adults' abilities in Kamikatsu can be broadly categorized into three types.

Divert Use of Wireless Telegraph for Equal Information Dissemination

First, the third-sector leaders made use of the existing system of wireless telegraph for dealing with disasters, as well as fax machines, for sending information about what kind of leaves were needed to all registrants at a time (Suzuki 2009: 5). For people living and working in scattered mountain areas, the simultaneous-broadcast wireless system has been utilized to inform townspeople of emergencies and other important matters. This time, a new system was organized by which the disaster fax service could be used to send out information to the leaf producers, forming a network that allowed everyone to quickly acquire information such as requests for shipments, etc. That way, information about seasonal leaves in demand, including the copy of leaf samples that help the producers easily adjust the form of a leaf, a color, or a size to a standard, is sent swiftly and simultaneously to all the farm households registered as leaf producers.

Producers who judged that they could supply sufficient leaves of the kind within a set period would then enter into a contract with the sector by making a phone call. After that, they take the packed leaves to the agricultural cooperative by the specified deadline. Only if a bid is placed does the order get finalized, however, so the old people of Kamikatsu always keep close tabs on the condition of the leaves growing on their mountains as they patiently wait for a fax to come in, acting very quickly until their phone call to make their bid goes through. Once, when I was interviewing one of the local women, she got a fax with an order request, whereupon she quickly dropped everything else to concentrate on the mountain leaves.

A Computer System for Older Adults to Communicate toward Decorative Leaf Production

Second, a user-friendly computer system especially designed for older people has been developed. It is extremely important for the leaf gatherers to get timely market information. Following consultations about the optimum hardware and software that should be provided for older people who may be using a computer for the first time, an easy-to-handle trackball, with the ball moved by the entire palm, was devised for older users who were unaccustomed to clicking a mouse. Training in the use of all of the new technological systems was conducted on a face-to-face basis, not just by simply distributing manuals. Training continued until users completely understood how to operate the systems.

What especially makes the leaf producers excited is getting constantly updated information about their own sales totals and sales rankings, as well as which kinds of leaves are hot sellers. With color-coded bar graphs depicting shipment targets and current shipment status, the leaf producers can instantly decide whether to ship seasonal items or those in constantly high demand. Every day, older adults lift up the protective cloth covers over their computer screens and pay rapt attention to them.

Another method developed to share information was Mr. Yokoishi's handwritten newsletter reminiscent of the bulletins used to exchange information at elementary school. The paper includes detailed information about leaves and is chock-full of stories about minor events in the town. Each issue, too, is distributed by fax. The townspeople are often highlighted in the newspaper, and they look forward to reading about each other's activities there (Suzuki 2013: 11).

Transportation of Older Adults by Paid Volunteer Taxies

Third, a new transportation for older adults has been prepared by taxi services given by paid volunteers. Manufactured leaves have to be supplied to an agricultural cooperative association by the fixed time. In a town without a public transportation facility except for a trunk road, reservation of transportation that older adults can easily use was a pressing need.

Kamikatsu applied to the government to develop the original system of helping aged and disabled people to move around town with volunteer-run, fare-charging taxis. The Project in Special District of Transportation with Fare-Charging Volunteers was approved through the government's policy of Special Districts in Structural Reform in May 2003 (Suzuki 2009: 5). This policy was efficient because residents devised an idea that is suitable to the region in which they live. Thanks to the system, older adults who cannot or do not drive are now able to ask someone else to transport them without hesitation.

The volunteer taxi service that was organized to help the work of the older adult can be provided by anyone who can drive, but necessary conditions for the drivers are living close to their customers and being familiar with narrow winding roads of the local mountainous areas. Thanks to the introduction of the small taxi system, both older adult and younger people have expanded their opportunity to talk with members in the vicinity. The small changes have led to an increase in the number of conversations, bringing about a sense of greater vitality to the town.

Changes in Older Adults' Lives

The way of life of the older residents, especially older women of Kamikatsu has changed significantly thanks to the new industry. Thanks to the stable income they earned through the "easy and clean work," they were able to enhance their lifestyles and build a sense of hope in the future. With their extra money, the first thing they did was to increase their avenues for amusement. Mrs. A said that although it seemed a small pleasure, she was relaxed and happy to have a cup of beer with her husband at suppertime after work. Her husband had been engaged in *sumiyaki* (charcoal making), but he had never got enough money from his hard work. Now they cooperate in collecting, coordinating, and shipping leaves. They feel so happy to have something to work for together and to talk and smile about. They even hope that their son's family will come back to the town and inherit their work.

In the case of older women, especially—those who had married into farmers' families or who had been housewives—a whole new life began, one in which they had income to spend freely for the first time.[7] Mrs. B, who was eighty-four years old in 2005, evenly split the income she made from collecting leaves with her daughter-in-law, who was helping her in her work. Although Mrs. B lost her husband a long time ago and lived with her son's family, she was proud of paying expenses when her family gathered for enjoyment or when her grandchildren living in a city bought a house.

The second thing the old people of Kamikatsu did with their extra money was to use it to invest in the future. Examples of that include people who have planted new trees with an eye to the kinds of leaves that are in high demand. Mrs. B, who has the nickname of "Ace," has been participating in this work from the very beginning of the project and has continued to plant new persimmon trees in anticipation of future harvests. While it takes some three years from the time a tree is planted until it can be harvested for its leaves, she says that she looks forward to it (Suzuki 2013: 12).

From the viewpoint of the investment, it is a new experience for the work colleagues to make bus trips to Kyoto for the purpose of study tours, not only for the sightseeing. On the tours, they can enjoy going to restaurants that buy their leaves to see how they are actually prepared and to taste dishes with the leaves in them. It provides a good opportunity for them to spark new ideas together.

The leaves have gone beyond merely being things that are "plucked" to things that are "made." The relation between such factors as sunlight and altitude with the color of leaves can only be predicted by those who have a lot of experience. What was formerly seen as the town's weak point—its unsuitability for planting crops because of the scarcity of flat land—is instead now recognized as its strong point, namely, the ability to get leaves of all sorts of colors. The whole town is now viewed as "shelves in a store," with the people totally absorbed in the task of caring for the nature of the forest.

The third change that came about was the increased number of opportunities for individuals in the community to "exist with visible faces." Many of the women, particularly, told me that for the first time they felt that they existed with a "visible face." Thanks to the information they get sent to them over the network, they can keep track of what their colleagues in the business are doing and learn about the market, even while they remain at home (Suzuki 2013: 12–13). Mrs. C is happy to do her work with her son, thanks to the growing accessibility of work. After being ill, her son is not strong enough for working outside, but he can drive to bring leaves for his parents.

The opportunity for people to meet others face-to-face has also expanded, because they have common topics of conversation. The townspeople use the renovated inn run by Kamikatsu for the purpose of exchanging new ideas. Those ideas will come in handy for an ongoing new project to energize the town (Suzuki 2009: 6).

New Projects toward Aging in Place of Every Generation

The changes in the lifestyle of the older adult in Kamikatsu led to changes in the atmosphere of the whole town, including the lifestyle of other generations and the way people interacted. Beginning in 1995, the town has been divided into five districts, each with six representatives (two of whom are women), serving on a thirty-member committee that makes proposals in relation to the town, including its environment. According to Mr. Yokoishi, the aim of the committee is to *Ki wo Sodateru* (foster the spirits) of the residents.

Transition to a "Clean Town" by the Efforts of Recycling

One stage for fostering spirits was the recycling center set up to support the town's economy and ecology. Since the town did not have an original garbage dump, garbage processing was an important subject of discussion. The townsfolk did not want to use tax money either to buy an incinerator or to ask another town to dispose of their waste materials. Searching for the good way to recycle, they solicited, over the internet, someone who could help them develop a feasible system of recycling for the town. They received an application from a young woman who had learned many ways of recycling in Denmark. She has lived in Kamikatsu since the summer of 2004 and has taken leadership as director of an NPO (nonprofit organization) called the Zero Waste Academy (Suzuki 2009: 8).

Recycling begins with carefully classifying waste. The newly hired recycling expert and the townsfolk developed a system to separate rubbish according to categories. The townsfolk have come to separate their rubbish into thirty or more groups at the center, with a clear explanation given of how the rubbish is to be recycled. The recycling center also resembles a small museum where children can learn about recycling. People now enjoy more opportunities than ever before to converse by consulting other older adults on the center's staff. A volunteer group that helps older adults with carrying their garbage was also formed. The rate of recycling in Kamikatsu is 80 percent, compared to just 19 percent overall in Japan (Kasamatsu and Sato 2008: 107).

The Zero Waste Academy publishes a journal called *Kurukuru*, a Japanese word describing a circular motion, to introduce its "eco-life," giving information to the townsfolk about how to make small articles from waste materials. Kamikatsu has been known for its efforts to recycle garbage to become a "clean town," which will enhance its image of growing "beautiful leaves" (Suzuki 2009: 8).

The recycling center has even become a kind of "new commons" where various activities are conducted. A meeting place called *Hidamari* (meaning a "cozy place in the sun") has been set up next to the center. The space is being utilized as a place for people to bring items they no longer need for recycling. Both the elderly and the young often use also the area during their free time to share their expertise in making new things, such as new shirts, bags, and hats out of material recycled at the center, as well as *koinobori* carp streamers. The latter, in particular, allows older people to pass on the technique of sewing old cloth such as *tafu* (which is made from the bark of the region during the winter).

A New Store for the Town

Another amenity that has been established for people has been the local grocery store, Ikkyu-jaya, which has served as the site for increased interaction and cooperation between young people coming from out of town and the town's older adults and housewives.[8]

Since 2000, young salesmen and saleswomen have been dispatched to Kamikatsu for a year at a time by an NPO in Tokyo. They select and sell the foods considered to be interesting from a stranger's viewpoint. In cooperation with the housewives, they sell a small amount of vegetables, homemade side dishes, the seasoning made from citrus fruits, and the traditional rice-cake sweets that are characteristic of the region. Some producers enjoy also providing information about the region, the source of ingredients, and recipes for eating edible wild plants that city dwellers might be happy to learn (Suzuki 2009: 8). On the second floor of the shop, both tourists and townspeople often enjoy healthy meals using local food at lunchtime as well.

Activities of the Younger Generation and a New Movement in the Town

Most people in Kamikatsu welcome returnees (u-turn people) and newcomers (i-turn people). For older adults and townspeople of Kamikatsu, various new plans have sparked a sense of discovery about new ways to use their leisure time, and that has led to the discovery of new jobs and activities for young people as well. Some young people, after a temporary stay, decided to continue to live in Kamikatsu.

Since 2005, a working-holiday scheme has been instituted in the town, with over one hundred persons participating by staying in farmers' homes. Since 2000, each year, one young person is sent from an NPO in Tokyo to work as a clerk at Ikkyu-jaya as a relocated person from the outside. The town pays for part of their living expenses, also supporting their lifestyle by providing low-rent apartments in a wooden building. That also provides a use for local timber, one of the resources in the town, which has promoted forestry. Ms. D, one young woman, chose to keep living in the town because people often talk to her and she can talk about various topics with them, unlike her experience in Tokyo (Suzuki 2009: 8). Young people have plenty of opportunity to try their ideas together with residents. By expressing their viewpoint as a "stranger," young people can gain a valuable place as a member of the town.

There are also those who apply experiences obtained in the town in new places. The woman who took charge of maintenance of a recycling center offers her experience now in another location near Tokyo. Thus, the experience cultivated and accumulated in Kamikatsu has been shared and utilized by people of other areas with similar challenges of aging and depopulation. People who have worked in town would share the same subject with and feel sympathy with people in other areas in Japan.

Although newcomers increased, the total population of Kamikatsu did not grow significantly. Older people have died, and some students have moved out of the town to go to school. However, the circulation of residents gives the town a chance for new conversations and ideas to grow. Thus, townspeople have made efforts to share resources with people living outside of the town as a means of offering urban dwellers the chance to visit a *tanada*, or "terraced field," in the town. Summer outdoor concerts have been held for the townsfolk and visitors at the *tanada*, now famous throughout Japan for its beautiful scenery (Suzuki 2009: 9). In former times, rice planting was conducted with the cooperation of community members of a settlement, and a rice-planting festival was held. Nowadays, *tanada* has been tended through the cooperation of townspeople and outsiders.

In order to realize their vision for the town, old and new residents alike are trying to find out how the factors once considered the disadvantages of a depopulated town have turned into advantages more recently. However, they do not have a vision of making Kamikatsu a "big town" or a tourist spot. The idea of maintaining and employing a town efficiently came to be shared by people through developing techniques and technologies of communication and sharing the town with newcomers. This involves the superimposition of each generation's life cycle as the culture of the district is being spun forth.

Conclusion

Kamikatsu was a depopulated town that aimed to promote an industry that took advantage of the region's special features and the practical knowledge of the older residents. Their innovations enabled the accessibility of work, which not only allowed older adults to participate, but also changed the lifestyle of the community, including other generations. The numerous innovations aimed at the district's revitalization created a new range of activities, in turn increasing the number of opportunities for everyone to better communicate with each other.

The older adults' feelings of happiness and sense of well-being were due not only to the money they earned, but also to social and cultural factors such as their place in their family and community having improved. This was because they no longer felt stereotyped as "objects of assistance," as their participation in a productive activity created the sense of being a full member of the district's community with a "visible face" and that being cared for is an important part of allowing them to continue with their work.

All the technologies have been learned through face-to-face communication until the users understood after much trial and error, not by simply distributing manuals. Such normalization processes have only taken shape by listening to wishes of each older adult as well as by looking into the environments where they have been leading their lives. This kind of effort is indispensable toward cultivating "a society without handicaps" (Suzuki ed. 2012: 1), a place where people are able to live performing what they would wish without feeling barriers.

The purpose of developing and applying technologies is not to make people live independently, but rather to get access to ideas of how to care for the town in which people of various positions would want to live and developing a more holistic system of care. For the people in the town, the act of building a relationship of interdependence—namely, depending on each other and helping each other out—for the purpose of letting others advance in their chosen field and accomplishing what they want done, leads to mutual recognition and the ability of each person to secure his or her niche in life.

In the past, mutual aid was practiced mostly within the family and among community members in a settlement to accomplish work such as rice planting, forestry, and roofing and to prepare the festival following harvesting, while taking advantage of common ground called *Iriaichi* that only qualified personnel could use.

At present, a greater variety of mutual cooperation is conducted by a diversified group of people by creating a new type of commons open to everyone. The new store selling locally produced goods served as a physical entrance or "channel" through which new young residents and tourists were attracted to the town. The recycling center has become multifunctional in nature and is now a place for people to both relax and socialize. Those "new commons," either publicly run by the town, such as the meeting hall and the recycling center, or commercial shops and restaurants, have two important features—they build upon a relationship to local cultural resources such as using organic vegetables of the region, and anyone can access the information needed to participate.

The residents of Kamikatsu noticed that it was not only economics or governmental administration that gave people power to think about what they value in their everyday lives and in the future, but also the time they had for pleasure and regeneration, often on occasions of new types of events shared with various people. Producing local foods and newly invented handicrafts by making use of the resources of the area, townspeople now enjoy communicating with visitors and have discovered the meaning of sharing leisure time to continuously develop ideas and reconsider their values. This promotes the resilience and flexibility of the community and the well-being of people living in as well as visiting the district.

Finally, the following two challenges must be faced in relation to the future of the town in order to transform it into a resilient place having various commons. The first is the challenge of secession of land ownership (sell or lease). It is still difficult for the residents of the town to decide to sell or even lend their land to those who wish to settle in the town as permanent residents even though they have been happy to hire young people from outside. Since the farmers are not sure if they could sell the land that their ancestors took care of to people other than family members, they sometimes leave their land as a *yūkyūnōchi*, farmland that becomes rough because it has not been well plowed. In rural Japan, people have often been buried in the corner of their own land, and this seems to make it more difficult for them to sell or lend their land to others. Thus, cultural resources that residents of the town have long cultivated might discourage them from change. In order to garner more resilience to share resources with others, discussion among the people involved in town and developing a way to save the current situation and people's memories in a form that can be referenced at any time will be essential.

The second challenge is that of sustaining valued family patterns of support. A change in lifestyle is seen in the homes where younger family members have inherited the new industry. A growing number of people in their eighties and nineties who had once been actively involved in the work for such industry have opted to enjoy their retirement in newly built assisted-living residences or nursing homes in town rather than being taken care of at home. They enjoy talking with their son and daughter-in-law after their work on a common topic that all of them are familiar with almost every evening, yet the former pattern of co-residence is lost. Instead of being unilaterally given nursing care by their son and daughter-in-law, they still cooperate with the younger generation by creating good ideas.

Developing resilience has enhanced accessibility and communication for people to participate in generating ideas to care for the place they live in as well as in regenerating themselves through the development of cultural capital and new forms of commons.

Acknowledgments

I would like to thank Dr. Philip B. Stafford of Indiana University for his conceptual and editorial assistance. Phil's valuable comments, which I considered repeatedly, gave me important new insights based on my fieldwork experience. I wish to express my deep appreciation to Mr. Tomoji Yokoishi for providing stimulating source materials through his lectures and interviews about the town's resources and the way the town's industry was promoted by enlisting the strength of older adults in Kamikatsu Town. I would also like to thank the decorative leaf producers as well as the younger generation, who gave me information about their work, discoveries related to new commons, and the ways in which they changed their lives.

This article publicizes research achievements of projects promoted by the Grant-in-Aid for Scientific Research (representative: Nanami Suzuki) in

Japan: International Collaborative Research Project: Ideas and Practices for Creating "Age-Friendly Communities" (July 2014–March 2017 JSPS KAKENHI Grant Number 26310109, in the domain of a special field research: "Neo Gerontology"); Historical Anthropology of the Creation of Multifunctional Spaces for Welfare and Education in Multicultural Aging Societies (April 2009–March 2012 JSPS KAKENHI [B] Grant Number 21320166).

Nanami Suzuki is professor of anthropology at the National Museum of Ethnology (NME) in Osaka, National Institutes for the Humanities, and professor of the Graduate University for Advanced Studies. She was interested in people's communal and healing activities for the life cycle by extending relationships with humans and the universe in changing societies and wrote *Historical Anthropology of Childbirth* (Shinyosha, 1997) and *Historical Anthropology of Healing* (Sekai Shisosha, 2002); received the Aoyama Nao award for women's history in 1998 for *Historical Anthropology of Childbirth*; and edited *Healing Alternatives* (SER120, NME, 2012), focusing on alternative medical movements in the United States in the nineteenth century. She proceeded to look into various communications to support the well-being of multi-generations in super-aged societies and edited *The Anthropology of Aging and Well-Being: Searching for the Space and Time to Cultivate Life Together* (SES80, NME, 2013), *The Anthropology of Care and Education for Life: Searching for Resilient Communities in Multicultural Aging Societies* (SES87, NME, 2014), and *Aging-Friendly Communities in Super Aged Societies: Exploring Diverse Options for Aging in Place* (NME, 2018), which includes Dr. Phil Stafford's keynote lecture "The Missing Ingredient in the Age-Friendly Community Movement: Aging with a Sense of Place" given at the international symposium Exploring Age-Friendly Communities: Diverse People Aging in Place held at NME on 25 February 2017 based on the research supported by JSPS Kakenhi JP26310109: International Collaborative Research Project: Ideas and Practices for Creating "Age-Friendly Communities" 2014–2016 (representative: Nanami Suzuki).

Notes

1. This essay is a revised version, slightly modified from *Aging and Anthropology Quarterly* (*Aging and Anthropology* since 2014) 33, no. 3 (2012): 87–96, copyright, 2012 (Suzuki 2012), with permission from the Association for Anthropology and Gerontology, with added information on changing aspects of the town based on my interviews and participant observation conducted in March 2014 after I presented the paper above in 2012. Regarding the findings of fieldworks I conducted from 2005 to 2013, I also refer to certain writings in my essay (Suzuki 2009, 2013), as indicated.

2. In fact, in Japan, the concept of an age-friendly community is currently beginning to attract attention from the viewpoint of reconsideration of the improved well-being of all generations by making the most of the potential of older adults as well as the younger generation related to a region when considering the challenges of disaster areas and rural depopulated areas.
3. The childbearing age of women is on an upward trend, and the average age of the mother at the time of first birth was 30.1 years in 2012, topping 30 years for the first time ever in Japan.
4. In previous research, I examined the process by which older adults in Kamikatsu have been able to continue making use of their abilities and their local material resources, culminating in the promotion of a new industry (Suzuki 2005, 2009).
5. The word "commons" has been used to mean land called *Iriaichi* that only specified people could use, especially for farming work, throughout Japan's history. The research on commons in Japan have mostly paid attention to sustainable use and control of local resources in the field of environmental management. However, in recent years, based on research on commons in North America (Ostrom et al. 2002), more discussion has been conducted regarding the share of resources and the aspect of "open space" that is accessible to everyone living there (Mamiya and Hirokawa 2013: i–ii; Koiso et al. 2014: 8). Especially after such a disaster as the Great East Japan Earthquake, the term "commons" is considered a key to making use of limited resources through cherishing trust relationships among people.
6. *Ido* means "well." "At *idobata*" is translated as "at the well."
7. A chapter in Coleman (2015) focuses on the experiences of an older woman working for decorative leaf production.
8. *Chaya* or *jaya* is a place for rest and to have food. It has been common from the Middle Ages through the modern period. People who traveled on foot had a break at *chaya* at mountain paths or near posting stations, enjoying sweets and tea. Nowadays, *chaya* is often found in tourist destinations, popular among people who enjoy local food and a pleasant time in a nostalgic atmosphere.

References

Caro, Francis G., and Kelly G. Fitzgerald. 2016. *International Perspectives on Age-Friendly Cities*. New York: Routledge.
Coleman, Joseph. 2015. *Unfinished Work: The Struggle to Build an Aging American Workforce*. New York: Oxford University Press.
Honma, Yoshito. 2007. *Chīki saisei no jōken* [The requirements for regenerating a regional community]. Tokyo: Iwanami Shoten.
Kamikatsu-cho. 1979. *Kamikatsu-cho shi* [A history of Kamikatsu Town]. Tokushima: Kamikatsu-cho shi Henshu Iinkai.
Kasamatsu, Kazuichi, and Yumi Sato. 2008. *Jizoku kanō na machi wa chiisaku utsukushii* [Sustainable town is small and beautiful]. Kyoto: Gakugei Shuppansha.
Koiso, Shuji, Takeshi Kusakari, and Manami Sekiguchi. 2014. *Commons: Chīki no saisei to sōzō, Kita kara no kyōsei no shisō* [Commons: Towards the reconstruction and creation of a region: Thoughts of coexistence from the north]. Sapporo: Hokkaido University Press.

Maeda, Nobuhiko. 2006. *Active aging no shakaigaku* [Sociology of active aging]. Kyoto: Minerva Shobo.
Mamiya, Yosuke, and Yuji Hirokawa, eds. 2013. *Commons to kōkyō kūkan* [Commons and public space]. Kyoto: Showado.
Matsumoto, Yoshiko, ed. 2011. *Faces of Aging: The Lived Experiences of the Elderly in Japan*. Palo Alto, CA: Stanford University Press.
Matsutani, Akihiko, and Iwao Fujimasa. 2002. *Jinkō genshō shakai no sekkei* [Life design in the depopulating society]. Tokyo: Chuōkōron-sha.
Miyamoto, Tsuneichi. 1984. *Kakyo no oshie* [Lore from home]. Tokyo: Iwanami Shoten.
Miyata, Noboru, Kenji Mori, and Fusako Amino, eds. 2000. *Rōjuku no chikara* [Power of older adults in maturity]. Tokyo: Waseda Daigaku Shuppanbu.
Oe, Masaaki. 2008. *Chīki no chikara* [The power of local communities]. Tokyo: Iwanami Shoten.
Ono, Akira. 2005. *Sanson kankyo shakaigaku josetsu* [Introduction to sociology on environment of mountain villages]. Tokyo: Nousangyoson Bunka Kyōkai.
Ostrom, Elinor, Thomas Dietz, Nives Dolšak, Paul C. Stern, Susan Stonich, and Elke U. Weber, eds. 2002. *The Drama of the Commons*. Washington DC: National Academy Press.
Phillipson, Chris. 2011. "Developing Age-Friendly Communities: New Approaches to Growing Old in Urban Environment." In *Handbook of Sociology of Aging*, ed. R. Settersten and J. Angel. New York: Springer.
Scharlach, Andrew E., and Amanda J. Lehning, eds. 2016. *Creating Aging-Friendly Communities*. Oxford: Oxford University Press.
Stafford, Philip B. 2009a. "Aging in the Hood." In *The Cultural Context of Aging*, ed. J. Sokolovsky. Westport, CT: Praeger.
———. 2009b. *Elderburbia: Aging with a Sense of Place in America*. Santa Barbara, CA: Praeger (ABC CLIO).
Suzuki, Nanami. 2005. "Kakinoha wo tsumu kurashi: Normalization wo koete, Bunkajinruigaku [Discovering a new old age through persimmon leaves: Living more than a "normalized" life]." *Japanese Journal of Cultural Anthropology* 70(3): 355–78.
———. 2009. "Creating a New Life through Persimmon Leaves: The Art of Searching for Life-Design for Greater Well-Being in a Depopulated Town." *Kyoto Working Papers for Area Studies*, G-COE Series 76: 1–14. Kyoto: Center for Southeast Asian Studies, Kyoto University. http://hdl.handle.net/2433/155753.
———. 2012. "Creating a Community of Resilience: New Meanings of Technologies for Greater Well-Being in a Depopulated Town." *Anthropology & Aging Quarterly (Aging and Anthropology since 2014)* 33(3): 87–96.
———. 2013. "Carrying Out Care: An Exploration of Time and Space in Cooperative Life Design." In *The Anthropology of Aging and Well-Being: Searching for the Space and Time to Cultivate Life Together*, SES (Senri Ethnological Studies) 80, ed. N. Suzuki, 1–19. Osaka: National Museum of Ethnology. http://hdl.handle.net/10502/4962.
———, ed. 2012. *Shogai no nai shakai ni mukete* [Toward a "society without handicaps": Reconsidering well-being and normalization]. SER (Senri Ethnological Reports) 102. Osaka: National Museum of Ethnology.
Thang, Leng Leng. 2001. *Generations in Touch: Linking the Old and Young in a Tokyo Neighborhood*. Ithaca: Cornell University Press.

Yokoishi, Tomoji. 2007. *Sōda, happa wo urō* [Let's sell leaves]. Tokyo: Sofbank Creative.
———. 2009. *Shogai genki shakai no tsukurikata* [Towards a society of people having an active social life all through their lives]. Tokyo: Softbank Creative.
Yuzawa, Yasuhiko. 2003. *Data de yomu kazoku mondai* [Reading issue of the family by data]. Tokyo: NHK Shuppan.

PART V
Being Well Enough in Old Age

AS AN ETHNOGRAPHER MYSELF, I am prone to be fond of research and practice that springs from a relationship in which the researcher/practitioner and the subject/client are active partners in the co-creation of meaning. I am pleased to see growing support for participatory approaches to research, practice, policy, governance, and technology/service/environmental design. This approach, indeed, even gives new meaning to the phrase *public art* as "art with" not "art for" the people (Manzini 2015; Hamdi 2004). I believe the democratic impulses underlying a surging sharing economy may be emerging from the same appreciation of the commons, brought to our attention by the Nobel Prize–winning Elinor Ostrom (1990).

Collaborating with older adults as active agents in the creation of meaning, Marian Barnes and her team are able to point to critical understandings of the lifeworld of their older co-researchers. It is exactly these kinds of insights that emerge from a research model in which older adults' lived experiences are taken as serious data points. In chapter 12, a fitting conclusion to this book, Barnes provides a wonderful example of co-creation, where three forms of knowledge (practice, research knowledge of academics, and experiential knowledge of older adults) coalesce and mutually inform. She describes the manner in which the research project, because it seriously includes older adults as co-researchers, was transformational for all concerned:

> It is no longer unusual to involve older people in research or in discussions about services or policies. But those initiatives do not always demonstrate what I have called "deliberating with care" . . . , a way of being attentive to lived experience and taking responsibility for action in response to what people say about their lives.

While the original goal of the project was to develop learning resources for practitioners, it provides extremely important insights for the age-friendly community movement. It demonstrates a way to define an age-friendly community through a bottom-up, co-design approach, closely tied to place and associated social relationships. It also cautions against a ready-made set of indicators that might not relate to the lived experiences and goals of older adults, a caution echoed in a recent blog for the Age-Friendly Innovation Exchange of the International Federation on Aging (2017). Citing Barnes again:

> In offering yet another set of indicators for an age-friendly city, it is vital not to lose sight of the fact that older people's well-being in any particular place cannot be separated from a sense that they are valued by others and they can remain connected to things that matter to them and that they value. It is too simplistic to suggest that what older people value can be encompassed by notions of choice and control that dominate UK policy discourse. Those things are likely to change as people move into older age. But they can also be changed by opportunities to take part in projects like this one that can enable recognition and opportunities for development. This should remind all of us of our collective responsibilities to enable well-being in older age.

Not losing sight of the importance of this issue to service personnel across the board, Barnes argues for an "ethics of care" that also acknowledges the relational character of not only health, but also health *care*:

> In contrast to much work on well-being that views this as an individual state, strongly impacted by the degree of choice and independence experienced by people as they grow older, our research suggests the importance of understanding well-being as generated through relationships. . . . And we need to understand care as a relational practice, and "good care" as embodying ethical understandings of what is necessary to live well and that recognize care giver and care receiver as jointly engaged in the dynamic process of care.

References

Hamdi, Nabeel. 2004. *Small Change: About the Art of Practice and the Limits of Planning in Cities.* London: Earthscan.
Manzini, Ezio. 2015. *Design, When Everybody Designs.* Cambridge: MIT.
Ostrom, Elinor. 1990. *Governing the Commons.* Cambridge: Cambridge University Press.

12 RELATIONAL WELL-BEING AND AGE-FRIENDLY CITIES

Marian Barnes

Introduction

ALONGSIDE THE DEVELOPMENT OF THE concept and practice of "age-friendliness," social and public policy during the first two decades of the twenty-first century have prioritized "well-being" as a focus for and outcome of policy for older people (and others). Both concepts reflect the necessity for going beyond purely material indicators of quality of life. Both concepts are subject to disputed interpretations and can lead to different types of policy initiative. Where we start from in terms of the concepts and ideological underpinnings of these will influence how we proceed and where we arrive. My starting point in this chapter is well-being, rather than age-friendliness. I consider how we understand what well-being means in old age and reflect on the implications of this for age-friendly cities. I do this by critiquing dominant conceptions of well-being and discussing how research with older people enabled an alternative way of thinking, with positive and potentially transformative practical applications. The research has been discussed in detail elsewhere, and my purpose here is not the reporting of research findings. Rather the aim is to contribute conceptual and methodological insights that can inform the diverse practices associated with creating age-friendly cities. But first it is necessary to describe briefly the research and the translational project that developed from this.

The Research

The project on which my argument is based involved collaborative research undertaken between university researchers, the local Age UK (a voluntary sector organization that both offers services and campaigns on behalf of older people), and a group of older people who were recruited to work with us as "co-researchers." The aim of the research was to understand what well-being means to older people and how this is generated (see Barnes, Taylor, and Ward 2013; Barnes, Gahagan, and Ward 2018; and Ward and Barnes, 2016 for details of the research and a translational project building on this). It was undertaken in Brighton and Hove, a city on the south coast of England with a strong youth-oriented culture and identity, which nevertheless embarked on the process of seeking recognition as an age-friendly city soon after the completion of the research. The initial impetus for the age-friendly city application came from the Older People's Council (OPC), an elected body of older people who are a key focus for consultation by the city council on issues relating to older age. Two members of the OPC were among the group of co-researchers on the well-being project, although the research project predated that initiative locally and was not framed by reference to it. The OPC is unusual in terms of forums that aim to reflect or represent older people's views to public authorities in England. Its constitution requires election of representatives by anyone over the age of sixty who lives or works in Brighton and Hove. Other types of forum exist across the country but usually cannot claim to be based on a formal process of election and thus representation (Barnes, Harrison, and Murray 2012).

The context of the research is important. Brighton has an active voluntary and community sector, and the University of Brighton has an established commitment to working closely with community organizations in relation to research. The well-being research was jointly funded by Age UK in Brighton and Hove and by the university. The nature of the funding and the freedom this gave to developing the research collaboratively with older people was significant in terms of how we were able to focus it, the way in which we carried it out, and the time period over which we conducted the work. This is important in the context of considering what is necessary for and what are the characteristics of an age-friendly city. We can suggest that an institutional willingness to collaborate and commit resources to innovative work involving older people is an important indicator of and resource for this.

Following the completion of the research, we made a successful application to the Economic and Research Council for "Follow On" funding in order to translate research findings into video training materials for social workers, occupational therapists, and others working with older people in different service contexts ("social care" services in the UK). A more formal funding regimen meant we were operating within a more restricted time scale in producing the filmed learning resources we had committed to generate.[1] But the strength of the relationships that had already developed through the research process enabled us to successfully achieve what we set out to do in this translational phase of the work. In this chapter I draw on both the research and the translational work.

What Is Well-Being and How Do We Recognize It?

Our decision to research well-being reflected the profile this concept had achieved in social policy and our sense that it was being rather uncritically adopted by some of those organizations charged with "delivering" it. Well-being used to be a conceptual add-on to "health" in much policy discourse. Since it has come out of the shadow to be recognized as something with significance in its own right, there has been a huge expansion in research designed to identify, measure, and assess the distribution of and changes in well-being (e.g., Searle 2008). Well-being has been associated with a range of other concepts, including a positive quality of life, satisfaction, and happiness, and it is often hard to distinguish one from another in both research and policy. For example, following the election of the Coalition Government in the UK in 2010, the government invested £2 million in a National Well-Being Project for the Office for National Statistics (ONS) to compile a "happiness index" (Evans 2011). The ONS included four questions in the 2011 Integrated Household Survey (IHS) that were intended to measure the degree of well-being among the population:

- Overall, how satisfied are you with your life nowadays?
- Overall, how happy did you feel yesterday?
- Overall, how anxious did you feel yesterday?
- Overall, to what extent do you feel the things you do in your life are worthwhile?

The survey enabled researchers to draw conclusions about the distribution of well-being according to geography, social group, and age (ONS 2012). Other research has adopted more sophisticated ways of measuring well-being that rely rather less on the nebulous and transient notion of happiness to assess population well-being or changes resulting from specific policy and practice interventions with specific groups (see, e.g., Bowling and Stenner 2011 for an approach to defining and measuring well-being with older people). Nevertheless, however sophisticated the measure, the concept of well-being remains rather elusive and seems to be only understandable by reference to other similarly elusive concepts, such as quality of life. And however sophisticated the attempts to define and conceptualize well-being, the dominant way of understanding this is as an absolute quality of individuals who should be striving toward achieving this. An example of this comes from work by Ryan and Sapp (2007: 71), who argue:

> Well-being concerns a person's capacity for optimal functioning and encompasses not only the issue of physical health, but also a sense of interest in one's surroundings, a confidence in being able to formulate and act to fulfil

goals and the motivation and energy to persist in the face of obstacles. A well being is able to maintain its vitality and to thrive within its everyday ecological environment.

While it might be hard to argue against this in general terms, this way of viewing well-being holds problems, in particular when we think about well-being in old age. It is a definition that emphasizes a rational, purposive actor striving toward goals and having intrinsic capacities to realize these. It has nothing to say about the structural contexts and resources that might contribute to or hinder well-being, nor about the social and personal relations within which and through which striving toward goals must take place. The future-oriented focus is problematic at a time of life when "looking forward" can itself be problematic (Clarke and Warren 2007). And, in view of the greater prevalence of health problems among older people compared with younger people, the emphasis on energy and vitality might seem to rule out the possibility of "being well" to many who are only too aware of the depletion in such resources as they grow older.

When we embarked on the research, we were aware of these conceptual and political critiques of well-being. Nevertheless, we also recognized the significance of the concept within policy discourse, and our voluntary sector partner was working with this concept in developing its own services and in dialogue with other agencies. Therefore, when we had the opportunity to carry out research, we decided to explore what well-being meant to older people themselves. We did not start (or end) with a definition, nor did we attempt to measure the extent to which older people in Brighton and Hove might be considered to "be well." Rather we wanted to understand what well-being means to older people and what, in their experience, generates this. Our starting point thus involved a perspective on well-being as a generative concept (Taylor 2011) and an approach to research that recognizes older people as experts in their own lives and generators of new ways of understanding (e.g., Holstein and Minkler 2007), hence our decision to work with older people as co-researchers in this study.

Researching Well-Being with Older People

We started out with a team of twelve co-researchers recruited via the local Age UK volunteering program. When we started, team members were aged from early sixties to late eighties—the oldest at that stage was eighty-seven, and by the time our work concluded two team members were in their nineties. The co-researchers contributed to all aspects of the research based on their own preferences and skills and in the context of other commitments.

Following training that aimed to recognize existing skills as well as develop new ones, some carried out interviews and focus groups, and others were involved in transcription and coding of data, producing written outputs, and presenting findings. All were involved in developing the research design, interpretation, and analysis of the findings during team meetings.

The co-research project included one-to-one interviews with thirty older people and seven focus groups in which another fifty-nine older people took part. The group decided that sixty-five should be the youngest age for inclusion in the project, and half of those who took part in one-to-one interviews were aged eighty-five or older, including five who were in their nineties. Twenty were women, and ten were men. We started with fifteen people who used Age UK services, and others were recruited using snowballing methods to include older people in a diverse range of circumstances. While we could not claim to have generated a "representative" sample of older people in the city, we did manage to include people whose material circumstances varied substantially, from "struggling over basics" to "comfortable," in the terms we invited people to describe their circumstances to us. One man we interviewed was openly gay, and one woman had learning disabilities. One focus group and one interview were with black older people. So we were able to explore at least some of the differences in the way in which people talk about well-being and what is important in generating this in relation to the diverse lives of older people. The age range of participants also meant that we could consider what might be involved in the process of sustaining well-being over a period of some thirty years. We produced a full report of the research (Ward et al. 2012), and a subgroup of co-researchers also produced a guide for other older people based on research findings. They called this *As Time Goes By*.

The topic guide for interviews and focus groups was designed to explore what older people themselves considered important about well-being. Interviewees were asked to reflect on what this meant to them, what contributed to a feeling of well-being, and how this might have changed as they grew older. While prompts were offered based on team discussions about what well-being might involve, interviewees and focus group participants were able to reflect on issues that the team themselves might not have identified as important; to discuss why things were important to them and what precisely it was about issues that made a difference in terms of their well-being.

When it came to analysis, some team members offered to code data, and they then brought this to meetings to introduce discussions on how and why they had coded the transcripts in the way they had. Team discussions enabled collective interpretation of the significance of what people had said to us. The whole process took approximately three years. By the end of this time, one team member had moved away, and one had decided not to carry on because she found much of what was said by interviewees upsetting. This woman had decided not to carry out interviews but had offered to transcribe them. We wondered if this work, carried out alone, made it harder to deal with some of the difficult issues people spoke of than was the case in the more social setting of an interview. Two others, the youngest members of the team, worked with us to the end of the research project but decided not to take part in the work to produce learning resources.

Other co-researchers worked with us on the Follow On project to produce learning resources based on research findings. They were joined at this stage by two older people from a senior's forum in a neighboring local authority and by local authority and voluntary sector practitioners working in older people's services. This group met over a period of a year to discuss the empirical material from the well-being research and to reflect on its significance for the practice of workers in different older people's services. We then developed case studies that were translated into scripted scenarios that were acted and filmed using a professional production company. We also filmed some of our team members talking about their experiences of being involved in the project and what it meant to them.

This brief description conceals both the huge amount of work involved in carrying out the research and the "translation" project, but also both the significance of and the learning from working together to understand well-being in older age. I can only summarize these issues here before considering the substance of research findings and their significance for age-friendly cities.

Well-Being through Working Together

My colleagues Lizzie Ward and Bea Gahagan have written about the way in which we sought to develop relationships and work with co-researchers (Ward and Gahagan 2010). We found it useful to draw on the ethics of care as we reflected on what was necessary to enable the older people who were working with us to experience well-being in our work together (see, e.g., Barnes 2012 for a discussion of care ethics and its applications). The ethics of care was also an important framework within which we could make sense of what the older people who took part in interviews and focus groups were saying to us. There was a way in which we were seeking to "live" the ethical and relational understanding of well-being that was emerging from the data as we worked together to make sense of what people had told us in the interviews and focus groups. The process was transformative for those taking part as well as generating outputs that we have tried to use to help transform the practice of others. The majority of co-researchers continued to work on other collaborations when the project came to an end and spoke of its importance as a source of personal learning and recognition from others (see Barnes et al. 2018). The translational project involved new people with different perspectives together with those who had already been working together to carry out the research. This, plus the shorter time frame, meant it was harder to sustain the relationships that had developed in the research team. However, by that point the strength of the relationships between co-researchers and ourselves, the willingness of the practitioners to take part in a rather unfamiliar way of working, and our collective confidence in the value of the research we had undertaken contributed to our capacity to realize the objectives of this new stage of the project.

This translational project had been defined, in line with funders' expectations about such initiatives, as a "knowledge exchange" project. It was designed to bring together the practice knowledge of social workers, occupational therapists, and voluntary sector practitioners, the experiential knowledge of older people, and the theoretical and research knowledge of academics. The aim was to use these different knowledges in applying research findings to practice. However, we concluded that understanding this as a process of exchanging knowledge was not the most useful way of characterizing the important things that were happening in the discussions that took place. Rather, we needed to understand the spaces in which we were meeting with older people and with practitioners as spaces in which we might deliberate both about and with care (Barnes 2008). They were spaces in which we could not only co-construct knowledge, but in which moral imagination could be stimulated and applied and assumptions deriving from practice discourse could be questioned. And in order to achieve this, the distinct identities with which we started—academic researcher, older person, practitioner—needed to be recognized for what they were—only one way of describing individuals who were all growing older and who all shared responsibilities for enabling old age to be a time when people can be well enough.

Thus the learning that came from the process of working together enabled important insights into the type of relationships that can generate well-being, and these insights are equally relevant to ways in which older people can be involved in work toward achieving an age-friendly city. The substance of what we learned about well-being is also highly relevant. I offer a brief summary of what we learned from the research and our interpretation of findings from a care ethics perspective. I then focus more specifically on what older people said about the significance of place in order to suggest links between well-being and age-friendliness.

What Is Being Well Enough in Old Age?

In contrast to much work on well-being that views this as an individual state, strongly impacted by the degree of choice and independence experienced by people as they grow older, our research suggests the importance of understanding well-being as generated through relationships. Those relationships include family, friends, strangers, and health and social care workers, as well as the places in which older people live—both their immediate home environment and the surrounding city and its environs. Care, while occupying an ambivalent position within many narratives, was fundamental to an understanding of what generates well-being for many older people. These findings may appear little more than common sense. But when we compare the way well-being was discussed by the older people in our study with the dominant discourses of public policy identified above, it suggests some rather different ways of viewing the world.

I have noted that to make sense of the way in which older people talked about relational well-being, we have drawn on work on the ethics of care (Barnes 2012). The ethics of care is based in an understanding of human beings not as autonomous individuals, but as necessarily existing in relation to others. Care is of relevance to all of us, not only those usually thought of as having assessable needs for care. Rather than thinking of care as a commodity to be allocated only to those defined as "dependent" or "needy," we should recognize that care is something we all need in order to survive, feel nurtured, and experience well-being, albeit that there are times when all of us are more likely to need to be cared for than others. We can be both care givers and care receivers at different, and sometimes at the same, times. And we need to understand care as a relational practice, and "good care" as embodying ethical understandings of what is necessary to live well and that recognize care giver and care receiver as jointly engaged in the dynamic process of care.

In the early 1990s Joan Tronto published an influential book in which she set out her thinking about care as political as well as personal and relational. In that book she cited a definition of caring that she and Berenice Fisher had developed (Tronto 1993: 103):

> On the most general level, we suggest that caring be viewed as a species activity that includes everything that we do to maintain, continue, and repair our "world" so that we can live in it as well as possible. That world includes our bodies, our selves, and our environment, all of which we seek to interweave in a complex, life-sustaining web.

This definition seems very relevant to an understanding of what is necessary to well-being—which surely encompasses living in the world as well as possible. And the breadth of the relevance of care ethics from this perspective—not only referring, for example, to the intimate care necessary when frailty or illness means we are dependent on others for basic personal care, but to the way we interact with our physical and social environment—also suggests its value when we consider well-being in the context of the drive to create age-friendly cities.

Talking about Well-Being

When the interviewees in this project were invited to reflect on what well-being meant to them and to offer examples of circumstances in which they experienced this, they reflected on their lives not only as they were now, but as they had been, what had changed and how this had affected them. Many reflected on health problems they were experiencing and the limitations this placed on their lives. Many of the older people who took part were objectively quite "unwell," but this did not necessarily mean they did not experience well-being. They had important things to say about what can help you "be well" when you are "unwell."

People spoke of other difficult aspects of growing older. In particular they spoke of losses—of friends, loved ones, roles, or capacities—and of how they dealt with these. They spoke of the impact of giving and receiving care as they became frailer or as a partner suffered illness, but also of the satisfactions of caring for others, including both partners and grandchildren. They spoke of the need to adapt their way of living as their mobility became problematic or as activities they used to enjoy became closed to them for different reasons. They spoke of changes in the world around them—in the behavior and attitudes of others—and of how their own attitudes had changed. They spoke about their homes and the hard decisions they had to make to move when these no longer worked for them. And they also spoke about the place they lived in, what they enjoyed about this, and the difficulties of sustaining connections with the places that meant a lot to them as well as with others who were no longer physically close.

Overall, as they reflected on what well-being meant, they were speaking about what mattered to them (Sayer 2011). They spoke of what they valued and the extent to which they were able to sustain their connections with things that mattered or felt overwhelmed by the struggle to do so. Through the interviews they were both constructing what well-being meant to them and demonstrating the processes through which they sought to maintain and develop their own well-being and contribute to that of others, in changing and often difficult circumstances. They identified personal, interpersonal, and material resources that made a difference to their capacity to sustain well-being. But they also identified how the actions, inactions, attitudes, and behaviors of others were also crucial to this. For many, uncertainty about financial security constrained both present and future well-being. This was not just a matter of living on limited income. Anxiety about having enough money for a future of uncertain length impacted on decisions about how to live in the present.

Our understanding of well-being from these accounts reinforced the need to move away from abstract, universalist conceptualizations in order to reflect the concrete, embodied insights into those things that contribute to and those things that detract from older people's well-being.

People and Places

If we look in more detail about the significance of places and spaces in older people's accounts, we can understand how the spatial and the interpersonal interact in the lives of older people to impact well-being (see also Ward 2014).

Sheila Peace and her colleagues have considered the way in which both "home" and close and more distant external environments are important in terms of people's identities as they grow older (Peace et al. 2006). Our research offers a related perspective on the importance of environment to well-being—which is itself linked to older people's capacities to sustain a sense of a valued identity that is recognized by others. If we start with "home" and one of the key issues that was important in terms of home and well-being, that of security, we immediately encounter the need to think about how spatial and relational factors are both associated with this. Thus Connie, who was eighty-seven and lived alone following the death of her husband, said:

> I'm not at all worried about being on my own. And they've got keys—my neighbors have got keys . . . but I know that unless they see my bedroom window open they are in here like a shot. So I am not nervous about being alone. But I think if one didn't have that, you could be nervous.

For others who could not identify close neighbors who could help out in times of need, this absence undermined the security necessary to well-being. For one woman, the experience of having a late evening crisis and not being able to identify anyone nearby who could help was a factor in her decision to move to sheltered housing.

Keeping their home environment "nice" was important not only in maintaining the quality of their environment, but also in sustaining a person's sense of themselves. Both are important to well-being. Grace, a 97-year-old widow who lived alone, proudly announced that she did all her housework herself, doing it "in bits" to make this manageable and to "keep up a standard." The converse of this was that anxiety about maintenance could detract from home as a source of well-being. Kathleen, a disabled woman living alone who at sixty-seven was one of our younger interviewees, experienced anxiety because of not being able to trust people who came in to do repair work. What she wanted to enhance her well-being was someone she could trust who would "take over" and supervise the work.

Anxiety about repair costs, the uncertainty about the time period over which a house or apartment would need to be maintained, as well as anxiety about being confident in those who might be employed to do the work were all factors in reducing a sense of well-being in relation to home. But so, too, were things happening beyond their front doors. At ninety-six, Ethel had already moved into sheltered accommodation, but

> you see all the ones that were in where I lived, they've all gone. . . . I would just like to have a few more friends or a few more people to meet and discuss things, unluckily as I say in my flat now everybody that was there when I went there twenty years ago they've more or less all died. The new people with husbands and all that, they say hello and all that but you don't have anything to do with them.

Or as another said, "We're reaching the stage where we're running out of friends and relations . . . they're just dying off."

These factors are significant wherever people live and grow old. But what about how they felt about the specific place of Brighton, the city with the avowedly "alternative" culture that attracts many of the young people who come to one of the two universities to stay on? Two important characteristics of the geography of Brighton and Hove are that it is a city by the sea and it is a very hilly city. Both factors are important in thinking about the role of place in older people's well-being.

Iris, aged eighty-eight, spoke for a number of others when she talked about this:

> I love the sea and I would love to do what I used to do and go down and walk by the sea, but I can't do it any more because it is such a long walk, terrifically long walk. I can't think of any bus that would go there either. There isn't one that goes down to the front, the promenade. I used to be able to do it every day, but I can't do it now. It's a shame that I'm longing to be by the sea.

The significance of the seafront encompassed different issues relevant to well-being. It embodied memories of good times that were past, it is a public space where interaction between people of different ages can take place spontaneously, and it is somewhere where just sitting is not only acceptable but expected. Ironically in view of the inability of some to access it because public transport did not go there, the promenade is also a flat area accessible to those who themselves or whose friends or partners used wheelchairs.

The physical geography that made it hard for many to get about as they would wish could also offer the possibility of interacting visually with their environment in ways that contributed to well-being. Jennifer, whose husband had had a stroke and who had already moved to a smaller house that they could manage more easily, recognized that there was likely to come a time when they would have to move into a flat. But she was clear that this would need to be a flat with a view because this was necessary "for her soul." And Richard said:

> We can from here, from the upstairs of this house, we can see the sea, we can see the Palace Pier and the seafront. . . . [The hills] are an awful nuisance for us when we are older, but the views and the pleasure they give . . .

Being connected to the outside world is important even if reduced mobility limits this. Else at eighty-one had spoken about the reduced confidence she had in walking following a stroke. But:

> So what I did was, opened the door, because the sun comes right through here ... what I normally do is take a chair, sit it out there and just sit and relax and I think, oh this is beautiful, this is lovely. I can see the sea, I can see people walking along, makes me a bit sad thinking I used to walk along.

So a number of people talked about difficulties in physical access to parts of the city, difficulties that could have been reduced by bus routes that took in the sea front and more public seating to enable them to rest. Many were also reluctant to go to the city center at night because it was too rowdy and busy. But maintaining a connection with the city and with the life of this was recognized as important to well-being. This was evident in Margaret's reference to the range of free cultural activities that are available in the city and in Kathleen's reference to her love of theater and the quality of plays at a local theater. For Peter, a gay man who had been born and brought up in a very different cultural environment, sharing his love of theater with younger friends was important to his well-being.

Intimate and Distant Relationships

Experiences of interaction with the physical place in which they live are interconnected with relationships with others. If we turn to look at what older people said more directly about the importance of interpersonal relationships to well-being, we can understand more about the interaction between people, place, and well-being.

The relationships that people spoke of were both "close" and "distant" in terms of degrees of intimacy and geography. What we have referred to as "stranger" relationships (Barnes et al. 2013) comprise interactions between older people and those they encounter when they move into public spaces: conversations at the bus stop, with the doctor's receptionist, at the checkout counter of supermarkets, for example. These are important for different reasons. They might be the only conversation someone has that day; they have the potential to confer at least some sense of recognition from others, and they can be an opportunity for an older person in turn to offer recognition that others may not "be well." And if such interactions are regular, they create the possibility that the older person would be missed if they became unwell or died. What might be considered trivial to those for whom regular interaction with others is unproblematic can become important when human contact becomes more limited. And they have practical implications for those designing and using different "public" environments—if shop assistants are entirely replaced by automated checkouts, this removes one possibility for human interaction.

As Connie, above, indicated, knowing that neighbors are there who can help out in an emergency is important, and some spoke about the importance of someone who would be aware if their curtains weren't opened or they had not been seen for some time. Casual chats over a balcony or a shared cup of tea can break up a somewhat isolated life. The absence of such opportunities for interaction, even in contexts like sheltered housing where people had expected they would have neighbors they would get to know, was detrimental to well-being. In part this was because more intimate relationships are often lost in old age:

> But I have lost seven people since I moved, which is quite extraordinary. People who were meaningful friends. Very, very sad and you can't replace them quickly you know. So I feel that gap enormously. (Kathleen)

Others also reflected that the suggestion to join in new activities in order to make new friends did not recognize the particular quality of friendships that rely on shared histories to give them their value:

> But I do desperately need, and there's no point in saying, oh, join an evening class or join this and that because people are not, I don't actually think they're actually joining things with the objective of making any sort of firm friendships. I mean, I get this at the poetry group, you go in and the recitals are over and everybody is up and away, you know, quickly, they don't hang around to pass the time of day or anything else.

The type of relationship that older people spoke most about when discussing well-being were those with family—those who were both physically present and distant. For those able to learn new technologies, distance did not necessarily mean it became impossible to give or receive care within the family when children lived far away. For those whose health or physical frailty meant that they were in regular contact with health and social care services, relationships with service providers were also significant. Thus, caring relationships occupied a significant place in the narratives of many interviewees. Some identified themselves as carers, and their narratives were constructed around the centrality of this role. They talked of the restrictions it placed on what they could do individually or with their ill or disabled partner, but also the satisfactions that can derive from knowing that you are caring well for another. For Eddie, whose wife had experienced long-term mental health problems, being able to secure good quality care in a residential home enabled him not only to care for himself, but also to feel satisfied at having done well for his wife. Jennifer, who spoke of multiple losses associated with the impact of her husband's stroke, also spoke with some pride of becoming a spokeswoman for others in a similar position.

Others talked of their need for care and of both positive and negative experiences of the way this was offered. One example illustrates how the presence or absence of care within a "helping" relationship can make a substantial difference to well-being. I have already introduced Grace, who was ninety-seven years old, lived alone, and had very limited mobility, so in order to go out she needed to be taken by car. She contrasted the way help to enable her to do her shopping was provided by her son with her experience of being taken shopping by a young male friend. Her son appeared to want to do the shopping as quickly as possible to ensure she had enough food in the house. In contrast, her young friend understood the importance of shopping as an outing that was important for Grace. Thus, he would take time to show her things she might be interested in, discuss prices, and generally make much of her and their time together. Grace said of him:

> He treats me. I just feel like the queen! You know, he says, "Don't you dare open the car, I'll do all that." Opens the car, gets the . . . I say, "Darling I can put my seatbelt on, I'm not helpless," and he says, "You'll do as you're told when you're out with me." And he treats . . . it's just wonderful, he's such a darling.

Elsewhere in her interview Grace demonstrated a fierce independence, but this was perhaps a response to the way she experienced her son's behavior when he was with her. She said she would rather "crawl on the floor" than ask for his help around the house. But in this context, where going shopping is about the only time she gets out of her flat, her friend's treatment transforms a functional activity into an experience of being cared for and made to feel special. We suggest that this may be an example of the "positive dependency" that Taylor (2011) suggests may contribute to rather than detract from well-being.

Care is thus characterized by complexity and ambivalence in older people's stories. On the one hand, skilled, sensitive care is fundamental to well-being, as is the confidence that good care will be available when it is needed and that people can easily find out where they can get help. On the other hand, older people have been well schooled into thinking that to seek help involves becoming a burden. The concern that they may be seen as "burdens" can itself detract from well-being.

Interviewees had both positive and negative things to say about those in paid caring roles whose help was important to them. In part this reflected the emotional and psychological impact of poor health or disability—those who could help sustain well-being in this context were those who recognized such impacts and demonstrated that people did not have to shoulder the problems alone. It was evidence of qualities such as reliability, reassurance, trust, and respect that made the difference in terms of older people's experiences of service providers and whether this helped sustain their well-being through difficult times. Connie's experience of help from her new GP as her husband was dying is a positive example of proactive help leading to confidence and trust:

> He [GP] was due to start that week and I remember he phoned on the Monday morning, introduced himself and said, "Can I come to see you at one o'clock?" And he was with me the whole time [husband] was ill, because I had him upstairs with the hospital bed, the nurses and what have you. When [husband] died, I thanked him and said, "I don't know what I would have done." And he said, "Now that is over I am going to look after you," and he has.

But this was not typical and most accounts referred to inconsistencies and what amounted to an absence of care from health workers.

Applying Learning from the Research

It was this emphasis on the importance of connection, of recognition, and of "good care" that provided the focus of the work we did with older people and practitioners to translate research findings into learning resources that could be used by those working in statutory and voluntary social care agencies and that could also be useful to older people's organizations. Our research convinced us that thinking of well-being as an individual characteristic, something that could be measured by the application of a standard instrument, however sophisticated, was not a good basis for practices and policies aiming to enhance well-being. Learning to be well enough in old age is a process that requires older people to engage in substantial emotional and organizational labor (Ward, Barnes, and Gahagan 2012). It includes reflections on what is important in terms of values, relationships, and priorities and dealing with a sense of declining visibility and lack of recognition of one's strengths. "Being well-enough," even when they are unwell or facing the losses that often accompany growing older, is not something that older people can achieve through individual will or by solely pursuing choice and independence. It includes learning how to receive care and how to respond to changes in the nature and balance of close relationships. For those working directly with older people and engaged in policy initiatives such as age-friendly communities, the objective should be to understand what generates well-being and what we all need to be doing to contribute to this. The work that needs to be done should not and cannot only be done by older people.

Because health-care services and social care services are important to older people's well-being, an age-friendly city will be one in which such services are provided in ways that reflect what matters to older people. What we sought to do in producing learning resources was to apply insights from this research to scenarios that frontline workers might face in working with older people and also to introduce them to ideas from the ethics of care that would be useful in focusing on what matters to those older people and how to help them sustain well-being through difficult times. Thus, for example, we combined Grace's contrasting experiences of help from her son and her friend with Elsie's loss of confidence about getting out following a stroke, to create a scenario in which a visiting social care worker is attentive both to the imagined character's emotional distress and her need for practical help. In the first of six films, and in the accompanying handbook, we introduce the dimensions of care articulated by Joan Tronto (1993)—attentiveness, responsibility, competence, and responsiveness—and suggest how working with these could offer a frame within which to understand what might enhance well-being in different contexts. These resources were directed toward both statutory and voluntary sector workers in Brighton and Hove, but also beyond.

Both the method of generating these resources, working collectively with practitioners and older people, and the nature of the resources themselves aimed to embody as far as possible what we had learned about the importance of relationships in generating and sustaining well-being. It is no longer unusual to involve older people in research or in discussions about services or policies. But those initiatives do not always demonstrate what I have called "deliberating with care" (Barnes 2008, 2012), a way of being attentive to lived experience and taking responsibility for action in response to what people say about their lives. The initial freedom that we had to design and conduct the research together with older people, rather than having to produce a proposal that met funder's requirements and could only involve older people at a later stage, was important in creating the context in which we could develop care ethical practice. The support of institutions within the city for this type of collaborative work helped significantly.

The involvement of workers and older people in this translational process also encouraged other public officials to give attention to what we had produced, including the group established to plan toward Brighton becoming an age-friendly city. I was invited to become a member of this group in order to contribute the learning generated from our work on well-being. In this context I sought to find a way of translating research findings into something that would help those working within a "measurable outcomes" framework. Thus, drawing on the complete findings from the well-being research, I suggested the following indicators. An age-friendly city would be one characterized by the following:

1. Older people feel able to sustain and develop relationships with friends and family and explore new relationships as others are lost or become more limited due to illness and/or distance.
2. There is opportunity for everyday encounters in public spaces to sustain older people's sense of being acknowledged, recognized, and valued and enable them to recognize others.
3. Older people feel that public spaces are not only physically accessible but are also designed with older people in mind and are spaces that are not dominated by young people.
4. Older people feel able to travel to all parts of the city by public transport.
5. Public officials are attentive to older people in the diverse contexts in which they encounter them—for example, from reception and inquiry desks, to detailed discussion about housing needs and circumstances, to interactions in libraries and leisure centers.
6. Both public and commercial services and facilities provide face-to-face service and do not rely entirely on technology.
7. Older people feel a sense of relational security in their homes. They feel there are people nearby they can call on for help and who would notice if they became unwell or were in difficulty.
8. There are trustworthy sources of help available to enable older people to maintain their homes when this becomes difficult.
9. Older people who become unwell receive help that enables them to adapt so that poor health does not inevitably detract from well-

being. Older people do not feel that they have to deal with health problems on their own.
10. Older people feel confident that health-care services and social care services will be available if they are needed and that asking for help will not label them as "burdens," and they feel confident that using such services will enhance rather than detract from well-being.
11. There is a range of different living options for older people who feel they can no longer manage in their own homes, including positive possibilities for shared or collective living that can reduce loneliness, isolation, and insecurity.
12. There is help available to support people in making the difficult decision about moving from home.
13. Leisure, voluntary, artistic, faith-based, and other activities and resources enable older people with diverse interests, cultures, and identities to take part in ways that enable them to use existing skills and develop new ones.
14. Support is available to enable older people to use new technologies to maintain and develop communication and relationships with others.
15. Older people are able to use their experience, knowledge, and wisdom in shaping policies and services and generating new knowledge through research and working with others in community projects and campaigns.
16. The diversity of experiences of growing older are recognized in relation to class and levels of financial security; identities with respect to learning disability, physical disability, or experience of living with mental illness; family and/or relationship status; caring responsibilities; gender; sexuality; and ethnicity.

Work on developing age-friendly cities encompasses both "top-down" and "bottom-up" initiatives and reflects both acceptance and critique of the active aging origins of the movement (Buffel, Phillipson, and Scharf 2012; Lui et al. 2009). Our insights into the importance of relational well-being reflect both a starting point in lived experience of old age and an ethical and political perspective on the interdependence of what it is to be human. In offering yet another set of indicators for an age-friendly city, it is vital not to lose sight of the fact that older people's well-being in any particular place cannot be separated from a sense that they are valued by others and they can remain connected to things that matter to them and that they value. It is too simplistic to suggest that what older people value can be encompassed by the notions of choice and control that dominate UK policy discourse. Those things are likely to change as people move into older age. But they can also be changed by opportunities to take part in projects like this one that can enable recognition and opportunities for development. This should remind all of us of our collective responsibilities to enable well-being in older age.

Acknowledgments

The research on which this chapter is based was carried out with Dr. Lizzie Ward, University of Brighton; Dr. Beatrice Gahagan, Age UK Brighton and Hove; Bunty Bateman, Marion Couldery, Nick Drury-Grahame, Julie Frayne, Jeanie Hawkins, Jack Hazelgrove, Joyce Laverpreddy, Dorothy Lewis, Diana Owen, Liz Ray, and Francis Tonks.

It is with sadness that I learned of Joyce Laverpreddy's death as I was finalizing this chapter.

Marian Barnes is professor emeritus in social policy at the University of Brighton, England. Throughout her career she has worked with people living with mental health problems, with carers, and with older people to research their lives and experiences of using services. She has studied and supported collective action by service users and carers and new forms of democratic practice. In her work she has sought to apply feminist care ethics to the political and personal experiences of struggle and transformative social relations involved in such action.

Note

1. *Older People, Wellbeing and Participation*, University of Brighton, accessed 19 August 2018, https://www.brighton.ac.uk/research-and-enterprise/groups/social-science-policy/research-projects/older-people-wellbeing-and-participation.aspx.

References

Barnes, Marian. 2008. "Passionate Participation: Emotional Experiences and Expressions in Deliberative Forums." *Critical Social Policy* 28(4): 461–81.
———. 2012. *Care in Everyday Life: An Ethic of Care in Practice*. Bristol: Policy Press.
Barnes, Marian, Beatrice Gahagan, and Lizzie Ward. 2018. *Re-imagining Old Age: Care, Wellbeing and Participation*. Wilmington, DE: Vernon Press.
Barnes, Marian, Elizabeth Harrison, and Lesley Murray. 2012. "Ageing Activists: Who Gets Involved in Older People's Forums?" *Ageing and Society* 32: 261–80.

Barnes, Marian, David Taylor, and Lizzie Ward. 2013. "Being Well Enough in Old Age." *Critical Social Policy* 33(3): 473–93.

Bowling, Anne, and Paul Stenner. 2011. "Which Measure of Quality of Life Performs Best in Older Age? A Comparison of OPQOL, CASP-19 and WHOQOL-OLD." *Journal of Epidemiology and Community Health* 65: 273–80.

Buffel, Tine, Chris Phillipson, and Thomas Scharf. 2012. Ageing in Urban Environments: Developing 'Age-Friendly' Cities. *Critical Social Policy* 32: 597–617. doi: 10.1177/0261018311430457.

Clarke, Amanda, and Lorna Warren. 2007. "Hopes, Fears and Expectations about the Future: What Do Older People's Stories Tell Us about Active Ageing?" *Ageing and Society* 27(4): 465–88.

Evans, Joanne. 2011. "Findings from the National Debate on Well-Being." Office for National Statistics. Accessed 15 January 2012. http://www.ons.gov.uk/ons/guide-method/user-guidance/well-being/wellbeing-knowledge-bank/understanding-wellbeing/well-being-reports-and-articles.html.

Holstein, Martha B., and Meredith Minkler. 2007. "Critical Gerontology: Reflections for the 21st Century" In *Critical Perspectives on Ageing Societies*, ed. Miriam Bernard and Thomas Scharf, 13–26. Bristol: Policy Press.

Lui, Chi-Wai, Jo-Anne Everingham, Jeni Warburton, Michael Cuthill, and Helen Bartlet. 2009. What Makes a Community Age-Friendly: A Review of International Literature. *Australasian Journal on Ageing* 28: 116–21.

ONS (Office for National Statistics). 2012. "Fi ONS Annual Experimental Subjective Well-Being Results." Office for National Statistics. Accessed 16 August 2012. www.ons.gov.uk.

Peace, Sheila, Caroline Holland, and Leonie Kellaher eds. 2006. *Environment and Identity in Later Life*. Maidenhead, NY: Open University Press.

Ryan, Richard, and Aislinn Sapp. 2007. "Basic Psychological Needs: A Self-Determination Theory Perspective on the Promotion of Wellness across Development and Cultures." In *Wellbeing in Developing Countries: From Theory to Research*, ed. Ian Gough and J. Allister McGregor, 71–92. Cambridge: Cambridge University Press.

Sayer, Andrew. 2011. *Why Things Matter to People: Social Science, Values and Ethical Life*. Cambridge: Cambridge University Press.

Searle, Beverley. 2008. *Well-Being. In Search of a Good Life?* Bristol: Policy Press.

Taylor, David. 2011. "Wellbeing and Welfare: A Psychosocial Analysis of Being Well and Doing Well Enough." *Journal of Social Policy* 40(4): 777–94.

Tronto, Joan. 1993. *Moral Boundaries: A Political Argument for an Ethic of Care*. London and New York: Routledge.

Ward, Lizzie. 2014. "Negotiating Well-Being: Older People's Narratives of Relationships and Relationality." *Ethics and Social Welfare* 8(3): 293–305.

Ward, Lizzie, and Marian Barnes. 2016. "Transforming Practice with Older People through an Ethic of Care." *British Journal of Social Work* 46(4):906–22.

Ward, Lizzie, Marian Barnes, and Beatrice Gahagan. 2012. *Well-Being in Old Age: Findings from Participatory Research*. University of Brighton and Age UK Brighton & Hove. https://www.brighton.ac.uk/_pdf/research/ssparc/wellbeing-in-old-age-full-report.pdf

Ward, Lizzie, and Beatrice Gahagan. 2010. "Crossing the Divide between Theory and Practice: Research and an Ethic of Care." *Ethics and Social Welfare* 4(2): 210–16.

INDEX

AARP, 127
accessibility, 233, 237, 240, 242
Actors Fund, 131
Administration for Community Living, 9
adolescents, 58–59, 62, 70, 75–77
AdvantAge Initiative, 7, 128–130, 134
    domains of, 128–129, 132
    framework of, 128, 132
advocacy
    evaluation of, 41–47
    intergenerational, 159
    training for, 38–40
Africa
    aging in, 189–192
age and ability-friendly communities, 51
age-friendly community (communities), 229, 243–244
age-friendly development
    in developing nations, 22
    implementing, 22–25
    obstacles to, 21–22
    policies towards, 23
Aging
    assets and, 81, 172, 232, 237
    chronic illness and, 2, 3
    civic participation and commodification of, 4
    crime and, 20
    demographics of, 1, 141–143
    empowerment and, 169, 176
    environment and, 5, 6
    families and, 160–161, 194–195
    gentrification and, 18
    in Japan, 229
    as lifestyle, 4
    livability and, 83
    migration and, 20, 216
    and organizations, 109, 156–157
    place and, 19
    poverty and, 171
    segregation and, 16, 18, 145–146
    successful, 4
    youth migration and, 2
agricultural cooperative (cooperatives), 233–234
alienation, 56
Alinsky, Saul, 34, 35
Appreciative Inquiry, 197
area agencies on aging, 9

baby boomers, 5
Benson, Peter L., 64
Berry, Wendell, 10, 61
buffered bike lanes, 65
built environment, 54, 57, 64

care, 229, 240–242
    being cared for, 240
    care for the place, 242
    care for the town, 241
    holistic system of care, 241
caring, 230, 236
    caring for and educating children, 230
    caring for nature, 236
Center for Home Care Policy and Research, 127
Centers for Disease Control, 9
cities
    age-friendly policies and, 81
    Atlanta, 219
    Berlin, 105
    Bloomington, 211
    inequality and, 17
    Manchester, 15
    New York, 127
    Portland, 8, 78
    sustainable, 81
    world, 17

citizen advocacy, 32
citizenship
    Urban, 23–24
civic engagement, 217
children, 230, 233, 238
children and youth, 54–59, 61–65, 67, 69–77
commons, 229–231, 238, 241–242
    land as (Iriaichi), 231, 241
    local, 230
    new commons, 231, 238, 241
    new forms of commons, 242
communities
    all age, 37, 149–150
community, 54, 77, 230, 237, 240–241
community building
    intergenerational, 153–154
community change and development
    disaster and, 181–183
    grassroots, 186
    intergenerational, 198
    models of, 33–34
computers, 234–235
cooperation, 231, 238, 240, 241
crime, 71
cultural resources (cultural capital), 229, 231, 241–242

depopulated areas, 244
depopulated town, 229–231, 240
depopulation, 229–230, 239
depression, 55–56, 58–59, 72
disability
    aging and, 38
    intellectual, 36
    persons with, 35–36
    physical, 36
disaster
    isolation and, 171
    resilience and, 171
Durkheim, Emile, 57

ecology, 237
economic development
    aging and, 199–200, 212–214, 232, 237
    small towns and, 214
environment(s), 230, 237, 240
    natural environment, 230
environmental equality, 229

environmental management, 244
environmental protection, 229
eyes on the street., 66, 67

face-to-face, 234, 237, 240
Fainstein, Susan S., 32, 49
farming, 232–233, 244
fertility rate, 229–230
festival(s), 232, 240–241
food(s), 232–233, 238–239, 241, 244
    food decorations, 23
    local food(s), 239, 241, 244

Gangadharan, 1
generation(s), 229–231, 237, 239–240
    multiple generations, 229
    younger generation(s), 230–231, 239
Genkai Shuraku (region in limit situation), 230, 232
gerontology, 5, 6, 18
    ecological, 84–85
grandchildren, 236

happiness, 240
Harlow, Harry, 55
health
    definition of, 256
    elders talking about, 257–258
    as a relational concept, 252
    well-being as, 251
health care
    critique of, 4–5, 252
    expenditures for, 3
    good care and, 263–265
    relationships and, 263
home, 233, 237, 239, 242
housing
    affordable, 107
    health and, 89–90
    high-rise, 56
    policy and, 87–92, 106–107
    social housing, 108
    sustainable development and, 87–89

Ibasho
    attributes of, 174
    lessons of, 184–185
    principles of, 173–174
income, 236
independent mobility, 64–65

Indiana
    Governor's Council for People with Disabilities, 36, 48
indigenous, 231, 233
    indigenous leaves, 233
    indigenous products, 231
Industrial Areas Foundation (IAF), 34–35, 49
industry, 230–233, 235, 240, 242
information, 234–235, 237–238, 241
interdependence, 241
isolation of older adults, 230
i-turn people (new comers), 239

Japan, 229–230, 232, 238–240, 242
just city, 32
justice
    equity and, 86
    spatial, 26
juvenile delinquency, 56, 74, 77

kaiseki, 232
Kamikatsu-cho (Kamikatsu Town), 229–241

land use, 54, 57, 67
Lawton and Nahemow, 5, 84
leaf production, 232–238, 244
    indigenous leaves, 233
    seasonal leaves, 232, 234
leisure time, 231, 239–240
life cycle, 240, 243
lifestyle, 231, 236–237, 239–240, 242
    changing lifestyle, 231
    lifestyle of the older adult, 4–5, 237
livable communities, 31, 33, 35, 36, 38, 42
local, 229–230, 232, 234–235, 238–239, 241, 244
    local community, 230
    local cultural resources, 229, 241, 244
    local culture, 229
    local food(s), 239, 241, 244
    local material resources, 244
    local vegetation, 232

mental health, 54, 56, 59, 61, 70, 74, 74
migration, 232
    out-migration, 232
mixed-use neighborhoods, 55, 57, 66, 70

natural environment, 230
nature, 236
    caring for nature, 236
neighborhoods, 25
    age-friendly, 103–104
    health and, 123
    relations in, 118–121, 230
Netherlands, 70
newcomers (i-turn people), 239–240
NORC (naturally occurring retirement community, 17
Normalization, 240
North American, 70
Norway, 70
nursing homes, 242

older women, 233, 235–236
Ostrom, Elinor, 244

participation, 233, 240, 241, 242
pension systems, 3
physical health, 54, 56, 59, 60, 61, 63, 67, 70
pit latrines, 203
place
    aging in, 17, 237
    home as a significant, 258
    importance of public, 260
    public, 117, 54–77
    shared spaces and, 159
planning
    lifetime community district, 219–220
    and public health, 211
    theories of, 31 (*see also* theory)
    urban, 25
play streets, 65

recycling, 231, 237, 238, 239, 241
region, 230–231, 235, 238, 240, 241, 244
relationships
    intergenerational, 195, 230
    intimate and distant, 260–262
    person-environment, 5
research
    action, 196
    collaborative, 249–250
    co-researchers in, 250
    evaluation, 121–123, 151
    focus group, 109–110, 128, 253
    knowledge exchange as, 255

narrative inquiry, 198
participatory, 197
qualitative, 84, 253–254
socio-spatial, 116
survey, 128–130
resilience, 229, 241–242

Scharlach, A. E., 21
semipublic joint venture (third sector), 230, 233
social anxiety syndrome, 59
social capital, 55, 59–61, 67, 71–71, 74–75, 145–148
social compact
John Gardner and, 143
social disorder, 61
social immune system, 59, 60
social interaction, 54–57, 63–68
social isolation, 54, 55, 57–59
social movements, 31
social networks, 54, 56, 59, 67–68, 70–71
social skills, 55, 58–59, 61–62
special district(s), 230, 235
stress, 60–61, 74, 76
suburbs, 56, 57–59, 65, 67, 70
super-aged society, 229, 243
support, 233, 237, 242–243
suicides, 56, 57, 59, 72–73
sustainability
community development and, 79–80, 199, 231, 244

tanada (terraced field), 239, 240
technologies, 231, 233, 239–241
theory
life course, 143–145
lifespan, 143
planning, 31 (*see also* planning)
third places, 67
third sector (semipublic joint venture), 230, 233, 234
time, 231, 233, 238–241, 244
Tokushima, 229, 231, 232
Tokyo, 238, 239

training
accessible, 41
approach, 39–41
content, 38–39
evaluation, 41
transportation planning, 54, 57, 65
true urbanism, 66, 70
trust, 56, 61, 63
tsunami
Japanese, 169
silver, 2

urbanism
lean, 218
urban design, 54, 76
urban dwellers, 239
urbanization, 15
urban theory, 31, 48
u-turn people (returnees), 239

visitors, 240, 241
volunteer(s), 235, 238

walkability, 39, 54–56, 58, 60, 61, 63, 68–75
well-being, 71, 75–76, 229–231, 240–241, 243
work, 230–233, 235–237, 239–242
accessibility of work, 237
"real work," 233
work of the older adult, 233, 235
World Health Organization
age-friendly framework, 7, 8, 229
World War II, 231

youth, 58–59, 61–62, 64, 72, 77, 229–231, 239, 242, 244
as agents of change, 204–205
African, 192
assets of, 193–194
voluntarism of, 200–204

zoning, 57

www.ingramcontent.com/pod-product-compliance
Lightning Source LLC
Chambersburg PA
CBHW070914030426
42336CB00014BA/2404